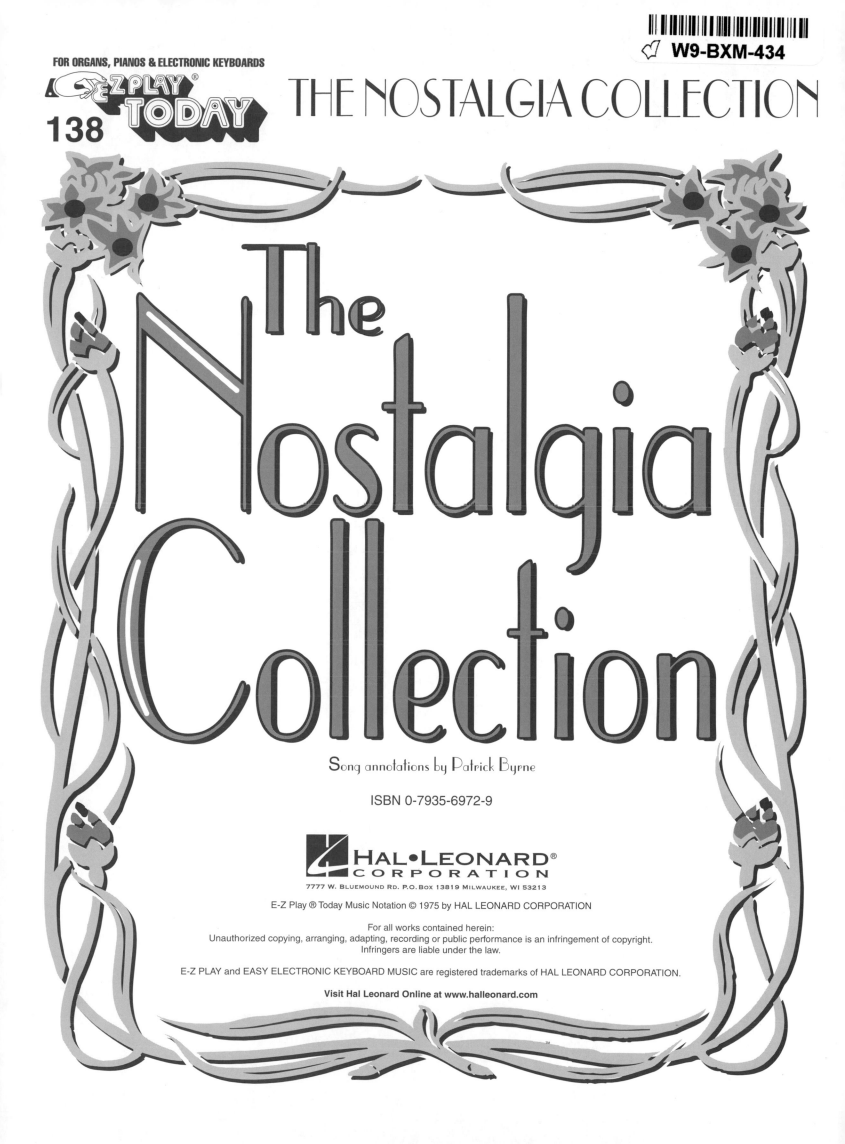

FOR ORGANS, PIANOS & ELECTRONIC KEYBOARDS

E-Z PLAY® TODAY

138

THE NOSTALGIA COLLECTION

The Nostalgia Collection

Song annotations by Patrick Byrne

ISBN 0-7935-6972-9

HAL•LEONARD®
CORPORATION

7777 W. BLUEMOUND RD. P.O. BOX 13819 MILWAUKEE, WI 53213

E-Z Play ® Today Music Notation © 1975 by HAL LEONARD CORPORATION

For all works contained herein:
Unauthorized copying, arranging, adapting, recording or public performance is an infringement of copyright.
Infringers are liable under the law.

E-Z PLAY and EASY ELECTRONIC KEYBOARD MUSIC are registered trademarks of HAL LEONARD CORPORATION.

Visit Hal Leonard Online at www.halleonard.com

W9-BXM-434

THE NOSTALGIA

COLLECTION

ABA DABA HONEYMOON

Words and Music by Arthur Fields and Walter Donovan

Chart Highlights
#1 in 1914
#9 in 1950
#3 in 1951

"Aba Daba Honeymoon" first became a hit when vaudevillian Ruth Roye began singing it at the legendary Palace Theatre in New York City in 1914. The song was later used for the film *Two Weeks With Love* (1950) starring Debbie Reynolds. The nineteen-year-old Reynolds earned a gold record for her hit recording of the song. In fact, five other recordings of "Aba Daba Honeymoon" made the Top 40 that year. *Two Weeks With Love* has long been forgotten, but Reynolds' performance of "Aba Daba Honeymoon" with Carleton Carpenter has been preserved in the block-buster musical anthology *That's Entertainment* (1974).

AFTER YOU'VE GONE

Words by Henry Creamer
Music by Turner Layton

Chart Highlights
#2 in 1918
#1 in 1919
#7 in 1927
#6 in 1937

An immense favorite ever since it was written in 1918, "After You've Gone" was often a featured part of the acts of two long-lived entertainment legends: Al Jolson and Sophie Tucker. The song's initial success came when it was a hit for singers Henry Burr and Albert Campbell in 1918 and songstress Marion Harris the following year. Harris' recording held onto the top of the charts for three weeks. "After You've Gone" became a jazz standard with recordings in the twenties and thirties by the likes of Bessie Smith, Paul Whiteman, Louis "Satchmo" Armstrong, and Lionel Hampton. In 1935, The Benny Goodman Trio — Goodman joined by pianist Teddy Wilson and drummer Gene Krupa —played "After You've Gone" on one side of their first recording together. You can still see and hear Goodman play "After You've Gone" in the film *Make Mine Music* (1946). Armstrong performed it in the film *The Five Pennies* (1959) and, as recently as 1979, the film *All That Jazz* featured this truly all-time hit.

ALABAMA JUBILEE

Words by Jack Yellen
Music by George Cobb

Chart Highlights
#2 in 1915
#28 in 1951
#14 in 1955

"Alabama Jubilee," written in 1915, was one of the last big hits to come out of the minstrel shows. The practice of blackfaced white performers impersonating blacks had existed in America since the early 19th century. In the 1840s Dan Emmett came up with the idea of building an entire show around this style of entertainment when he formed the Virginia Minstrels. Emmett's own songs became a central part of the minstrel repertoire: "Old Dan Tucker," "The Blue-Tail Fly (Jimmy Crack Corn)," and, of course, "Dixie," which Emmett wrote in 1859. Many of the most memorable songs of both Stephen Foster and James Bland were originally written for minstrel shows. During Reconstruction and into the 20th century minstrel shows ranked with vaudeville as one of the most popular forms of entertainment in America. Although the basic premise of the minstrel show was patently racist, many tuneful minstrel melodies, from the days of Dan Emmett right up to the early career of Al Jolson, have become part of our musical heritage.

ALEXANDER'S RAGTIME BAND

Words and Music by Irving Berlin

Chart Highlights
#1 in 1911
#3 in 1912
#17 in 1927
#9 in 1935
#12 in 1937
#1 in 1938
#20 in 1947

Not many songs can match the lasting popularity of "Alexander's Ragtime Band," Irving Berlin's first giant hit. Although "Alexander's Ragtime Band" is not really a rag (see Scott Joplin's "Maple Leaf Rag" of 1899 for the *real* thing), Berlin's use of the term "ragtime" in the title helped earn him the title 'King of Ragtime' and made ragtime an international craze. Among the performers who have had hit recordings of "Alexander's Ragtime Band" are: Bessie Smith (1927); Louis Armstrong (1935); Bing Crosby (1938); and the duo of Bing Crosby and Al Jolson (1947). Of course, Hollywood also eagerly capitalized on the song's immense popularity first with the movie *Alexander's Ragtime Band* (1938) and then in the film *There's No Business Like Show Business* (1954).

ALICE BLUE GOWN

Lyric by Joseph McCarthy
Music by Harry Tierney

Chart Highlights
#1 in 1920
#7 in 1940

This beautiful waltz was introduced by Edith Day in the title role of the Broadway musical *Irene* (1919). Day's recording of "Alice Blue Gown" topped the charts in 1920. The song refers to the favorite style of dress and color — light blue — of Alice Roosevelt Longworth, the daughter of the recently deceased former president, Theodore Roosevelt. In 1940 a film version of *Irene* was made which led to hit recordings of the song by Frankie Masters, Ozzie Nelson, and Glenn Miller. *Irene* returned to the Broadway stage in a 1973 revival starring Debbie Reynolds in the title role.

ALOHA OE

Words and Music by Queen Liliuokalani

Chart Highlights
#10 in 1924

Written in 1878 by Queen Liliuokalani of Hawaii, "Aloha Oe" was already almost fifty years old when it became a hit record in 1924. Despite competition from Tin Pan Alley tunes like "Oh, How She Could Yacki, Hacki, Wicki, Wacki, Woo," "The Honolulu Hicky-Boola-Boo," and "They're Wearing Them Higher In Hawaii," "Aloha Oe" remains the restful musical image most of us have of our fiftieth state.

ANCHORS AWEIGH

Words and Music by Alfred Hart Miles and Charles A. Zimmerman

Chart Highlights
#13 in 1921
#18 in 1930

"Anchors Aweigh" was originally written for the Army-Navy football game in 1906 by Lieutenant Charles A. Zimmerman and Midshipman Alfred H. Miles. At that time, Zimmerman was the director of music at the United States Naval Academy and Miles was a senior. Zimmerman had composed a football marching song for each graduating class. In 1906, cheered on by Zimmerman and Miles' new march, which was originally called "Sail Navy Down The Field," Navy defeated its long-time rival Army for the first time in many years. The title was later changed to "Anchors Aweigh" and new words were added in 1930.

BABY, WON'T YOU PLEASE COME HOME

Words and Music by Charles Warfield and Clarence Williams

Chart Highlights
#6 in 1923
#13 in 1928
#20 in 1932

Once W.C. Handy had brought the blues into the mainstream with his "St. Louis Blues" (1914), a number of other composers kept the style popular. Spencer Williams got his start — as a boy — playing in the Storyville honky tonks of New Orleans. "Baby, Won't You Please Come Home" was his first big hit. He wrote the song in 1919 when he was twenty-one years old. His own recording of "Baby, Won't You Please Come Home" in 1928 reached the number thirteen position on the charts. Five years earlier Bessie Smith, with Williams playing piano, had a number-six hit with the same song. Throughout his long musical career, Williams accompanied some of the best blues singers of his day, often working with Smith and Ethel Waters. Williams was also the musical director of Okeh Records, the first label to record a black singer performing a solo blues when it recorded Mamie Smith singing "Crazy Blues" on August 10, 1920.

BALLIN' THE JACK

Words by Jim Burris
Music by Chris Smith

Chart Highlights
#1 in 1914

"Ballin' The Jack" is one of the first popular songs to describe the movements of a dance. In the slang of the day *ballin' the jack* meant to *go full speed*. The saying came from a phrase used by lumberjacks and railroaders for full-throttle: *high ballin'*. The dance described in "Ballin' The Jack" featured suggestive bumps and grinds which shocked parents for over a decade until the dance faded from popularity in the late 1920s. "Ballin' The Jack" had been introduced in vaudeville by Billy Kent and Jeanette Warner in 1913, and a year later it was interpolated into the musical *The Girl From Utah* (1914). The renewed popularity of "Ballin' The Jack" was greatly aided by its revival in several Hollywood musicals: *For Me And My Gal* (1942); *On The Riviera* (1951); and *That's My Boy* (1951).

BEALE STREET BLUES

Words and Music by W.C. Handy

Chart Highlights
#5 in 1917
#21 in 1921
#16 in 1927
#20 in 1932
#20 in 1942

William Christopher Handy was born in Florence, Alabama in 1873. The son of a pastor, Handy's earliest musical urges were thwarted by his father who told his son: "I'd rather see you in a hearse than have you become a musician." Nevertheless, Handy purchased his first trumpet from a visiting circus musician and soon joined a traveling minstrel show. The hardships of the traveling life eventually led him home where his family convinced him to abandon music for the more stable profession of teaching. But the call of music was too strong to be put off for very long. In the 1890s Handy was back on the road pursuing his first love, music. "Beale Street Blues" is named for the street that Handy lived on in Memphis, Tennessee. It became the theme song of jazz trombonist Jack Teagarden and was featured in the film *St. Louis Blues* (1958) starring Nat 'King' Cole in the role of W.C. Handy.

BECAUSE

Words by Edward Teschemacher
Music by Guy d'Hardelot

Chart Highlights
#10 in 1910
#4 in 1913
#4 in 1948
#16 in 1951

"Because" is a high-brow, quasi-operatic love song that is still often sung at weddings. It has been recorded over fifty times since it was written in 1902. Enrico Caruso, Perry Como, and Mario Lanza all had hit recordings of "Because," and it was featured in the film *Three Smart Girls Grow Up* (1939) starring Deanna Durbin.

THE BELLS OF ST. MARY'S

Words by Douglas Furber
Music by A. Emmett Adams

Chart Highlights
#7 in 1920
#21 in 1946

In the 1920's a new vocal style called 'crooning' was pioneered by singer Rudy Vallee. Earlier popular vocalists invariably had to sing loud (jazz and vaudeville), high (Irish tenors), or both in order to be heard in the theaters and noisy dance clubs of the day. With the rapid development of recordings, microphones, and radio, a new, more intimate style of singing became possible. Vallee was the first singer to exploit this possibility. Because of his naturally weak voice — initially, his megaphone wasn't a gimmick; he *had* to use one to be heard — he would have never made it as a singer a generation earlier. But, thanks to radio in the 1920s, Vallee came across the airwaves with a soft, soothing sound that oozed romance and made him radio's first superstar.

The ultimate crooner was, of course, Harry Lillis Crosby of Tacoma, Washington. Crosby's nickname "Bing" referred to his reading habits; he was an avid fan of the newspaper cartoon "Bingville Bugle." Crosby soon eclipsed Vallee as a crooner, and by the mid-1930's he was well on his way to becoming an American institution both on record and on the silver screen. Before his death at the age of 73, in 1977, 'Bing' Crosby had sold a phenomenal 300 *million* records and had starred in over 50 movies. "The Bells Of St. Mary's" was used as the title song for the film of the same name in 1944, starring Crosby and Ingrid Bergman. The song was also part of the score for *The Godfather* (1972).

BY THE BEAUTIFUL SEA

Words by Harold R. Atteridge
Music by Harry Carroll

Chart Highlights
#1 in 1914

Vaudevillian Muriel Window performed "By The Beautiful Sea" in the *Passing Show of 1914*. The *Passing Shows* were an annual vaudeville review put on by the Shubert brothers between 1912 and 1924 in an attempt to compete with the trend-setting *Ziegfeld Follies*. "By The Beautiful Sea" was later featured in the films: *The Story Of Vernon And Irene Castle* (1939) and *Some Like It Hot* (1959).

BY THE LIGHT OF THE SILVERY MOON

Lyrics by Ed Madden
Music by Gus Edwards

Chart Highlights
#1 in 1910
#12 in 1942

"By The Light Of The Silvery Moon" had a very humble debut. Child vaudevillian Georgie Price, planted in the audience, stood up and sang the song as part of Gus Edwards' "School Boys And School Girls" sketch. The song quickly advanced from this hokey bit of theater to the *Ziegfeld Follies of 1909*. Lillian Lorraine, whom the ever-observant Florenz Ziegfeld once had described as the most beautiful woman he had ever seen, made "By The Light Of The Silvery Moon" the hit of the show. It eventually became Lorraine's personal theme song. Over the years several movies have helped keep "By The Light Of The Silvery Moon" popular: *Birth Of The Blues* (1941); *Sunbonnet Sue* (1945); *The Jolson Story* (1946); *Always Leave Them Laughing* (1949); and *Two Weeks With Love* (1950).

CARELESS LOVE

Anonymous

"Careless Love" is a traditional folk song that probably originated in the mountains of Appalachia during the early-19th century. With the rise of jazz around 1900 in New Orleans, "Careless Love," with its sad story of love gone wrong, was easily adapted to the blues. In 1921, W.C. Handy recorded his own arrangement of "Careless Love" and this version can be heard in his film biography *St. Louis Blues* (1958).

CHINATOWN, MY CHINATOWN

Words by William Jerome
Music by Jean Schwartz

Chart Highlights
#1 in 1915
#5 in 1932
#14 in 1935
#24 in 1952

"Chinatown, My Chinatown" was not an immediate hit for the team of William Jerome and Jean Schwartz. When they wrote the song in 1906, they had in mind a dreamy, romantic serenade. A few years later, when "Chinatown, My Chinatown" was interpolated into the revue *Up And Down Broadway* (1910), Eddy Foy sang it as an up-tempo dance number and the song became a hit. "Chinatown, My Chinatown" was later used in the films *Bright Lights* (1931); *Is Everybody Happy* (1943); *Jolson Sings Again* (1949); *The Seven Little Foys* (1955); and Woody Allen's *Radio Days* (1987).

COME, JOSEPHINE IN MY FLYING MACHINE (UP SHE GOES!)

Music by Fred Fisher
Words by Alfred Bryan

Chart Highlights
#1 in 1911

When brothers Orville and Wilbur Wright made their historic first flight at Kitty Hawk on December 17, 1903, they not only changed the world but they also provided Tin Pan Alley with a whole new topic to be exploited in song. "Come, Josephine In My Flying Machine" is the most memorable of the early aviation songs that dealt with the romantic potential of this new wave of technology. "Come, Josephine In My Flying Machine" was featured in two films: *The Story Of Vernon And Irene Castle* (1939); and the biography of Fred Fisher, the song's composer: *Oh, You Beautiful Doll* (1949).

CUDDLE UP A LITTLE CLOSER, LOVEY MINE

Words by Otto Harbach
Music by Karl Hoschna

Chart Highlights
#1 in 1908
#24 in 1942
#19 in 1943

"Cuddle Up A Little Closer" began life as a modest little number in a vaudeville sketch. It became a national hit after it was interpolated into the musical *The Three Twins* (1908) where it was sung by Alice Yorke. "Cuddle Up A Little Closer" was later used in a number of films: *The Story Of Vernon And Irene Castle* (1939); *Birth Of The Blues* (1941); *Coney Island* (1943); *Is Everybody Happy* (1943); and *On Moonlight Bay* (1951).

DANNY BOY (LONDONDERRY AIR)

Words by Frederick Edward Weatherly
Music is Irish Traditional

Chart Highlights
#5 in 1918
#17 in 1940
#10 in 1959

Frederick Weatherly's 1913 adaptation of the traditional Irish song "Londonderry Air" (1855) is near the top of the list of the 100 most recorded songs from the first half of the 20th century. Of the wide variety of musicians who have recorded "Danny Boy" over the years, the most notable performances have been by the big bands of William 'Count' Basie and Glenn Miller; the Irish crooners Bing Crosby and Dennis Day; the opera divas Ernestine Schumann-Heink, Eleanor Steber, and Eileen Farrell; and the country singers Conway Twitty and Ray Price. For many years singer-comedian Danny Thomas used "Danny Boy" as his personal theme song.

DARDANELLA

Words by Fred Fisher
Music by Felix Bernard and Johnny S. Black

Chart Highlights
#1 in 1920

"Dardanella" overcame its original lack-luster title — "Turkish Tom Toms" — to become the big hit of 1920. Ben Selvin's recording held the number-one position for thirteen weeks that year and became the first recording ever to sell over five million copies. Selvin's name is now generally forgotten but he probably still holds the record for making records. During his long career as a bandleader, Selvin made over 2,000 recordings with the likes of Benny Goodman, the Dorsey Brothers, Kate Smith, and Ethel Waters.

THE DARKTOWN STRUTTERS' BALL

Words and Music by Shelton Brooks

Chart Highlights
#2 in 1917
#1 in 1918
#12 in 1927
#29 in 1948
#7 in 1954

Vaudevillians Sophie Tucker and Blossom Seely made "The Darktown Strutters' Ball" a ragtime classic. Shelton Brooks had written the song in 1917 to commemorate a ball given at an Exposition in San Francisco. In the slang of the day, a "strutter" was a dancer. "The Darktown Strutters' Ball" can be heard in the films *The Story Of Vernon And Irene Castle* (1939); *Broadway* (1942); *The Dolly Sisters* (1945); and *Incendiary Blonde* (1945).

DOWN BY THE OLD MILL STREAM

Words and Music by Tell Taylor

Chart Highlights
#1 in 1911
#1 in 1912

"Down By The Old Mill Stream" was a giant hit with sheet music sales of around 5 to 6 million copies. How big a hit would that be today? Well, the U.S. population was only 92 million in 1910, the year "Down By The Old Mill Stream" was written. Today, there are over 250 million Americans. So, in order for one of today's pop hits to equal the impact of "Down By The Old Mill Stream" it would need to sell more than 16 million copies!

THE ENTERTAINER

By Scott Joplin

Chart Highlights
#3 in 1974

During the 1950s and 1960s, pianist Max Morath kept interest in ragtime alive through his performances on radio and educational television. In the early 1970s a scholarly ragtime revival began when musicologist Joshua Rifkin released an entertaining album of Scott Joplin. About that same time the New York Public Library put together the first collected edition of Scott Joplin's rags. "The Entertainer" was used as the theme for the Academy Award winning movie *The Sting* (1973). Composer Marvin Hamlisch received an Oscar for the film's score which featured adaptations of several Joplin rags. Suddenly, Joplin's music was again in the mainstream and "The Entertainer," a rag that Joplin had written in 1902, had finally become a hit.

EVERY LITTLE MOVEMENT (HAS A MEANING ALL ITS OWN)

Words by Otto Harbach
Music by Karl Hoschna

Chart Highlights
#1 in 1910

"Every Little Movement (Has A Meaning All Its Own)" was one of two hits from *Madame Sherry* (1910), the most memorable farce from the songwriting team of Otto Harbach and Karl Hoschna. The other hit from *Madame Sherry* was the interpolated "Put Your Arms Around Me Honey." "Every Little Movement (Has A Meaning All Its Own)" was later used in the movie *On Moonlight Bay* (1951).

FASCINATION (VALSE TZIGANE)

By F.D. Marchetti

Chart Highlights
#6 in 1914
#7 in 1957

Dick Manning added words to F.D. Marchetti's beautiful melody "Valse Tzigane (Gypsy Waltz)" in 1932. Twenty-five years later, another surge in popularity came when this melody was featured in the movie *Love In The Afternoon* (1957). Three recordings of "Fascination" made the charts that year: Jane Morgan (no. 7); Dinah Shore (no. 15); and Dick Jacobs (no. 17).

FOR ME AND MY GAL

Words by Edgar Leslie and E. Ray Goetz
Music by George W. Meyer

Chart Highlights
#1 in 1917
#3 in 1942
#17 in 1943

"For Me And My Gal" was by far George W. Meyer's biggest hit, selling over 3 million copies of sheet music. During The Great War it was popularized by such fabled vaudevillians as Al Jolson, Eddie Cantor, and Sophie Tucker. Twenty-five years later it was featured in a cinematic tribute to that era in *For Me And My Gal* (1942) starring Judy Garland and, in his motion picture debut, Gene Kelly. "For Me And My Gal" was also used in *Jolson Sings Again* (1949).

THE GLOW WORM

English Words by Lilla Cayley Robinson
German Words and Music by Paul Lincke

Chart Highlights
#1 in 1908
#1 in 1952

"The Glow Worm" was published in Germany in 1902 and introduced to America by May Naudain in the musical *The Girl Behind The Counter* (1907). Years later Johnny Mercer added lyrics and in 1952 the Mills Brothers had one of their greatest hits with Mercer's version of the song.

A GOOD MAN IS HARD TO FIND

Words and Music by Eddie Green

Chart Highlights
#2 in 1919
#8 in 1928

Pioneering blues singer Alberta Hunter introduced "A Good Man Is Hard To Find," but it was Marion Harris who had the first hit recording. The song was featured in the film *Meet Danny Wilson* (1952).

GOODBYE, MY LADY LOVE

Words and Music by Joseph E. Howard

Chart Highlights
#3 in 1904

"Goodbye, My Lady Love" is based on a melody published in 1900 called "Down South" composed by W.H. Myddleton. It was the first true ragtime song to cross over into the mainstream of American popular music. "Goodbye, My Lady Love" was later interpolated into two productions of the musical *Show Boat* (1927, 1946) where it was used to add some authenticity to the 1900s scenes. For the same reason the song was also used in both film versions of *Show Boat* (1936, 1951). Composer Joseph Howard's colorful life was the subject of a Hollywood biography in the film *I Wonder Who's Kissing Her Now* (1947).

Gypsy Love Song

Words by Harry B. Smith
Music by Victor Herbert

Chart Highlights
#1 in 1899
#14 in 1920

Born in Dublin, Ireland, raised in London, England, and receiving his classical musical training in Germany, composer Victor Herbert showed little sign of becoming one of the giants of American popular music before he quietly immigrated to the States in 1886. Herbert came to America because his wife, Theresa Förester, had been engaged to sing at the Metropolitan Opera. Herbert played cello in the opera orchestra and was soon well-known in New York City as both a soloist and a conductor. But it wasn't until Herbert received a commission from the first lady of American theater, Lillian Russell in 1893, that he considered making the transition from the concert hall to the Broadway stage. In 1898, after several successful operettas, Herbert's *The Fortune Teller*, opened on Broadway. With songs like "Gypsy Love Song," "Romany Life," and "Czardas," Herbert had taken his first step toward immortality.

Hearts and Flowers

Words by Mary D. Brine
Music by Theodore Moses Tobani

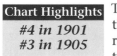
#4 in 1901
#3 in 1905

The release of the first silent movies around the turn of the century was followed by the rapid spread of nickelodeons throughout the country as everyone wanted to view this amazing new invention. Suddenly there was a need for background music to accompany the flickering action on the screen. "Hearts And Flowers" was one of the earliest of these movie instrumentals. It was used so often that it became a musical cliché. Countless pianists and organists used it to accompany melodramatic scenes such as when the sinister, mustache-twirling villain demanded the rent from a desperate, young widow…or else.

Hello! My Baby

Words by Ida Emerson
Music by Joseph E. Howard

#1 in 1899

Vaudevillians Joseph Howard and Ida Emerson were husband and wife when they wrote "Hello! My Baby," their biggest hit. According to legend, Howard got the idea for the song when he overheard a Black porter talking to his girlfriend on the new-fangled telephone.

(There'll Be) A Hot Time in the Old Town Tonight

Words by Joe Hayden
Music by Theodore M. Metz

Chart Highlights
#1 in 1896
#1 in 1897

Originally written in 1886 for a minstrel show, "A Hot Time In The Old Town Tonight" became one of the most popular songs of the Spanish-American War (1898). Supposedly, it was sung by Teddy Roosevelt's Rough Riders *during* their famous charge up San Juan Hill. Metz claimed to have been inspired to write the song when he witnessed a fire in Old Town, Louisiana.

How 'Ya Gonna Keep 'Em Down on the Farm?
(After They've Seen Paree)

Words by Sam M. Lewis and Joe Young
Music by Walter Donaldson

Chart Highlights
#2 in 1919

With three recordings in the top ten in 1919, "How 'Ya Gonna Keep 'Em Down On The Farm?" captured, in a light-hearted fashion, the universal sigh of relief that marked the conclusion of The Great War and the return of the doughboys. The song quickly became a staple of vaudeville with Sophie Tucker and Eddie Cantor leading the way singing their very different interpretations. You can hear Eddie Cantor singing "How 'Ya Gonna Keep 'Em Down On The Farm?" — although you'll *see* Keefe Brasselle moving his lips — in the film *The Eddie Cantor Story* (1953).

I Didn't Raise My Boy to Be a Soldier

Words by Alfred Bryan
Music by Al Piantadosi

Chart Highlights
#1 in 1915

The Great War began with the assassination of Austrian Archduke Ferdinand by a Serbian nationalist in Sarajevo on June 24, 1914. From the outset, most Americans wanted nothing to do with the war in Europe—the general feeling being that it was none of our business. President Woodrow Wilson's successful reelection campaign in 1916 rallied the country around the slogan: "He Kept Us Out Of War." While the war raged in the trenches of France, the mood of America at this time was definitely one of neutrality and pacifism. The *Pittsburgh Gazetter-Times* hailed "I Didn't Raise My Boy To Be A Soldier" as "the song that would end the war." With this kind of political atmosphere, it is not surprising that two different recordings of "I Didn't Raise My Boy To Be A Soldier" reached number one in 1915.

I Love a Piano

Words and Music by Irving Berlin

Chart Highlights
#1 in 1916

Irving Berlin wrote "I Love A Piano" for the Broadway musical *Stop! Look! Listen!* (1915). In the original staging of this show, the singer Harry Fox performed the song on a fantastic set made up of a gigantic piano keyboard that stretched across the entire stage. Also on stage with Fox were six pianists who played the song's melody. For many years Irving Berlin felt that this was one of his best songs. It can be heard in the film *Easter Parade* (1948).

I Want a Girl (Just Like the Girl That Married Dear Old Dad)

Words by William Dillon
Music by Harry von Tilzer

Chart Highlights
#2 in 1911

This is one of the all-time great barbershop quartet songs from the turn of the century. "I Want A Girl (Just Like The Girl That Married Dear Old Dad)" is used in the films *Show Business* (1944) and *The Jolson Story* (1946). During the 1950s and 1960s, ragtime pianist Jo Ann Castle helped revive "I Want A Girl" through her many appearances as a regular on the Lawrence Welk Television Show.

I Wonder Who's Kissing Her Now

Lyrics by Will M. Hough and Frank R. Adams
Music by Joseph E. Howard and Harold Orlob

Chart Highlights
#1 in 1909
#4 in 1910
#2 in 1947

The melody to "I Wonder Who's Kissing Her Now" was written by Harold Orlob while he was employed as an arranger for vaudevillian Joseph E. Howard who introduced the song in the Chicago production of *The Prince Of Tonight* (1909). Howard considered the song done 'for hire' and took full credit for writing it himself, making it his theme song. "I Wonder Who's Kissing Her Now," of course, became a tremendous hit and it earned Howard a small fortune in royalties. It wasn't until 1947, when the screen biography of Howard was being released, that Orlob came forward to file a suit to have himself named as the true composer of the song. The two old-timers reached an agreement in which Howard granted Orlob co-author status and Orlob dropped his claims on the many years of lost earnings from his song. "I Wonder Who's Kissing Her Now" can be heard in *The Time, The Place, And The Girl* (1946) and, of course, in Howard's screen biography *I Wonder Who's Kissing Her Now* (1947).

I'm Always Chasing Rainbows

Words by Joseph McCarthy
Music by Harry Carroll

Chart Highlights
#1 in 1918
#5 in 1946

The beautiful melody of "I'm Always Chasing Rainbows" is taken almost note-for-note from the slow, middle section of Frederick Chopin's *Fantaisie Impromptu in C# minor*. Tin Pan Alley composer Harry Carroll never denied the fact that he had plagiarized Chopin's melody, but he must have felt chagrined that the biggest hit of his career used another man's tune. Judy Garland sings "I'm Always Chasing Rainbows" with Charles Winninger in the film *Ziegfeld Girl* (1941). The song was later used in *Nobody's Darling* (1943), *The Merry Monahans* (1944), and the *Dolly Sisters* (1946). At the height of this revival of interest in "I'm Always Chasing Rainbows" in the 1940s, Perry Como had a million-selling hit with his recording of the song that was released just in time for Valentine's Day, 1946.

I'm Falling in Love with Someone

Words by Rida Johnson Young
Music by Victor Herbert

Chart Highlights
#1 in 1911
#9 in 1912
#4 in 1935

"I'm Falling In Love With Someone" was introduced by Orville Harold in the operetta *Naughty Marietta* which opened in New York on November 7, 1910. The three other hits from this, Victor Herbert's masterpiece, are "Ah, Sweet Mystery Of Life," "Italian Street Song," and "Tramp, Tramp, Tramp." *Naughty Marietta* was brought to the screen in 1935 with Jeanette MacDonald and Nelson Eddy in the leads, and "I'm Falling In Love With Someone" is also part of the score of *The Great Victor Herbert* (1939).

If I Had My Way

Words by Lou Klein
Music by James Kendis

Chart Highlights
#3 in 1914
#19 in 1936
#20 in 1939

"If I Had My Way" can be heard in the films *If I Had My Way* (1940) and *Sunbonnet Sue* (1945).

If You Were the Only Girl in the World

Words by Clifford Grey
Music by Nat D. Ayer

Chart Highlights
#14 in 1946

"If You Were The Only Girl In The World" began life as an uptempo fox-trot in the London musical *The Bing Boys Are Here* (1916). Many years later, singer Rudy Vallee came up with the idea of crooning it as a romantic waltz and sang it that way in his first film, *The Vagabond Lover* (1929).

Hubert Prior Vallee took the name 'Rudy' hoping to profit from the fame of legendary silent-screen sex symbol Rudolph Valentino who had died in 1926. Vallee and his band, the Yale Collegians, were given their first big break when they were booked to open at New York's Heigh-Ho Club on January 8, 1928. At the last minute the club's manager objected to Vallee's vocalist and threatened to cancel the engagement unless a new singer was found. Unable to find a replacement on such short notice, Vallee laid down his saxophone, grabbed a megaphone to amplify his weak singing voice, and stepped forward to save the day. Radio broadcasts from locations like the Heigh-Ho Club were just coming into vogue. Shortly after Vallee's successful debut as a singer, WABC began nightly broadcasts of his show. Vallee took on the role of on-air host beginning each broadcast with one of the medium's first catch phrases: "Heigh-ho, everybody!" The immense popularity that Vallee was to enjoy as radio's first sex symbol was already evident a year later when the police had to be summoned to maintain order at one of his performances. The twenty-eight-year-old crooner clearly led the way for later pop idols like Frank Sinatra, Elvis Presley, and The Beatles.

In the Shade of the Old Apple Tree

Words by Harry H. Williams
Music by Egbert Van Alstyne

Chart Highlights
#1 in 1905
#13 in 1933

Egbert Van Alstyne got the idea for "In The Shade Of The Old Apple Tree" while he was strolling through New York City's beautiful Central Park. Henry Burr's recording of the song held the top spot on the charts for seven weeks in 1905, and recordings by Albert Campbell and the Haydn Quartet both reached number two that same year. By comparison, Arthur Pryor's instrumental recording was a relative flop when it only reached number nine a few months later. The 1933 revival was by 'Duke' Ellington.

Indiana (Back Home Again in Indiana)

Words by Ballard MacDonald
Music by James F. Hanley

Chart Highlights
#8 in 1917
#19 in 1929

"Indiana" was the flip side of one of the most famous releases in the history of recorded sound: the first jazz record ever made. The group making this historic first was The Original Dixieland Jass Band led by cornetist Nick La Rocca. Musicians had just begun using the word "jazz" to describe the new, wilder dance music they were playing. This music and the term were so new that the spelling was still uncertain, as can be seen in the announcement of this ground-breaking release in the *Victor Records* catalogue of March 17, 1917: "Spell it Jass, Jas, Jaz, or Jazz—nothing can spoil a Jass band." The A-side of this historic recording was "The Darktown Strutters' Ball."

It's a Long, Long Way to Tipperary

Words and Music by Jack Judge and Harry Williams

Chart Highlights
#1 in 1914
#1 in 1915

A Long, Long Way To Tipperary" was written in England in 1912, but it did not become popular in America until the early days of The Great War. What had been written as a sentimental love ballad for the British music halls in 1912 was transformed into one of the most familiar marching songs of the War. "It's A Long, Long Way To Tipperary" was later featured in the films *For Me And My Gal* (1942) *Wait Till The Sun Shines, Nellie* (1952); and *What Price Glory?* (1952).

K-K-K-Katy

Words and Music by Geoffrey O'Hara

Chart Highlights
#3 in 1918

A huge hit during The Great War, "K-K-K-Katy" was originally billed as "The Sensational Stammering Song Success Sung By The Soldiers And Sailors." It was one of the many humorous songs that poked fun at the romantic adventures of the doughboys stationed in France. Jack Oakey gives the song a memorable performance in the film *Tin Pan Alley* (1940).

LET ME CALL YOU SWEETHEART

Words by Beth Slater Whitson
Music by Leo Friedman

Chart Highlights
#1 in 1911

In 1909, Beth Slater Whitson and Leo Friedman had written "Meet Me Tonight in Dreamland," a song that sold 2 million copies of sheet music. Unfortunately, the inexperienced authors had sold the song to a publisher for a small fee and received no royalties from these sales. They got another chance at fortune as well as fame with "Let Me Call You Sweetheart." Having learned a hard lesson in how heartless the music business can be, the songwriters worked out a much better deal for their second hit. This time they each made about $500,000 in royalties as "Let Me Call You Sweetheart" sold over 5 million copies of sheet music.

LET THE REST OF THE WORLD GO BY

Words by J. Keirn Brennan
Music by Ernest R. Ball

Chart Highlights
#2 in 1920

"Let The Rest Of The World Go By" was featured by the tenor Morton Downey on his popular radio show during the thirties. Downey, who billed himself as the "Irish thrush," was named in a national poll taken in 1932 as the best male singer on the air. This kind of popularity helped the Irish tenor earn around $250,000 per year during the Depression.

MANDY

Words and Music by Irving Berlin

Chart Highlights
#2 in 1919
#5 in 1920

Irving Berlin wrote "Mandy" as a minstrel number for his all-soldier show *Yip, Yip, Yaphank* (1918). Later the song was used in a post-war edition of the *Ziegfeld Follies* (1919). Berlin revived the song for his World War II show and movie *This Is The Army* (1942) — starring Kate Smith and future president Ronald Reagan — and Berlin, who was way ahead of his time in terms of recycling, again revived "Mandy" in *White Christmas* (1954).

MAPLE LEAF RAG

Music by Scott Joplin

Chart Highlights
#2 in 1907

Scott Joplin did not invent ragtime. It was already a vibrant musical style when he was hired as the pianist at the Maple Leaf Club in Sedalia, Missouri, in 1895. Joplin, 33 years old at the time, had already spent nearly twenty years playing piano in honky tonks, brothels, and social clubs from Louisiana to Chicago. Joplin published his first rag in 1899, and John Stark, the owner of the local music store, became interested in Joplin's music, especially a rag that Joplin had named after the Maple Leaf Club. Joplin had prophetically commented that this rag "will make me the king of ragtime composers." Stark paid Joplin $50.00 for the "Maple Leaf Rag" plus the promise of royalties on each copy sold. The "Maple Leaf Rag" went on sale in Stark's music store in September of 1899. Within a few years ragtime had become a national passion, and Joplin, the poor kid from Texarkana, Arkansas, had truly become its king.

MARCH OF THE TOYS

By Victor Herbert

Chart Highlights
#4 in 1911
#14 in 1939

Noting the success of Frank Baum's *Wizard Of Oz* (1903), Victor Herbert and lyricist Glen MacDonough set out to write their own fairy tale fantasy. Their creation, *Babes In Toyland*, opened at the Majestic Theater on October 13, 1903. While the story of the *Wizard Of Oz* lives on, the music from the Broadway show is now long forgotten, overshadowed by the totally new score that was written for the 1939 screen version. Just the opposite happened with *Babes In Toyland*. The songs, "March Of The Toys" and "Toyland," have far outlived the rest of the original show. The screen version of *Babes In Toyland* (1934)— which has since been renamed *March Of The Wooden Soldiers* — stars Laurel and Hardy.

MARCHETA (A LOVE SONG OF OLD MEXICO)

Words and Music by Victor L. Schertzinger

Chart Highlights
#5 in 1922
#8 in 1923
#12 in 1924

When he composed "Marcheta" in 1913, Victor Schertzinger was heavily influenced by Otto Nicolai's overture to the opera *The Merry Wives Of Windsor* which had been premiered in Berlin in 1849. In fact, Schertzinger probably had a copy of the score lying open on his piano while he was composing his one and only hit. Schertzinger certainly wasn't the first, nor will he be the last, composer to flatter a past master of classical music by swiping one of their best tunes.

MEET ME TONIGHT IN DREAMLAND

Words by Beth Slater Whitson
Music by Leo Friedman

Chart Highlights
#1 in 1910
#13 in 1938

The location of the rendezvous sung about in "Meet Me Tonight In Dreamland" is not some exotic, romantic hideaway. The song was inspired by the first Coney Island amusement park, *Dreamland*. This park had opened in 1902 at the then astronomical cost of $2,000,000. "Meet Me Tonight In Dreamland" is featured in the film *In The Good Old Summertime* (1949).

MEMORIES

Words by Gus Kahn
Music by Egbert Van Alstyne

Chart Highlights
#4 in 1916

"Memories" was the first hit from the pen of Gus Kahn, a thirty-year-old lyricist then newly arrived at Tin Pan Alley from Chicago. Working with several composers over the next twenty-five years, Kahn became one of the most successful lyricists of all time. Here are just a few of the memorable standards that are part of Kahn's incredible string of hits: "Ain't We Got Fun"; "Carolina In The Morning"; "Dream A Little Dream Of Me"; "I'll See You In My Dreams"; "It Had To Be You"; "Josephine"; "Makin' Whoopee"; "My Baby Just Cares For Me"; "My Buddy"; "Nobody's Sweetheart Now"; "Pretty Baby"; "Swingin' Down The Lane"; "Toot, Toot Tootsie (Goo' Bye)"; "The Waltz You Saved For Me"; and "Yes Sir, That's My Baby". It is no wonder that Kahn is the *only* lyricist to ever have his biography made into a movie: *I'll See You In My Dreams* (1951).

THE MERRY WIDOW WALTZ

Words by Adrian Ross
Music by Franz Lehar

Chart Highlights
#2 in 1907
#3 in 1908

After having conquered both Vienna (1905) and London (1906), *The Merry Widow* premiered on Broadway at the New Amsterdam Theatre on October 21, 1907. This first run lasted 416 performances. Subsequent revivals have introduced succeeding generations to Lehar's wonderful music. On the silver screen there have been three *Merry Widows* in 1925, 1934, and 1952.

MOONLIGHT BAY

Words by Edward Madden
Music by Percy Wenrich

Chart Highlights
#1 in 1912
#14 in 1951

Percy Wenrich was only 25 when he wrote "Moonlight Bay," one of the all-time great golden oldies. Since it was written in 1912, "Moonlight Bay" has been 'sung-along' countless times and was featured in the films *Tin Pan Alley* (1940) and *On Moonlight Bay* (1951).

MY GAL SAL

Words and Music by Paul Dresser

Chart Highlights
#1 in 1907
#11 in 1921

Paul Dresser left his unhappy home in Indiana in 1873, at the age of 16, to become a blackface performer in a traveling medicine show. A lowly start to be sure, but it gave Dresser a chance to try his hand at writing comedy songs and parodies. Eventually, Dresser made his way to the Big Time in New York as the end man in a minstrel show. It was about this time that he changed his name from Dreiser to Dresser. (The Dreiser family still made their mark through the writings of Paul's younger brother, the famed novelist Theodore Dreiser.)

In New York, Dresser turned from writing comedy songs to concentrate on composing sentimental ballads such as "I Believe It For My Mother Told Me So"; "The Letter That Never Came"; "The Pardon That Came Too Late"; etc. Dresser spent the fortune that he earned from these popular songs as fast as he made it. When sentimental balladry suddenly went out of fashion after the turn of the century, the high-living Dresser was soon ruined financially.

Dresser was thirty-nine years old when his life hit bottom, an emotionally broken man living again in poverty. But he still had one last, great sentimental ballad left in him. In it he would tell the story of Sally, a girl he had fallen in love with when he was a young man but had let slip through his fingers. The song, of course, was "My Gal Sal," and it became Dresser's greatest hit. Unfortunately, almost all of the song's success came after Dresser's death in 1906. "My Gal Sal" can be heard in Dresser's film biography *My Gal Sal* (1942).

MY LITTLE GIRL

Words by Sam M. Lewis and William Dillon
Music by Albert von Tilzer

Chart Highlights
#2 in 1915

The 1915 hit recording of this song was performed by the singing duo of Ada Jones and Will Robbins. The English-born Jones was by far the most popular female vocalist of the first two decades of the twentieth century. She had a strong contralto voice and her humorous delivery made the most of her ability to master ethnic dialects. She died in 1922, a few weeks shy of her fiftieth birthday.

My Melancholy Baby

Words by George Norton
Music by Ernie Burnett

Chart Highlights
#9 in 1915
#3 in 1928
#20 in 1935
#6 in 1936
#14 in 1939
#5 in 1947
#26 in 1959

Under its original title of "Melancholy," "My Melancholy Baby" was first performed at the Dutch Mill Club in Denver in 1912. Besides being recorded by everyone from Bing Crosby to Barbra Streisand, "My Melancholy Baby" has been used in at least two films: *Birth Of The Blues* (1941) and *A Star Is Born* (1954).

Oh! How I Hate to Get Up in the Morning

Words and Music by Irving Berlin

Chart Highlights
#1 in 1918

"Oh! How I Hate To Get Up In The Morning" was part of the all-soldier musical *Yip, Yip, Yaphank* (1918) that Irving Berlin wrote and performed in while he was stationed at Camp Upton, in Long Island, N.Y. Berlin repeated his performance when he used the song again for his second all-soldier show *This Is The Army* (1942). Berlin sang "Oh! How I Hate To Get Up In The Morning" in the film version of this show the following year, but he *didn't* sing it in the earlier film *Alexander's Ragtime Band* (1938). This honor went to Jack Haley. Berlin donated all of the royalties from this song to the Army Emergency Relief fund.

Oh Johnny, Oh Johnny, Oh!

Words by Ed Rose
Music by Abe Olman

Chart Highlights
#1 in 1917
#2 in 1939

"Oh Johnny, Oh Johnny, Oh!" was the only hit to come out of the Broadway musical *Follow Me* (1916) which closed after only 78 performances. Orrin Tucker and his orchestra, featuring singer "Wee" Bonnie Baker, saved "Oh Johnny, Oh Johnny, Oh!" from musical oblivion when they had a hit with it in 1939. "Oh Johnny, Oh Johnny, Oh!" became Baker's personal theme song.

Oh! You Beautiful Doll

Words by A. Seymour Brown
Music by Nat D. Ayer

Chart Highlights
#1 in 1912

"Oh! You Beautiful Doll" gained a second wave of popularity when it was used in the following films: *Wharf Angel* (1934); *The Story Of Vernon And Irene Castle* (1939); *For Me And My Gal* (1942); and, of course, *Oh! You Beautiful Doll* (1949). Antique car buffs may also recall that part of the melody of "Oh! You Beautiful Doll" was used on Gabriel-Trumpet car horns during the 1920s.

On Wisconsin!

Words by Carl Beck
Music by W.T. Purdy

Chart Highlights
#5 in 1915

The early decades of the twentieth century were the golden era of college fight songs. Many of these old songs are still being sung by fans to rally their teams almost a hundred years after the songs were written. In addition to "On Wisconsin!" the honor roll from these years would include: Yale's "The Whiffenpoof Song"; "The Notre Dame Victory March"; University of Michigan's "The Victors"; "Washington and Lee Swing"; the Naval Academy's "Anchors Aweigh"; and everyone's favorite "Sweetheart Of Sigma Chi."

Over There

Words and Music by George M. Cohan

Chart Highlights
#1 in 1917
#1 in 1918

"Over There" was written on April 8, 1917, just a day after President Woodrow Wilson had signed a declaration of War against Germany. For three years America had watched Europe tear itself apart, and the national sentiment had gradually shifted from the isolationist feelings expressed in the 1915 hit "I Didn't Raise My Boy To Be A Soldier" to those that were so brilliantly given voice to in Cohan's rousing patriotic anthem. By the end of the Great War in 1918, "Over There" had sold two million copies of sheet music and over one million records. "Over There" was originally featured in the musical *Zig Zag* (1917) and later revived for Cohan's musical biography *George M!* (1968).

Pack Up Your Troubles in Your Old Kit Bag and Smile, Smile, Smile

Words by George Asaf
Music by Felix Powell

Chart Highlights
#1 in 1917
#1 in 1918

"Pack Up Your Troubles In Your Old Kit Bag And Smile, Smile, Smile" was introduced by Adele Rowland in the Broadway musical *Her Soldier Boy* (1915, London 1916). While America observed the War from the sidelines, "Pack Up Your Troubles In Your Old Kit Bag And Smile, Smile, Smile" helped arouse sympathy for the Allies. When the United States finally entered the war in the Spring of 1917, "Pack Up Your Troubles In Your Old Kit Bag And Smile, Smile, Smile" became an instant hit. It can be heard in the films: *It's A Great Life* (1929); *What's Cookin'?* (1942); *Wait Till The Sun Shines, Nellie* (1952); *On Moonlight Bay* (1951); and *What Price Glory?* (1952).

Paper Doll

Words and Music by Johnny S. Black

Chart Highlights
#20 in 1942
#1 in 1943

The Mills Brothers recorded over a thousand songs between their first hit in 1931, "Tiger Rag," and their last one in 1968, "Cab Driver." None of these songs matched their smooth vocal style better than this, their theme song. "Paper Doll" had been written in 1915 but, surprisingly, it aroused very little interest at that time. Composer Johnny Black died in the 1930s with a rag-song, "Dardanella," being his only major hit. The Mills Brothers originally released "Paper Doll" in the Fall of 1942, and their recording reached only number twenty on the charts. Knowing that the song was better than that, they re-released it the following summer. This time, "Paper Doll" worked its way up to the top of the charts where it held the number one spot for twelve straight weeks, making it one of the top songs of the decade. Eventually the Mills Brothers' recording of "Paper Doll" sold over six million records.

Peg o' My Heart

Words by Alfred Bryan
Music by Fred Fisher

Chart Highlights
#1 in 1913
#7 in 1914
#1 in 1947

"Peg O' My Heart" was introduced in the *Ziegfeld Follies of 1913* where it was sung by José Collins. Fred Fisher, probably the only American composer who could also claim membership in the French Foreign Legion, wrote "Peg O' My Heart" after seeing Laurette Taylor in the Broadway play *Peg O' My Heart*. As huge a hit as "Peg O' My Heart" was in 1913 and 1914, it was an even bigger hit when it was revived in 1947: six different recordings of it made the top-ten that year. The classic interpretation from that year was by the Harmonicats, a recording which sold over a million copies.

Play a Simple Melody

Words and Music by Irving Berlin

Chart Highlights
#8 in 1915
#4 in 1916
#2 in 1950

"Play A Simple Melody" was introduced in the syncopated musical *Watch Your Step* (1914) where it was sung by Sallie Fisher and Charles King. In this duet Irving Berlin successfully married the sentimental-ballad style of the 19th century to the jagged rhythms of modern ragtime. This was quite a presumptuous undertaking since everyone in 1914 assumed that the two styles were both musically and morally incompatible. "Play A Simple Melody" was revived on vinyl in 1950 by Bing Crosby and his son Gary, and a few years later on film by Ethel Merman and Dan Dailey in the movie *There's No Business Like Show Business* (1954).

Poor Butterfly

Words by John L. Golden
Music by Raymond Hubbell

Chart Highlights
#1 in 1917
#12 in 1954

Giacomo Puccini's famous opera *Madama Butterfly* premiered at Milan's Teatro La Scala in 1904. The tragic story of Cio-Cio San and Pinkerton soon became well known even by those who had never set foot in an opera house. For an upcoming Hippodrome extravaganza, *The Big Show* (1916), John Golden and Raymond Hubbell were assigned the task of writing a topical song for an oriental singer. They assumed that the mystery singer would be Tamaka Miura, a Japanese diva who had recently achieved some fame singing the role of Cio-Cio San. With this singer in mind, Golden and Hubbell hit upon the clever idea of writing a song based on the operatic *Butterfly*. It was a clever idea, but the singer who showed up at the Hippodrome was not Miura but a Chinese vaudevillian with an awful voice. "Poor Butterfly" managed to survive several days of lackluster performances by the Chinese performer before Sophie Bernard could be brought in as a replacement. Bernard was neither Japanese nor an opera star, but she could put a song over, even in the cavernous, 5,000-seat Hippodrome. She made "Poor Butterfly" the hit of the show and helped it on its way to selling over four million copies of sheet music.

Pretty Baby

Words by Gus Kahn
Music by Egbert Van Alstyne and Tony Jackson

Chart Highlights
#1 in 1916

"Pretty Baby" was first heard as a minor chorus number in the musical *A World Of Pleasure* (1915). Showing some hit potential, the song was interpolated into the *Passing Show of 1916* where it was featured as a solo by Dolly Hackett. "Pretty Baby" has been used in a number of films, including *Rose of Washington Square* (1939); *Is Everybody Happy* (1943); *Broadway Rhythm* (1944); *Jolson Sings Again* (1949); and *I'll See You In My Dreams* (1951).

A Pretty Girl Is Like A Melody

Words and Music by Irving Berlin

Chart Highlights
#1 in 1919

"A Pretty Girl Is Like A Melody" was introduced in the *Ziegfeld Follies* (1919), and for the last seventy years it has been the one song most closely associated with Ziegfeld's glorification of feminine beauty. In the original production, John Steel sang the song surrounded by showgirls dressed in costumes representing famous classical music compositions.

Put On Your Old Grey Bonnet

Words by Stanley Murphy
Music by Percy Wenrich

Chart Highlights
#1 in 1909
#3 in 1910
#11 in 1937

Percy Wenrich made his way from his birthplace in Joplin, Missouri, to the big time via Chicago, Illinois and Milwaukee, Wisconsin. In 1909, the twenty-two-year-old composer visited the offices of New York music publisher Jerome H. Remick to personally plug his latest song: "Put On Your Old Grey Bonnet." Remick, at that time one of the most powerful men in music publishing, was not impressed by either the song or its youthful composer from the provincial Midwest. A few days later, however, Remick called Wenrich back to his office. It seemed that the simple melody of "Put On Your Old Grey Bonnet" had been running through the publisher's head ever since Wenrich had sung it for him. Remick commented: "Any song that even I can't forget must become a hit." He was, of course, absolutely right. "Put On Your Old Grey Bonnet" became one of the biggest hits of the decade, spending eleven weeks at the top of the charts and ringing up sales of over two million copies of sheet music. Remick's respect for the Midwest grew as he went on to publish two other giant hits by Wenrich: "On Moonlight Bay" (1912) and "When You Wore A Tulip" (1914).

Put Your Arms Around Me, Honey

Words by Junie McCree
Music by Albert von Tilzer

Chart Highlights
#1 in 1911
#19 in 1942
#4 in 1943

"Put Your Arms Around Me, Honey" was introduced in 1910 by Elizabeth Murray, but it was the interpretation of the famed vaudevillian Blossom Seely that made it a hit. "Put Your Arms Around Me, Honey" has been used in the following films: *Coney Island* (1943); *Louisiana Hayride* (1944); and *In The Good Old Summertime* (1949).

Ragtime Cowboy Joe

Words and Music by Lewis F. Muir,
Grant Clarke and Maurice Abrahams

Chart Highlights
#1 in 1912
#14 in 1939
#16 in 1947
#10 in 1949
#16 in 1959

The year 1912 was an important one for the good citizens of Arizona. On February 14, the Arizona Territory became the 48th state of the Union. Inspired by this event, Tin Pan Alley immortalized the new state with a novelty song about its most famous, albeit legendary, native son: "Ragtime Cowboy Joe." By the end of the year the song was number one and the whole country was singing about the "high fallutin', scootin', shootin', son-of-a-gun from Arizona." Thanks to performances by Paul Whiteman, Jo Stafford, and even The Chipmunks, "Ragtime Cowboy Joe" has maintained his popularity over the decades. The song was used in the films *Hello Frisco, Hello* (1942); and *Incendiary Blonde* (1945).

Rock-A-Bye Your Baby with A Dixie Melody

Words by Sam M. Lewis and Joe Young
Music by Jean Schwartz

Chart Highlights
#1 in 1918
#10 in 1956
#37 in 1961

One of Al Jolson's biggest hits, "Rock-A-Bye Your Baby With A Dixie Melody" was introduced by the legendary performer in the extravaganza *Sinbad* (1918). In addition to Wayne Newton, singers as diverse as Jerry Lewis (1956) and Aretha Franklin (1961) have kept this great song alive.

Rose of Washington Square

Lyric by Ballard MacDonald
Music by James F. Hanley

Chart Highlights
#3 in 1920
#10 in 1939

Fanny Brice introduced "Rose Of Washington Square" in the show *Ziegfeld Midnight Frolic* (1920) and the song soon became her theme song.

Row, Row, Row

Words by William Jerome
Music by Jimmie V. Monaco

Chart Highlights
#1 in 1913
#15 in 1940

"Row, Row, Row" was written for the *Ziegfeld Follies of 1912* where it was sung by the beautiful Lillian Lorraine. It was later used in the films *Incendiary Blonde* (1945); *Two Weeks With Love* (1950); and *The Seven Little Foys* (1955).

SCHOOL DAYS

Words by Will D. Cobb
Music by Gus Edwards

Chart Highlights
#1 in 1907
#3 in 1908

The early Twentieth Century was filled with mind-boggling technological changes. Within a little over a decade, telephones, horseless carriages, moving pictures, phonographs, flying machines, and the wireless had all become part of everyday life. By the 1920s, the Nineteenth Century had become a dim memory, especially for those who had moved from the family farm to the big city. The nostalgic tone of "School Days" struck a responsive chord as America experienced a wave of longing for the simplicity of its recent, rural days. It was written in 1906 to be part of a vaudeville skit: *Gus Edward's School Boys and Girls* (1907). In this famous skit, Gus Edwards played the role of a schoolmaster surrounded by a precocious class of juvenile singers, dancers, and comedians. "Schools Days" sold over three million copies of sheet music making it one of the most popular songs of this century. Bing Crosby portrayed Gus Edwards in the film *The Star Maker* (1939).

SHINE ON, HARVEST MOON

Words by Jack Norworth
Music by Nora Bayes and Jack Norworth

Chart Highlights
#1 in 1909
#5 in 1910
#9 in 1931
#19 in 1943

One of the most famous songs of this era, "Shine On, Harvest Moon" was introduced in the *Ziegfeld Follies of 1908* by Nora Bayes, the "Empress of Vaudeville." Bayes and her husband Jack Norworth were major stars of this era, and their life together is the subject of the movie *Shine On, Harvest Moon* (1944). "Shine on, Harvest Moon" was also interpolated by Bayes into the musical *Miss Innocence* (1908) and sung by Ruth Etting in the *Ziegfeld Follies of 1931*, the last show produced by the great Ziegfeld. "Shine On, Harvest Moon" was used for the movies *Ever Since Eve* (1937); *Nancy Goes To Rio* (1950); and *The Eddy Duchin Story* (1956).

SMILES

Words by J. Will Callahan
Music by Lee S. Roberts

Chart Highlights
#1 in 1918

"Smiles" was introduced by Nell Carrington in the *Passing Show of 1918*. According to Tin Pan Alley legend, composer Lee Roberts wrote the tune for this three-million seller and perennial favorite on the back of a pack of cigarettes. "Smiles" has been used in the films *The Dolly Sisters* (1945); *Somebody Loves Me* (1952); *Wait Till The Sun Shines, Nellie* (1952); and *What Price Glory?* (1952).

SNOOKEY OOKUMS

Words and Music by Irving Berlin

Chart Highlights
#4 in 1913

Irving Berlin wrote "Snookey Ookums" in 1913 while he was staying at the Hotel Sherman in Chicago. His fledgling publishing company, Waterson, Berlin and Snyder, needed a hit to help launch their Chicago office. Locked in his room, Berlin created "Snookey Ookums" from one of the day's catch-phrases: "I had thought what a laugh would be sent up by a song wherein a half-sized man gurgled baby-talk to a whale of a woman…"

SOME OF THESE DAYS

Words and Music by Shelton Brooks

Chart Highlights
#2 in 1911
#5 in 1923
#1 in 1927
#16 in 1932

Russian-born Sophie Tucker — her real name was Sonia Kalish — began her career in 1906 when, at the age of 18, she appeared in an amateur-night contest. A large woman with unattractive features, Tucker was advised to perform in blackface. One day, traveling the 'small time' vaudeville circuit, her trunk failed to arrive in time for an engagement at a burlesque house in Boston. Without her usual costume and blackface makeup, Tucker was forced to take the stage as herself. When she found that the audience loved her as she was, Tucker swore that she would never wear blackface again.

Turning from blackface also meant a change in repertoire from minstrel songs to ragtime. Tucker's earthy performances of this racier material soon earned her the title 'The Last Of The Red-Hot Mamas.' In 1910, Tucker's maid persuaded her to meet with songwriter Shelton Brooks and listen to some of his songs. The composer sang "Some Of These Days" for Tucker in her dressing room in a Chicago vaudeville theatre. Tucker, of course, loved the song and it became her theme song.

Unfortunately for Brooks, he never profited from the millions of copies of "Some Of These Days" that were sold thanks to Tucker's ceaseless promotion of his song. He had already sold his rights to the song for $30.00. Years later, after his death, Brooks' family successfully challenged the legality of this deal and royalty payments were rightfully restored to his heirs. "Some Of These Days" can be heard in the films *Animal Crackers* (1930); *Rose Marie* (1936); *Broadway* (1942); and *Follow The Boys* (1944).

ST. LOUIS BLUES

Words and Music by W.C. Handy

Chart Highlights
#4 in 1916
#9 in 1919
#1 in 1920
#3 in 1921
#9 in 1923
#3 in 1925
#11 in 1930
#2 in 1932
#15 in 1935
#20 in 1936
#11 in 1939
#18 in 1943
#24 in 1953

W.C. Handy began writing the blues in 1909, at the age of thirty-two. Even though he had already written the very popular "Memphis Blues," Handy was unable to find a publisher who would accept the "St. Louis Blues." So, in 1914, he formed his own publishing company in Memphis with the sole purpose of publishing "St. Louis Blues." When the song still failed to attract much attention, Handy figured that the other publishers had been right to reject it. Handy moved to New York City and convinced several stars, most notably Sophie Tucker, to feature "St. Louis Blues" in their acts. With these celebrity endorsements the song finally received the attention that it deserved.

By 1950 — after several decades of hit recordings — "St. Louis Blues" ranked second only to "Silent Night" as one of the most often recorded songs of all time. "St. Louis Blues" provided the title for two films (1928 and 1958). It also was used in the films *Is Everybody Happy* (1929 and 1943); *The Birth Of The Blues* (1941); *Jam Session* (1944); and *Glory Alley* (1952).

SUGAR BLUES

Words by Lucy Fletcher
Music by Clarence Williams

Chart Highlights
#2 in 1931
#6 in 1935
#27 in 1940
#4 in 1947

Guitarists may think that the wah-wah effect was newly invented by them in the sixties, but they would be wrong-wrong. Trumpeter Clyde McCoy was wah-wahing his way to fame and fortune in the twenties and thirties, and "Sugar Blues" was his theme song. McCoy recorded the song four times, and two of these recordings — from 1931 and 1935 — made it into the Top Ten.

SWANEE

Words by Irving Caesar
Music by George Gershwin

Chart Highlights
#1 in 1920

George Gershwin's "Swanee" almost didn't survive its opening night. As part of the grand-opening celebrations for the Capitol Theater in New York City on October 24, 1919, the song was performed by Muriel DeForrest in a lavish production number that featured sixty chorus girls dancing across a darkened stage wearing slippers illuminated by tiny electric lights. Gershwin's brilliant song was lost among the spectacle. Sometime after that fiasco, the virtually unknown composer played "Swanee" for Al Jolson, who was then at the height of his fame. Jolson agreed to try the song out at one of his concerts at the Winter Garden Theater. Jolson liked the audience response, and he had "Swanee" interpolated into *Sinbad* which he was touring with following its successful Broadway run. Jolson's recording of "Swanee" in 1920 was a tremendous hit, selling well over a million copies and catapulting George Gershwin into the forefront of American popular music.

THE SWEETHEART OF SIGMA CHI

Words by Byron D. Stokes
Music by F. Dudleigh Vernor

Chart Highlights
#3 in 1927
#8 in 1928

Fred Waring's Pennsylvanians made the fraternity song "The Sweetheart Of Sigma Chi" a national hit in 1927. Waring, whose professional career began when he was a member of a banjo ensemble on a Detroit radio station in the early 1920s, achieved lasting fame by blending a dance band with a glee-club style vocal group. Crooner Rudy Vallee and Waring helped maintain the vogue for things collegiate through the 1920s with songs like "Collegiate" (1925), "I Love The College Girls" (1927), and, of course, "The Sweetheart Of Sigma Chi." The last song had been written in 1912 to commemorate the 25th anniversary of the Sigma Chi fraternity chapter at Albion College in Michigan. In addition to being one of the most popular and admired musicians in America for four decades, Waring somehow found time to invent the food blender that still carries his name. The film *The Sweetheart Of Sigma Chi* (1946) starred Phil Regan and Elsye Knox.

SWEETHEARTS

Words by Robert B. Smith
Music by Victor Herbert

Contrary to the image promoted by MGM's publicity department, Nelson Eddy and Jeanette MacDonald, 'America's Sweethearts,' never really cared much for each other. They were united on screen for the first time in *Naughty Marietta* (1933). Seven more musicals in as many years created the notion of the Eddy and MacDonald embrace being the ultimate symbol of musical romance. "Sweethearts" was originally written for the operetta *Sweethearts* (1913) which starred Tom MacNaughton and Christie MacDonald. Nelson Eddy and Jeanette MacDonald starred in the film version of *Sweethearts* in 1938.

TAKE ME OUT TO THE BALL GAME

Words by Jack Norworth
Music by Albert von Tilzer

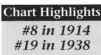

Sorry to say it, but Jack Norworth and Albert von Tilzer, whose song has epitomized America's national pastime for generations, were not baseball fans. In fact, neither of them had ever attended a game until years *after* they had written "Take Me Out To The Ball Game." Say it isn't so! Well, at any rate, "Take Me Out To The Ball Game" is now part of just about every baseball game's seventh-inning stretch and is sung by millions of true baseball fans every year. The film *Take Me Out To The Ball Game* (1949) starred Gene Kelly and Frank Sinatra.

THAT'S A PLENTY

Words by Ray Gilbert
Music by Lew Pollack

Chart Highlights
#8 in 1914
#19 in 1938

This dixieland classic was written in 1914 by Lew Pollack, a composer who apparently liked to pace himself, his big hits being spread out over three decades. "That's A Plenty" was followed by "Charmaine" (1926); "Diane" (1927); and "Two Cigarettes In The Dark" (1934). In the jazz slang of the day, the catch phrase 'that's a plenty' was a complement meaning *that is excellent!*

THEY DIDN'T BELIEVE ME

Words by Herbert Reynolds
Music by Jerome Kern

Chart Highlights
#1 in 1915
#8 in 1916
#15 in 1934

"They Didn't Believe Me" was Jerome Kern's first hit. It was so popular that it was interpolated into two successive musicals: *The Girl From Utah* (1914) and *Tonight's The Night* (1915), proving that the thirty-year-old Kern was ready to challenge George M. Cohan for the title of America's leading composer of Broadway musicals.

Kern had been born in New York City in 1885. His keen interest in music lacked the precociousness of a prodigy, and for a time it seemed that he would follow in his father's footsteps as a respected Newark businessman. But music's call became too strong for him to ignore, and the younger Kern bargained with his father to allow him to spend one year (1903-1904) studying classical music in Europe before he would dutifully return to tend to the family business.

As a student in London in need of some extra spending money, Kern took on a low-paying job as a staff composer at a music hall. This exposure to the exciting world of popular music lead Kern to abandon the symphonic path that he had been following and take up the one that eventually would lead him to Tin Pan Alley, the bright lights of Broadway, and away from the family business in Newark.

TIGER RAG (HOLD THAT TIGER)

Words by Harry DeCosta
Music by Original Dixieland Jazz Band

Chart Highlights
#1 in 1918
#14 in 1922
#8 in 1923
#10 in 1927
#1 in 1931
#6 in 1934
#23 in 1941
#2 in 1952

One of the earliest and most popular jazz standards, "Tiger Rag" has been recorded more than seventy times. The biggest hits were by the Original Dixieland Jazz Band (1918); the Mills Brothers (1931); and Les Paul and Mary Ford (1952). "Tiger Rag" was used in the films *The Big Broadcast* (1932); *Birth of The Blues* (1941); *Is Everybody Happy* (1943); *Nightclub Girl* (1944); and *Has Anybody Seen My Gal* (1952).

TILL THE CLOUDS ROLL BY

Words by P.G. Wodehouse
Music by Jerome Kern

Chart Highlights
#1 in 1917

"Till The Clouds Roll By" was written for the musical *Oh, Boy!* (1917). Thirty years later the song was still so popular that it was used as the title for Kern's screen biography *Till The Clouds Roll By* (1945).

TILL WE MEET AGAIN

Words by Raymond B. Egan
Music by Richard A. Whiting

Chart Highlights
#1 in 1919

"Till We Meet Again" is considered by many to be *the* sentimental ballad of The Great War. Richard Whiting's daughter, Margaret — the popular Big Band songstress — once reminisced about the creation of her father's greatest hit. In 1918, near the end of the War, the Remick Music Company, a Detroit music publisher that her father worked for at the time, was sponsoring a song contest. One day, Mr. Remick's secretary was cleaning out "my father's wastepaper basket and discovered a manuscript my father had thrown away…" The secretary liked the song and showed it to Mr. Remick who questioned Whiting about his discarded song. "It's not very good," the young composer replied, "so I threw it away." Remick, however, shared his secretary's enthusiasm for the song and asked Whiting for the song's title. "Auf Wiedersehen," came the unexpected response, the composer adding that the German title meant "till we meet again." Remick threw out the German title but not the song which he entered in the contest as "Till We Meet Again." Naturally, Whiting's song won first place in the contest, and eventually it would sell an estimated seven million copies of sheet music. As peace settled over the world in early 1919, "Till We Meet Again" broke into the top ten five times, with three recordings of the song quickly reaching number one. The duet version recorded by Henry Burr and Albert Campbell held the top spot for nine weeks in the spring of that year. Many years later, "Till We Meet Again" again eased the pain of war-time separation as Judy Garland sang it in the film *For Me And My Gal* (1942) during WW II, and Gordon MacRae and Doris Day sang it during the Korean War in *On Moonlight Bay* (1951).

TOO-RA-LOO-RA-LOO-RAL (THAT'S AN IRISH LULLABY)

Words and Music by James R. Shannon

Chart Highlights
#1 in 1914
#4 in 1944

Irish tenor and composer Chauncey Olcott introduced "Too-Ra-Loo-Ra-Loo-Ral (That's An Irish Lullaby)" on Broadway in the Gaelic musical *Shameen Dhu* (Black Jamie) (1914). Thirty years later Bing Crosby, in his Oscar-winning portrayal of Father Chuck O'Malley, revived "Too-Ra-Loo-Ra-Loo-Ral (That's An Irish Lullaby)" when he sang it in the movie *Going My Way* (1944). Crosby's recording of the song sold over a million records that year and has become the definitive performance of this song.

TWELFTH STREET RAG

By Euday L. Bowman

Chart Highlights
#7 in 1917
#14 in 1923
#19 in 1935
#1 in 1948
#23 in 1954

The "Twelfth Street Rag" had to wait thirty-one years before it reached the top of the charts. Frequent recordings by the likes of Earl Fuller (1917), Ted Lewis (1923), and Thomas 'Fats' Waller (1935) kept the rag popular, but none of them could match the million-selling success of Pee Wee Hunt's 1948 hit record.

WAITING FOR THE ROBERT E. LEE

Words by L. Wolfe Gilbert
Music by Lewis F. Muir

Chart Highlights
#1 in 1912

"Waiting For The Robert E. Lee" was popularized by, among others, the vaudevillians Ruth Roye, Fanny Brice, and Eddie Cantor. But the performer who was most closely associated with this song was the great Al Jolson who introduced it at the Winter Garden in New York City in *The Honeymoon Express* (1912). L. Wolfe Gilbert got the idea for this song after watching black stevedores unloading a Mississippi riverboat, the *Robert E. Lee*, in Baton Rouge, Louisiana. "Waiting For The Robert E. Lee" was probably the first song ever sung in a sound film when it was performed by Bobbie Gordon in *The Jazz Singer* (1927). It was later featured in the films *The Story of Vernon and Irene Castle* (1939); *Babes On Broadway* (1941); *The Jolson Story* (1946); and *Jolson Sings Again* (1949).

WHEN IRISH EYES ARE SMILING

Words by Chauncey Olcott and George Graff, Jr.
Music by Ernest R. Ball

Chart Highlights
#1 in 1913
#4 in 1917

"When Irish Eyes Are Smiling" is a classic Irish-American standard that has been recorded by many great popular singers since it was first introduced in the musical *The Isle O' Dreams* (1912). Some of the best recordings were made by Chauncey Olcott, Harry MacDonough, John McCormack, Dennis Day, Kate Smith, Bing Crosby, and Morton Downey, who claimed to have sung the song 'thousands of times.' "When Irish Eyes Are Smiling" has been the title song of two films, a silent movie in 1922 and a 1947 musical.

WHEN YOU WORE A TULIP (AND I WORE A BIG RED ROSE)

Words by Jack Mahoney
Music by Percy Wenrich

Chart Highlights
#3 in 1915
#19 in 1942

Written in 1914, "When You Wore A Tulip" was the third and last of Percy Wenrich's giant hits. The other two had been "Put On Your Old Grey Bonnet" (1909) and "On Moonlight Bay" (1912). The royalties from these three wonderful songs allowed the twenty-seven-year-old Wenrich to begin and enjoy an early and extended retirement. He died in 1952 at the age of 65.

THE WORLD IS WAITING FOR THE SUNRISE

Words by Eugene Lockhart
Music by Ernest Seitz

Chart Highlights
#2 in 1922
#2 in 1951
#24 in 1952

"The World Is Waiting For The Sunrise" is a ballad that was long favored by jazz musicians. Bandleader Isham Jones had a 1922 hit with an instrumental version of the tune. The 1951 revival of the song was led by the hit recording of Les Paul and Mary Ford. The following year, comedian Stan Freeberg satirized the earlier versions of "The World Is Waiting For The Sunrise" with a recording featuring Dick Roberts and Red Rountree on banjos.

YOU MADE ME LOVE YOU (I DIDN'T WANT TO DO IT)

Words by Joe McCarthy
Music by James V. Monaco

Chart Highlights
#1 in 1913
#25 in 1940
#5 in 1941

In the film *Broadway Melody of 1938*, a Hollywood newcomer — playing the role of Sophie Tucker's love-sick daughter — sings "You Made Me Love You" to a picture of Clark Gable. The newcomer, Frances Ethel Gumm, had been discovered by a talent agent just three years earlier while she was one of the Gumm Sisters of Grand Rapids, Michigan. A few minor parts and a name change lead up to Gumm's big break opposite heart-throb Gable's photo. When you watch this fifteen-year-old as she sings the 1913 standard "You Made Me Love You," you are witnessing the birth of the legendary star Judy Garland.

Another famous performer, Al Jolson, also got himself off to a great start when he introduced "You Made Me Love You," in the musical *The Honeymoon Express* (1913). This premiere also marked the first time that Jolson performed in blackface and got down on one knee — reportedly to ease the pain of an ingrown nail — with his arms outstretched to sing a song. Of course, the song, the makeup, and the gesture all became part of the Jolson legend.

This great old standard has been used in many films: *Wharf Angel* (1934); *Syncopation* (1942); *Private Buckaroo* (1942); *The Jolson Story* (1946); *Jolson Sings Again* (1949); and *Love Me Or Leave Me* (1955). "You Made Me Love You" also became the theme song of bandleader Harry James.

Aba Daba Honeymoon

Registration 4
Rhythm: Fox Trot or March

Words and Music by Arthur Fields
and Walter Donovan

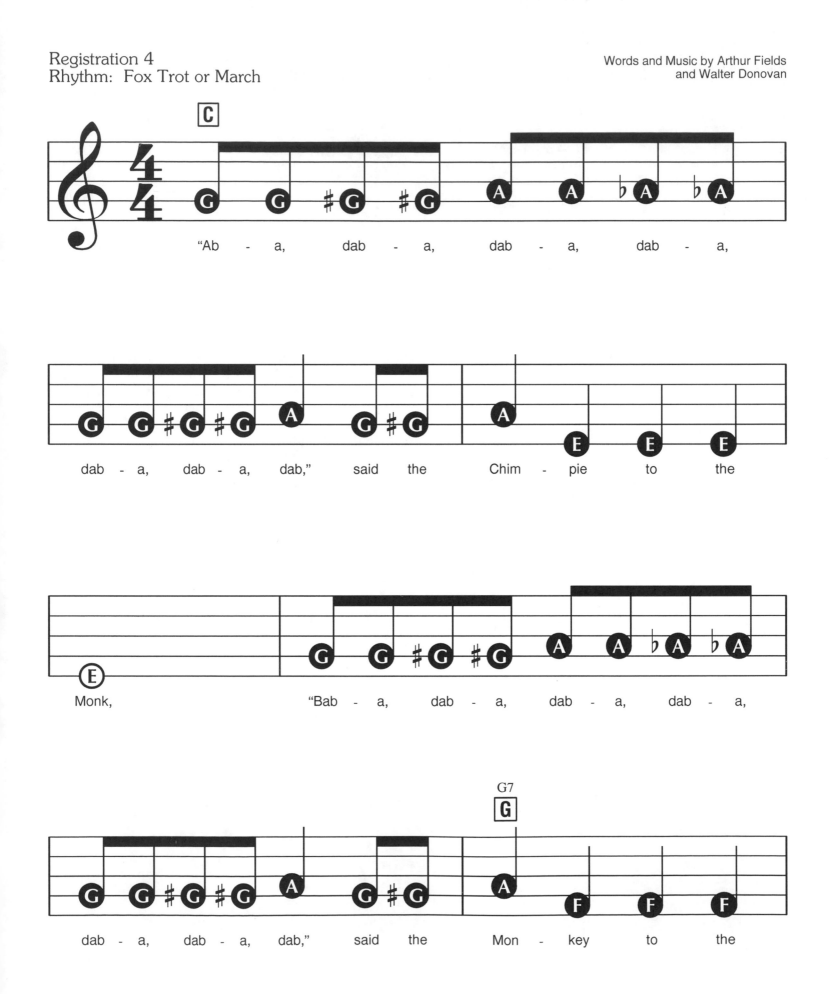

Copyright © 1996 by HAL LEONARD CORPORATION
International Copyright Secured   All Rights Reserved

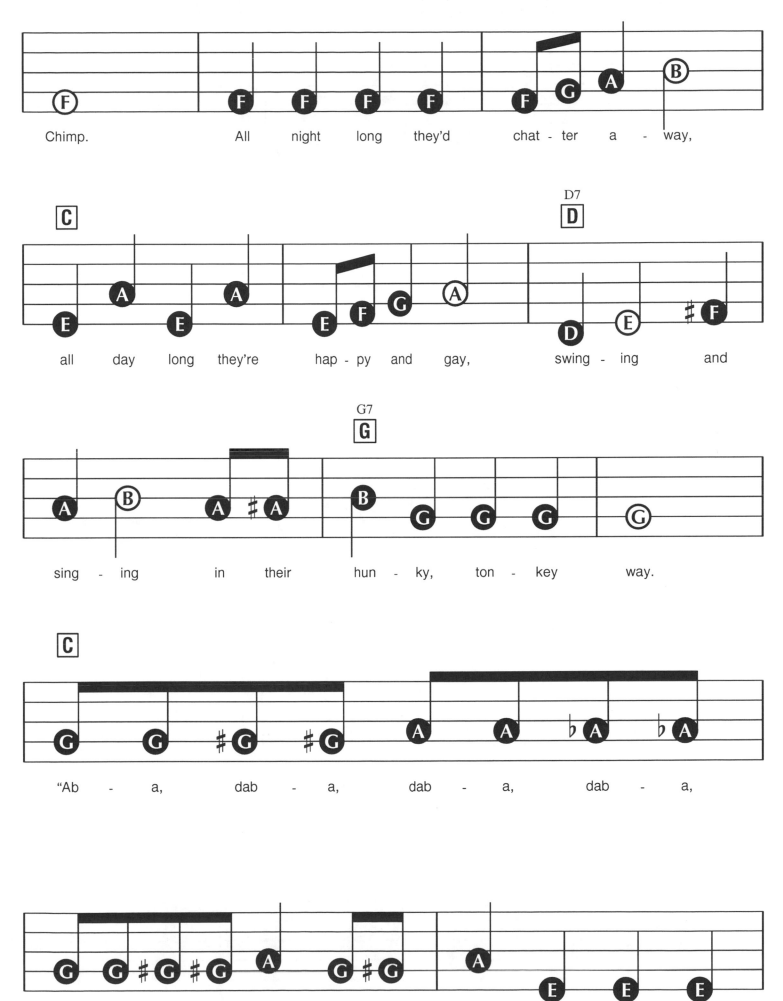

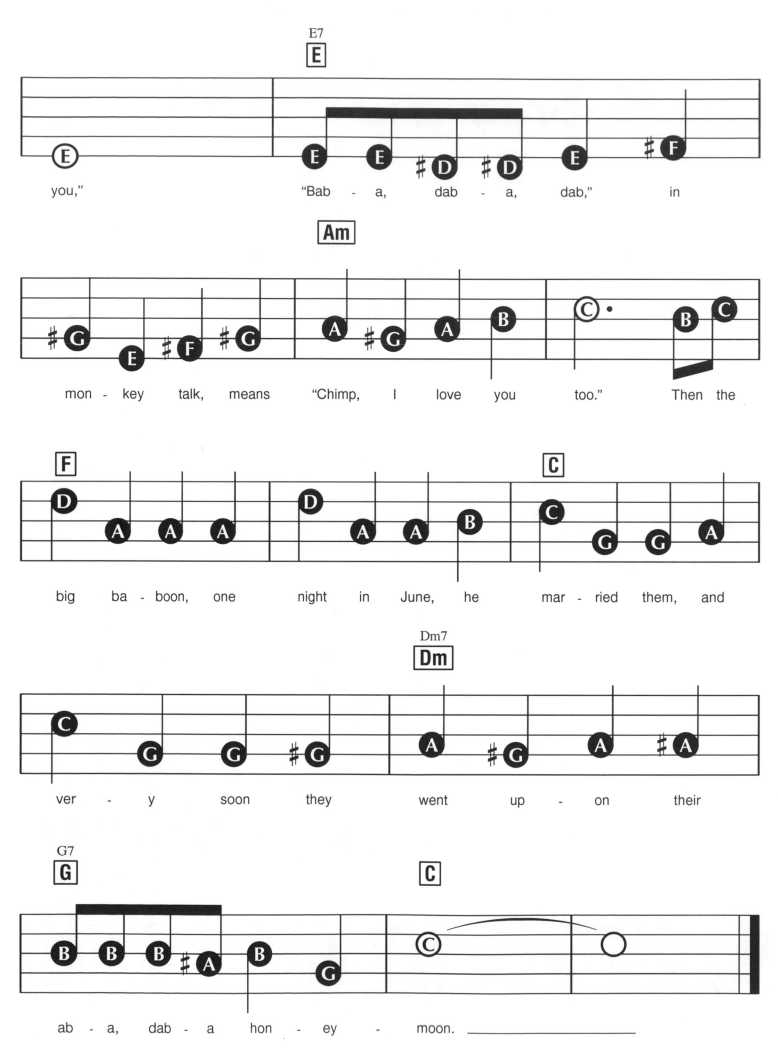

Beale Street Blues

Registration 4
Rhythm: March

Words and Music by
W.C. Handy

Copyright © 1994 by HAL LEONARD CORPORATION
International Copyright Secured All Rights Reserved

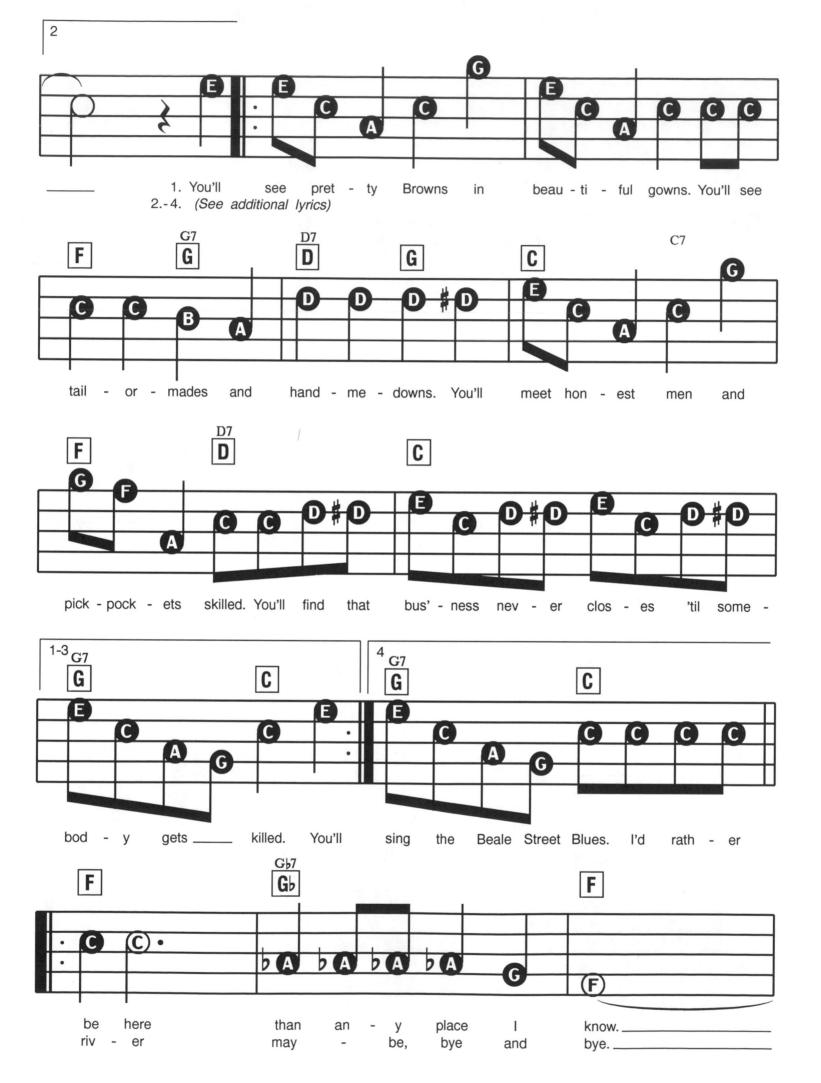

1. You'll see pret - ty Browns in beau - ti - ful gowns. You'll see
2.-4. *(See additional lyrics)*

tail - or - mades and hand - me - downs. You'll meet hon - est men and

pick - pock - ets skilled. You'll find that bus' - ness nev - er clos - es 'til some -

bod - y gets ____ killed. You'll sing the Beale Street Blues. I'd rath - er

be here than an - y place I know. ____
riv - er may - be, bye and bye. ____

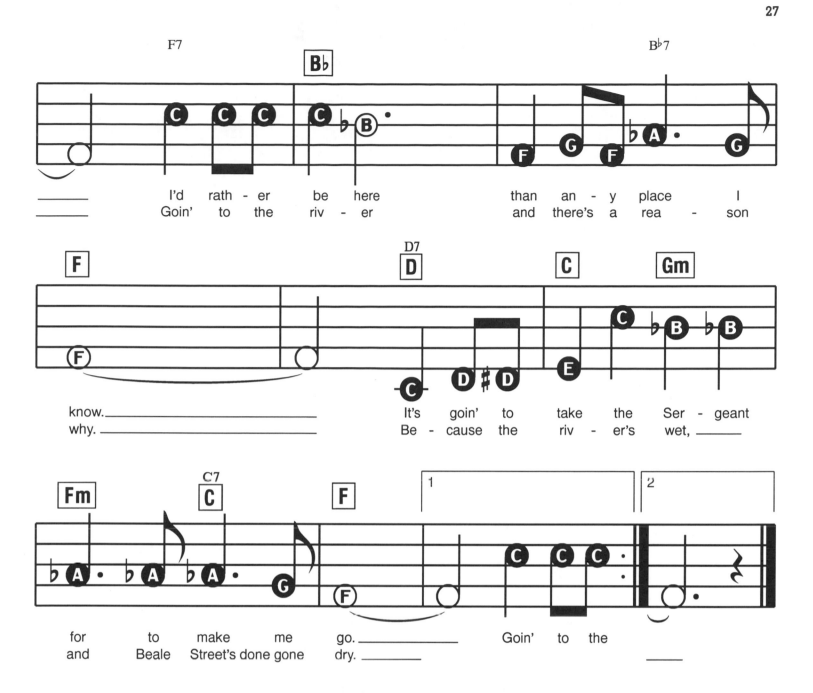

Additional Lyrics

2. You'll see Hog Nose rest'rants and Chitlin' Cafes.
   You'll see jugs that tell of bygone days
   And places once places now just a sham.
   You'll see Golden Balls enough to pave the New Jerusalem.

3. You'll see men who rank with the first in the nation
   Who come to Beale for inpiration.
   Politicians call you a dub unless you've been initiated
   In the Rickriters Club.

4. If Beale Street could talk, if Beale Street could talk,
   Married men would have to take their beds and walk,
   Except one or two who never drank booze,
   And the blind man on the corner who sings the Beale Street Blues.

After You've Gone

from ONE MO' TIME

Registration 8
Rhythm: Swing

Words by Henry Creamer
Music by Turner Layton

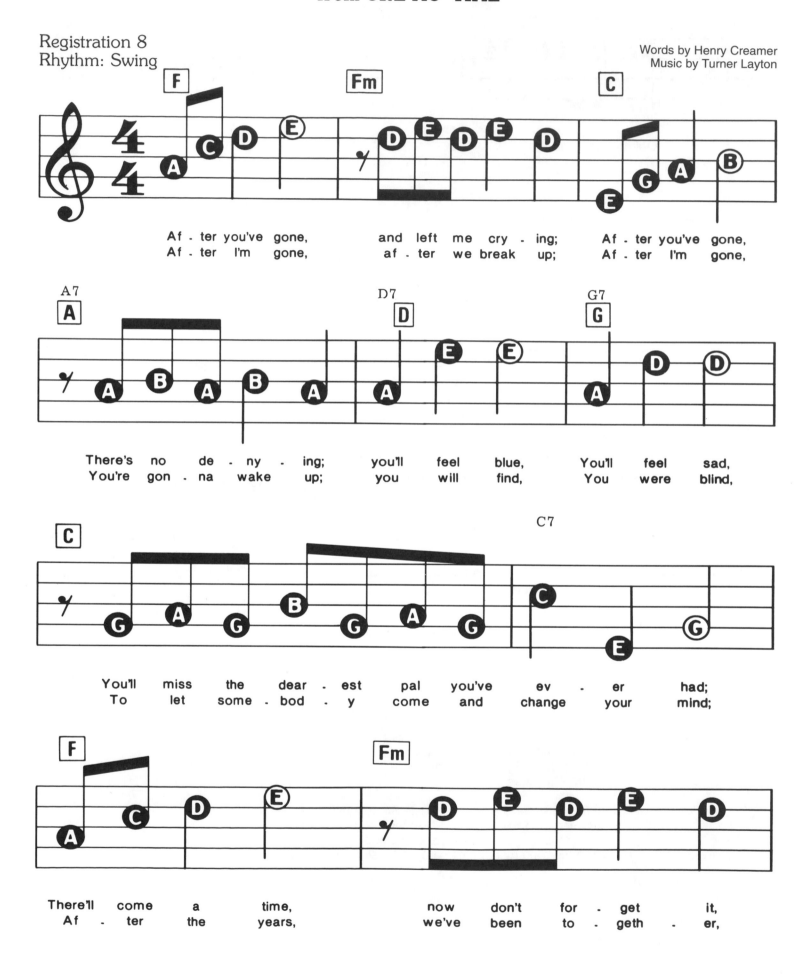

Af - ter you've gone, and left me cry - ing; Af - ter you've gone,
Af - ter I'm gone, af - ter we break up; Af - ter I'm gone,

There's no de - ny - ing; you'll feel blue, You'll feel sad,
You're gon - na wake up; you will feel find, You were blind,

You'll miss the dear - est pal you've ev - er had;
To let some - bod - y come and change your mind;

There'll come a time, now don't for - get it,
Af - ter the years, now we've been to - geth - er,

Copyright © 1994 by HAL LEONARD CORPORATION
International Copyright Secured   All Rights Reserved

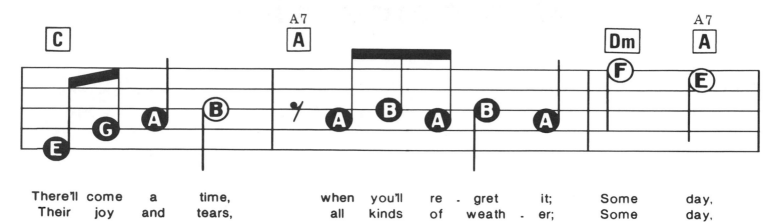

There'll come a time, when you'll re - gret it; Some day,
Their joy and tears, all kinds of weath - er; Some day,

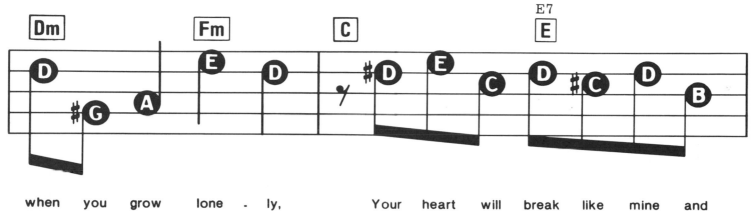

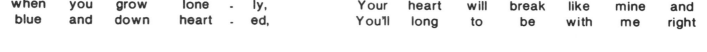

when you grow lone - ly, Your heart will break like mine and
blue and down heart - ed, You'll long to be with me and right

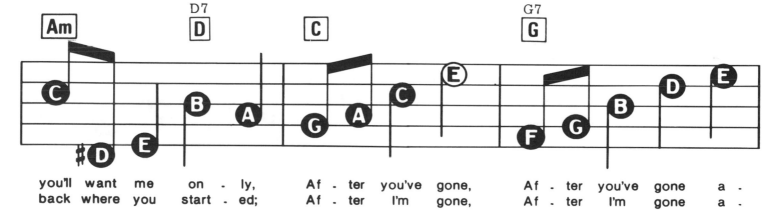

you'll want me on - ly, Af - ter you've gone, Af - ter you've gone a -
back where you start - ed; Af - ter I'm gone, Af - ter I'm gone a -

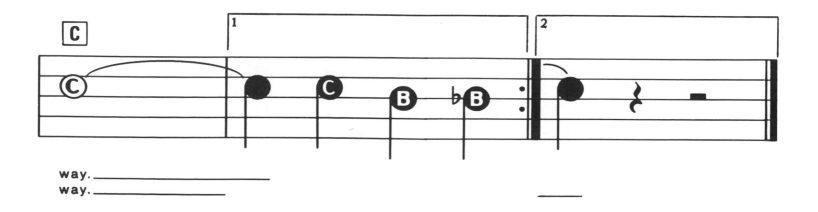

way._____
way._____

Alabama Jubilee

Registration 8
Rhythm: Swing

Words by Jack Yellen
Music by George Cobb

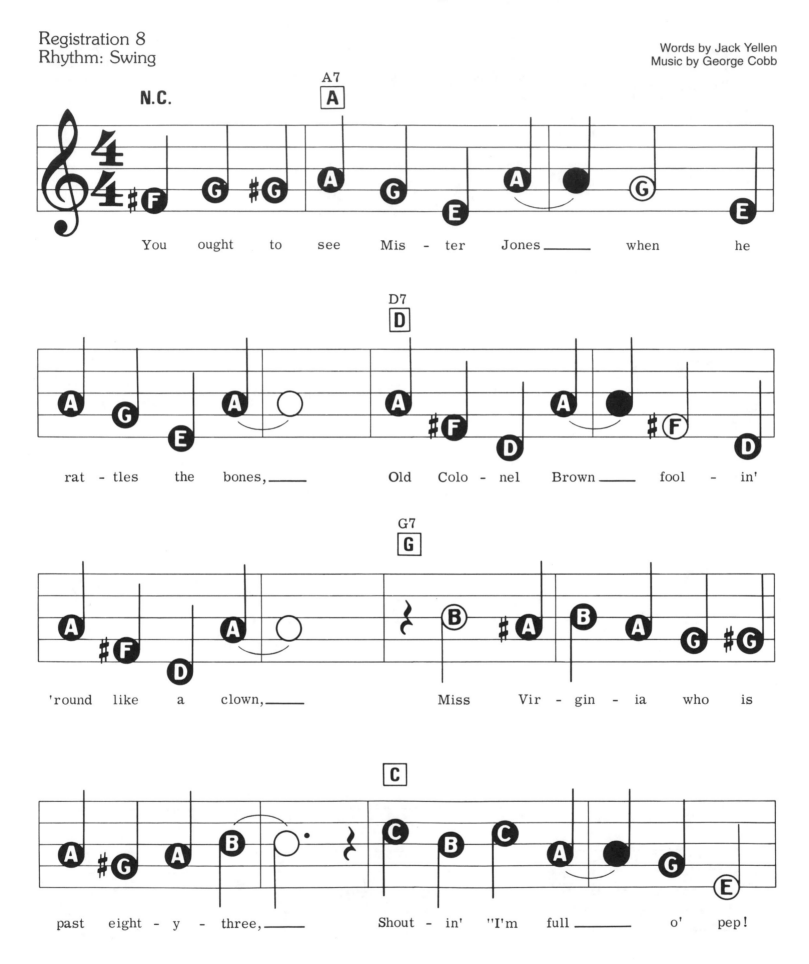

Copyright © 1996 by HAL LEONARD CORPORATION
International Copyright Secured   All Rights Reserved

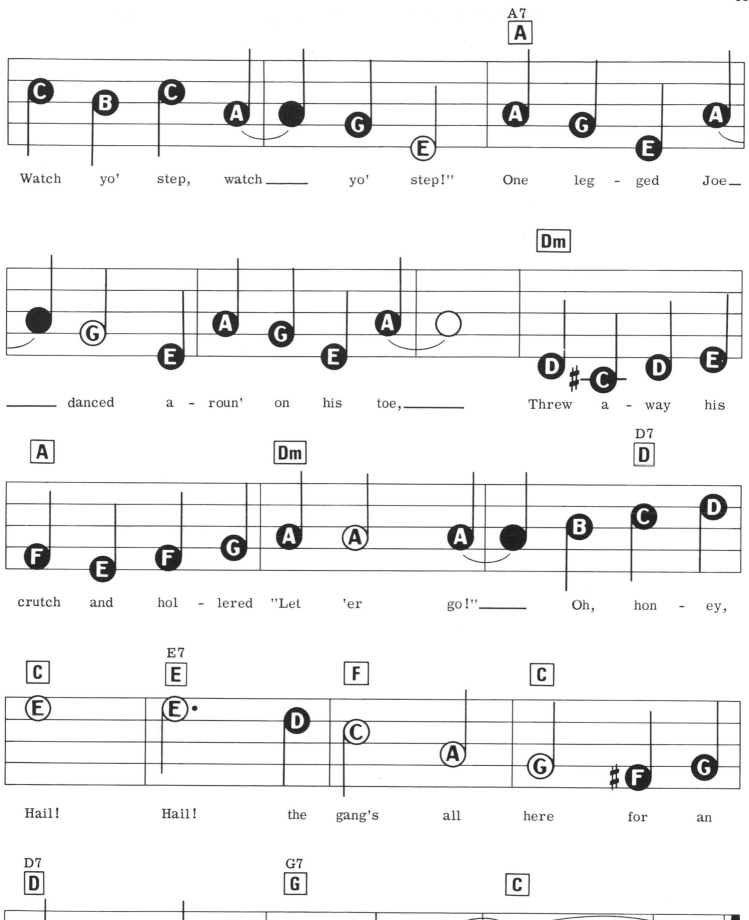

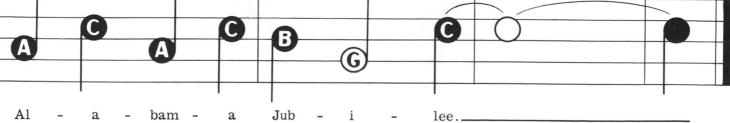

Alexander's Ragtime Band
from ALEXANDER'S RAGTIME BAND

Registration 5
Rhythm: Fox Trot or Swing

Words and Music by
Irving Berlin

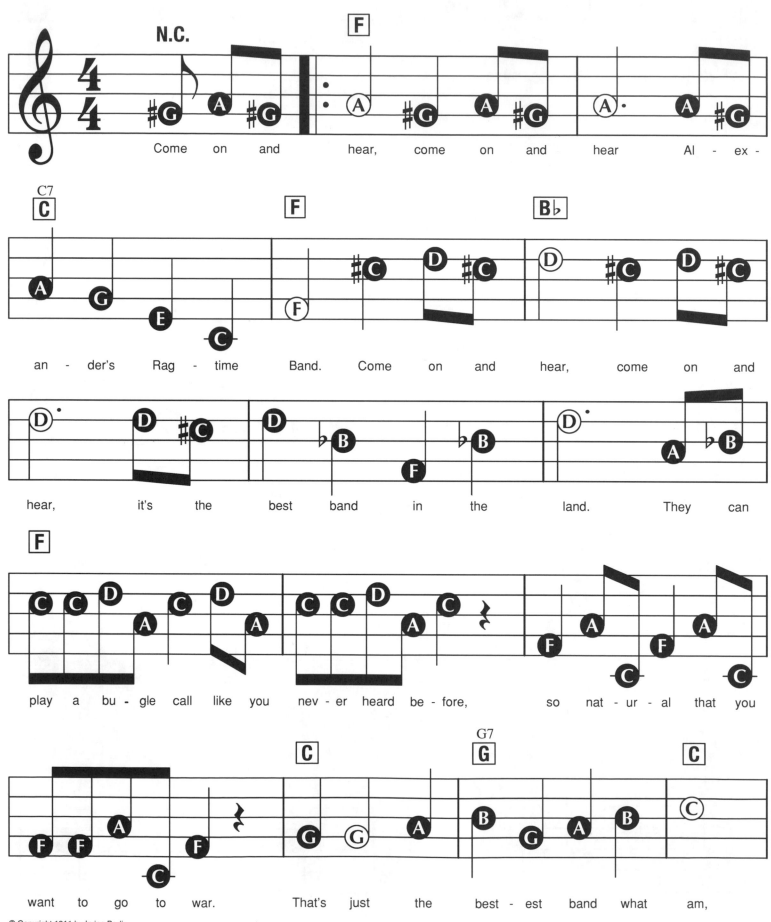

© Copyright 1911 by Irving Berlin
© Arrangement Copyright 1938 by Irving Berlin
Copyright Renewed
International Copyright Secured   All Rights Reserved

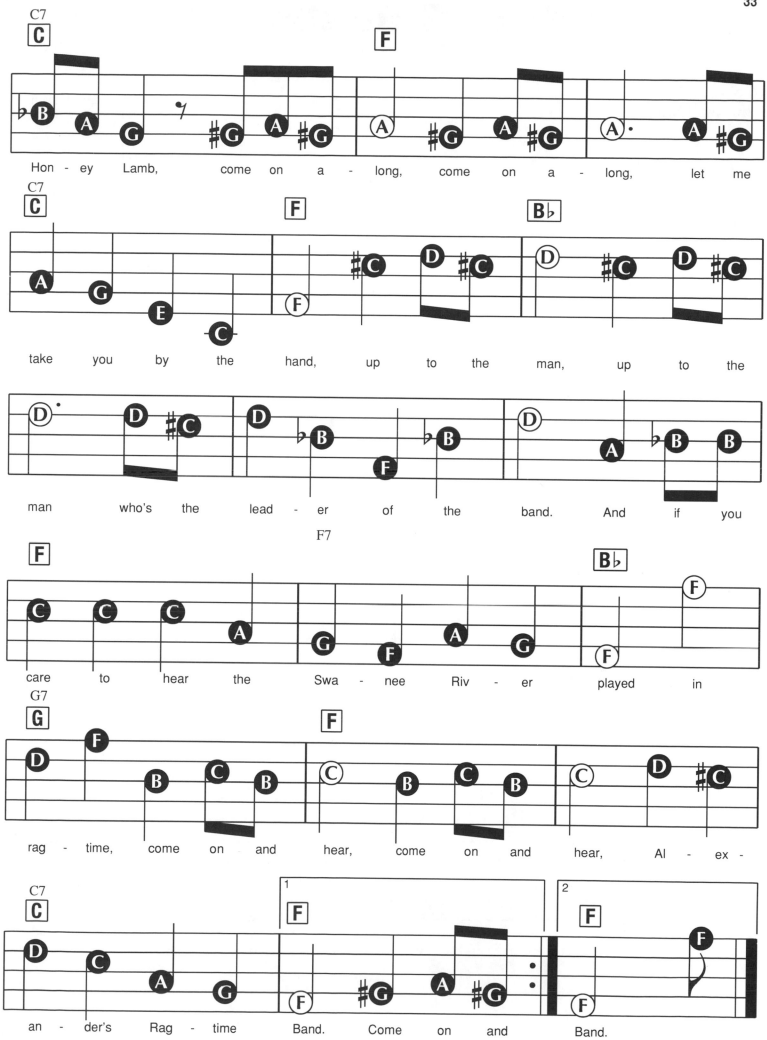

Alice Blue Gown

from IRENE

Registration 4
Rhythm: Waltz

Lyric by Joseph McCarthy
Music by Harry Tierney

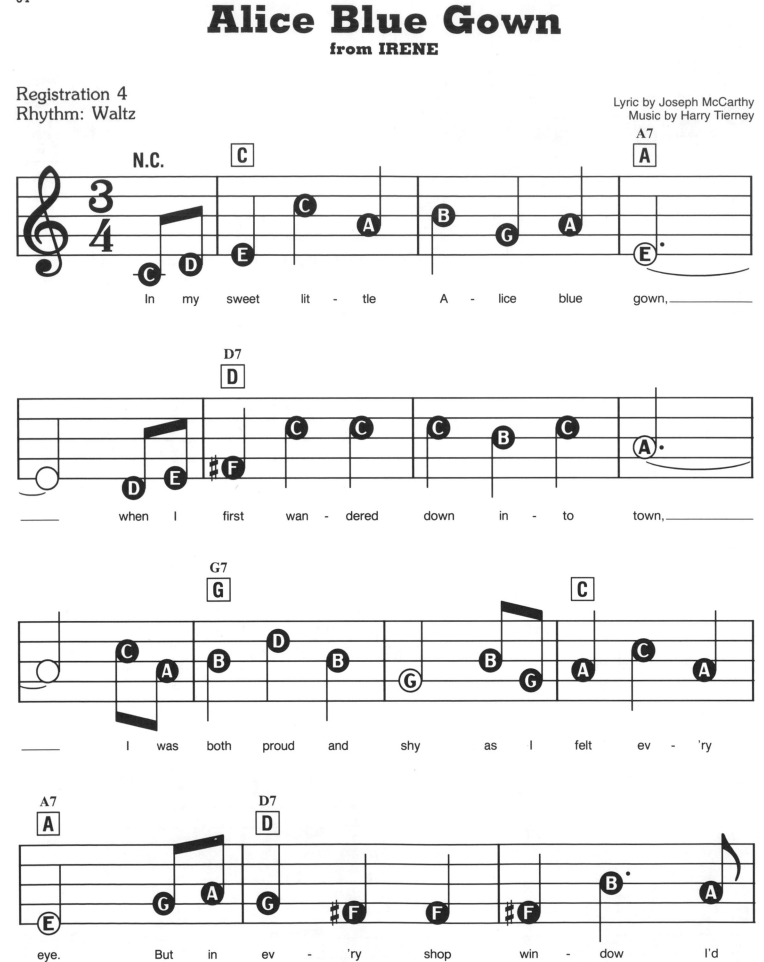

Copyright © 1996 by HAL LEONARD CORPORATION
International Copyright Secured   All Rights Reserved

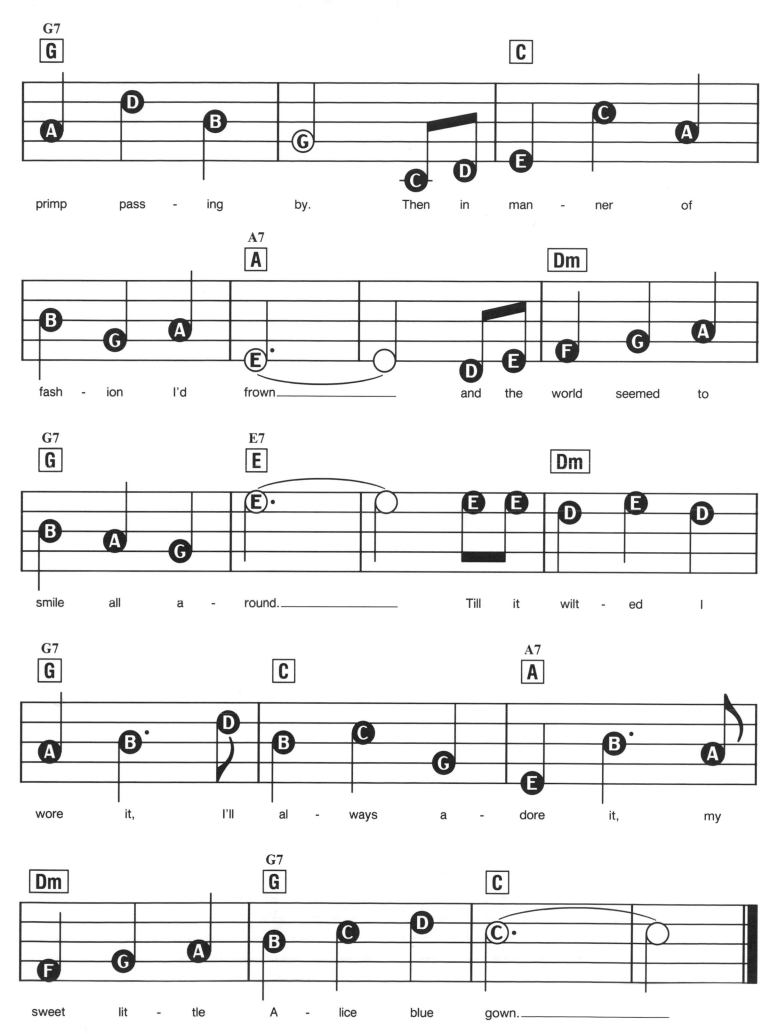

Aloha Oe

Registration 2
Rhythm: Swing

Words and Music by
Queen Liliuokalani

Fare - well, dear love. I'll dream of

you. No pass - ing grief is this my heart is

feel - ing. I love you so. Be -

fore you go, I'll say "Dear

Copyright © 1993 by HAL LEONARD CORPORATION
International Copyright Secured   All Rights Reserved

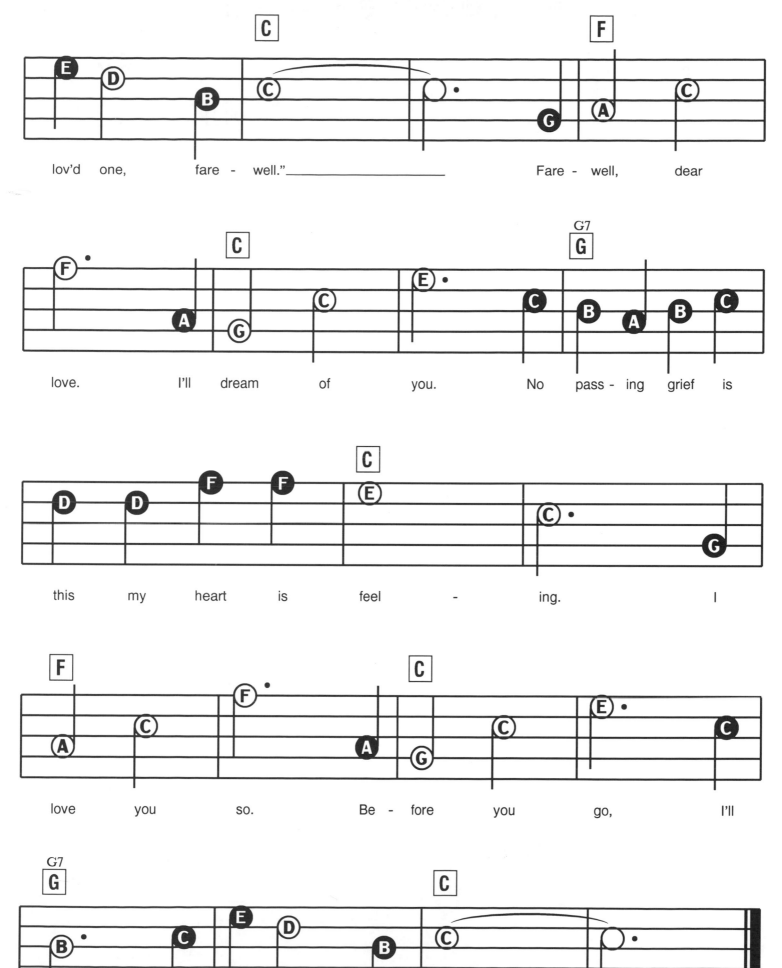

Anchors Aweigh

Registration 4
Rhythm: March

Words and Music by Alfred Hart Miles
and Charles A. Zimmerman

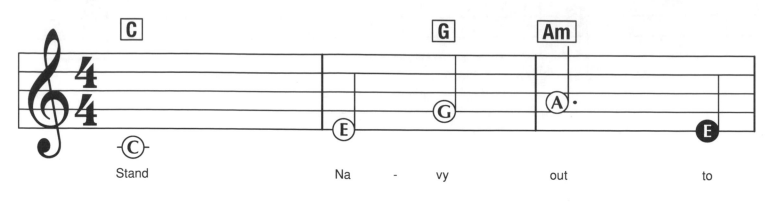

Stand   Na - vy   out   to

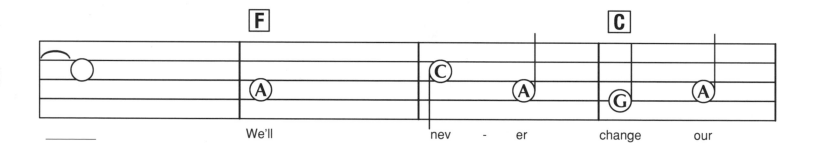

sea,   Fight   our   bat - tle   cry,_____

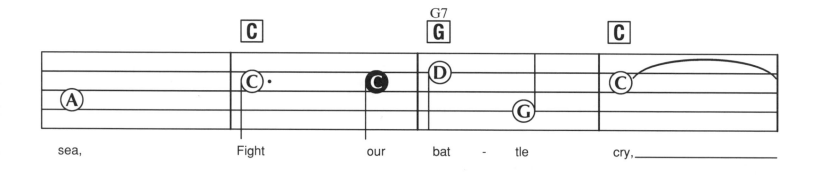

_____ We'll   nev - er   change   our

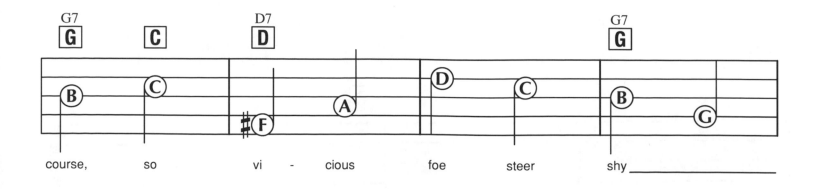

course,   so   vi - cious   foe   steer   shy_____

Copyright © 1994 by HAL LEONARD CORPORATION
International Copyright Secured   All Rights Reserved

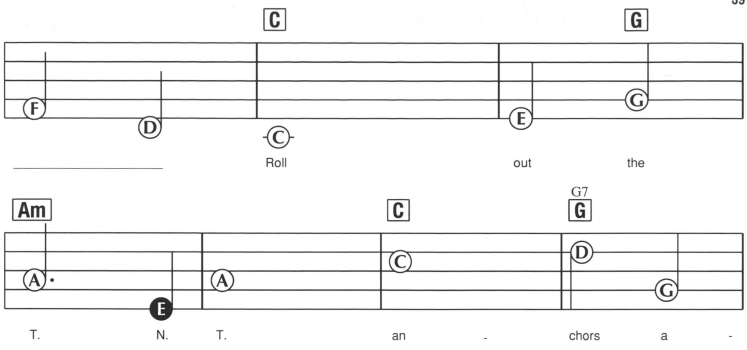

Roll out the

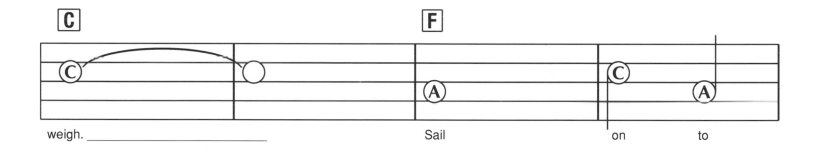

T. N. T. an - chors a -

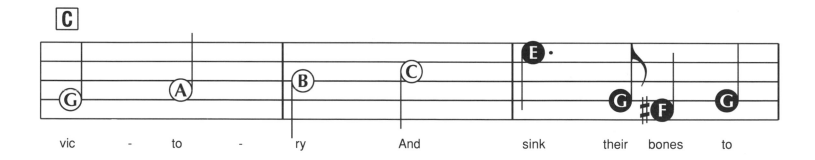

weigh. Sail on to

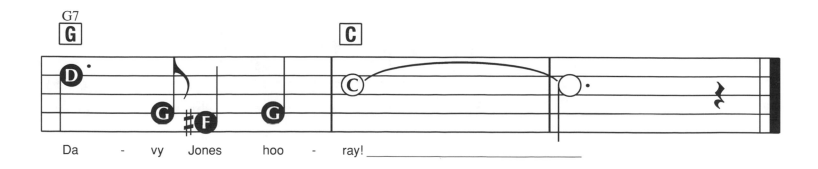

vic - to - ry And sink their bones to

Da - vy Jones hoo - ray!

Baby, Won't You Please Come Home

Registration 7
Rhythm: Fox Trot or Swing

Words and Music by Charles Warfield
and Clarence Williams

Copyright © 1996 by HAL LEONARD CORPORATION
International Copyright Secured   All Rights Reserved

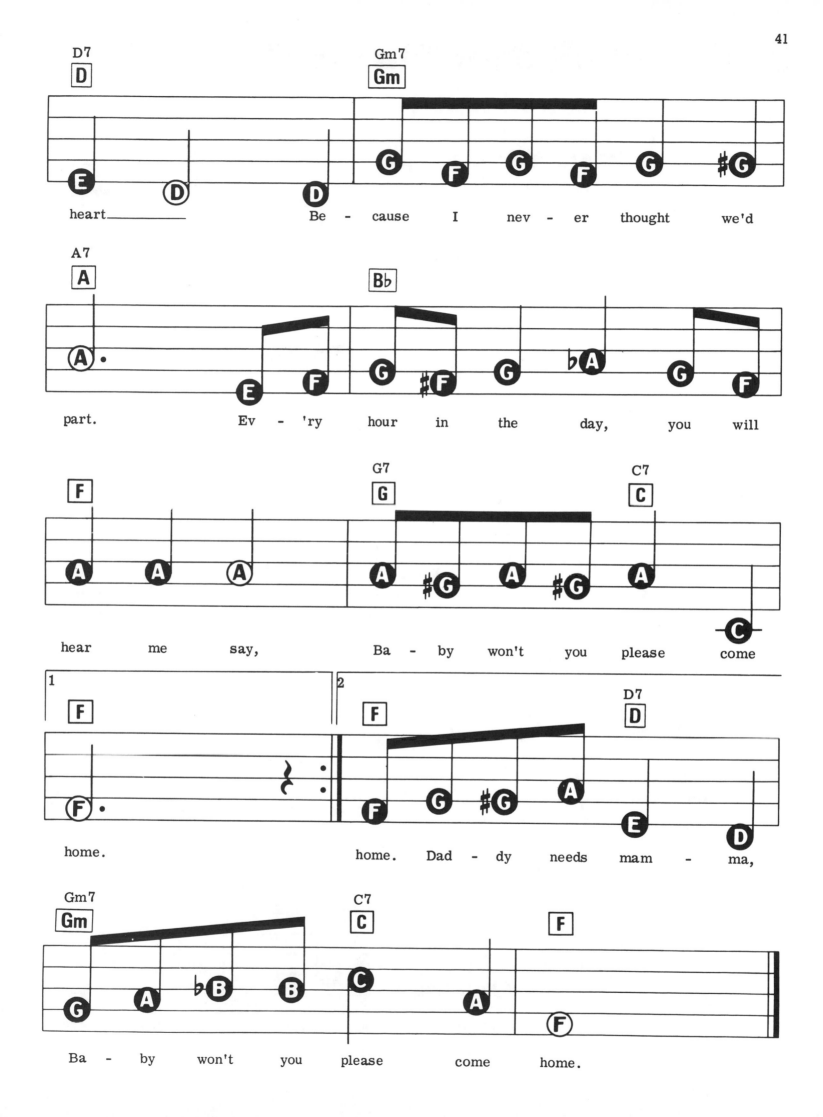

Ballin' the Jack

Registration 9
Rhythm: Swing or Fox Trot

Words by Jim Burris
Music by Chris Smith

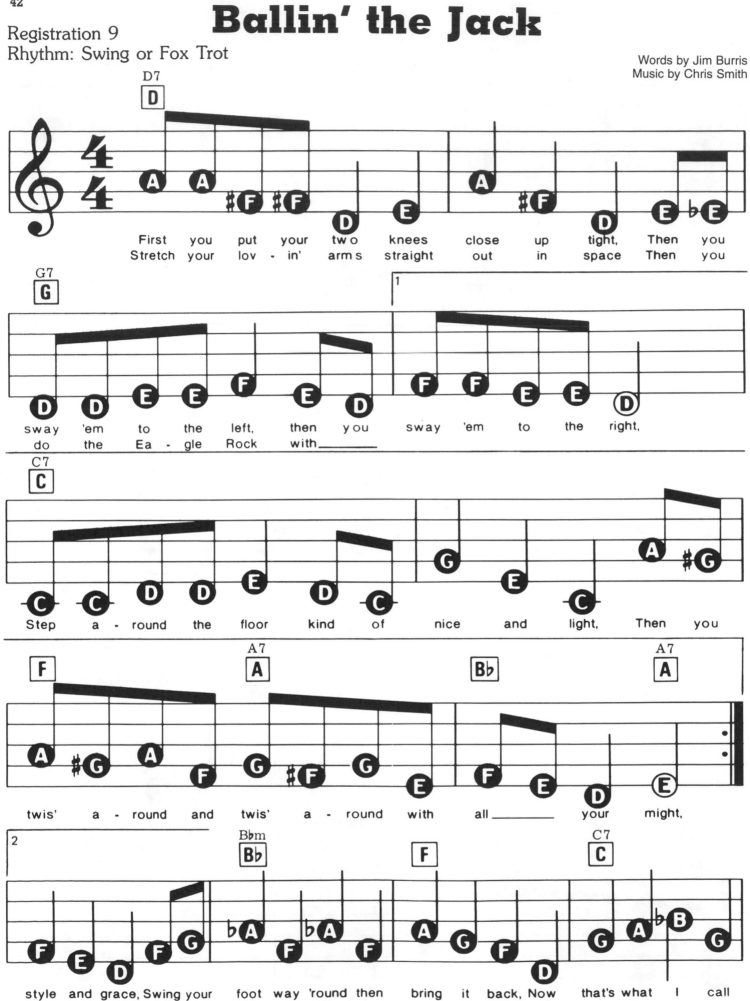

Copyright © 1994 by HAL LEONARD CORPORATION
International Copyright Secured   All Rights Reserved

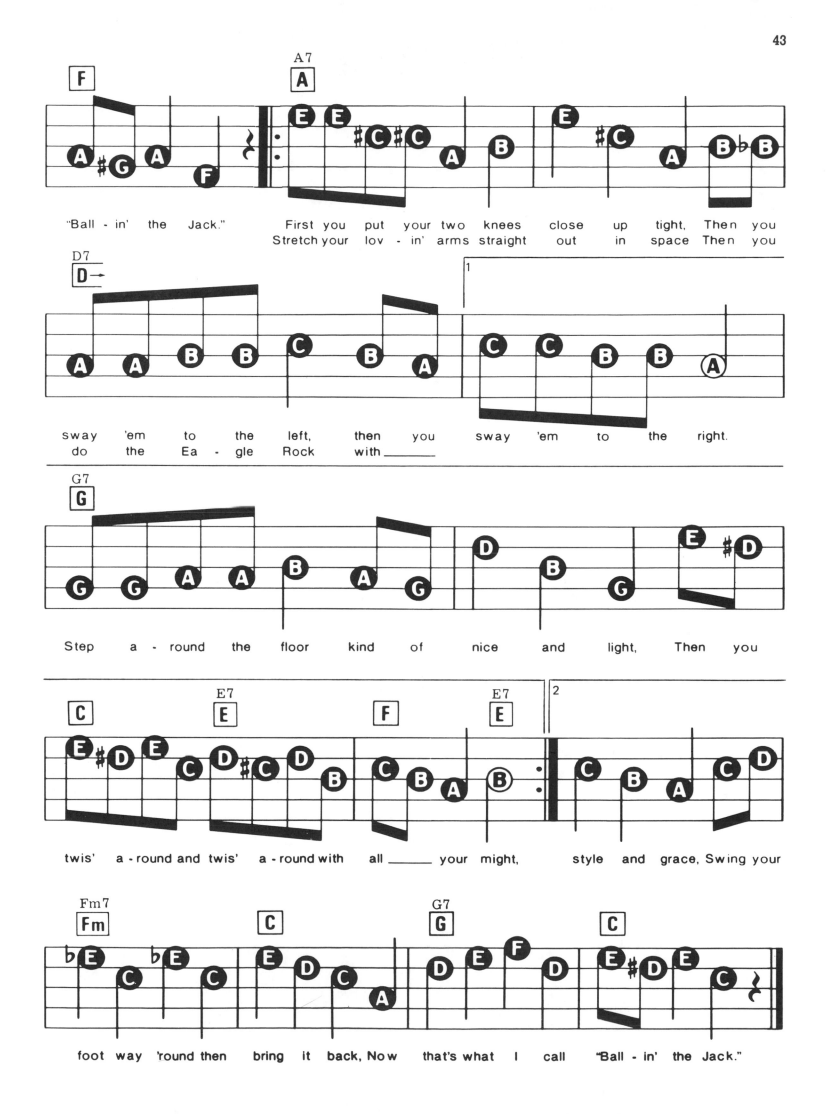

Because

Registration 6
Rhythm: Fox Trot

Words by Edward Teschemacher
Music by Guy d'Hardelot

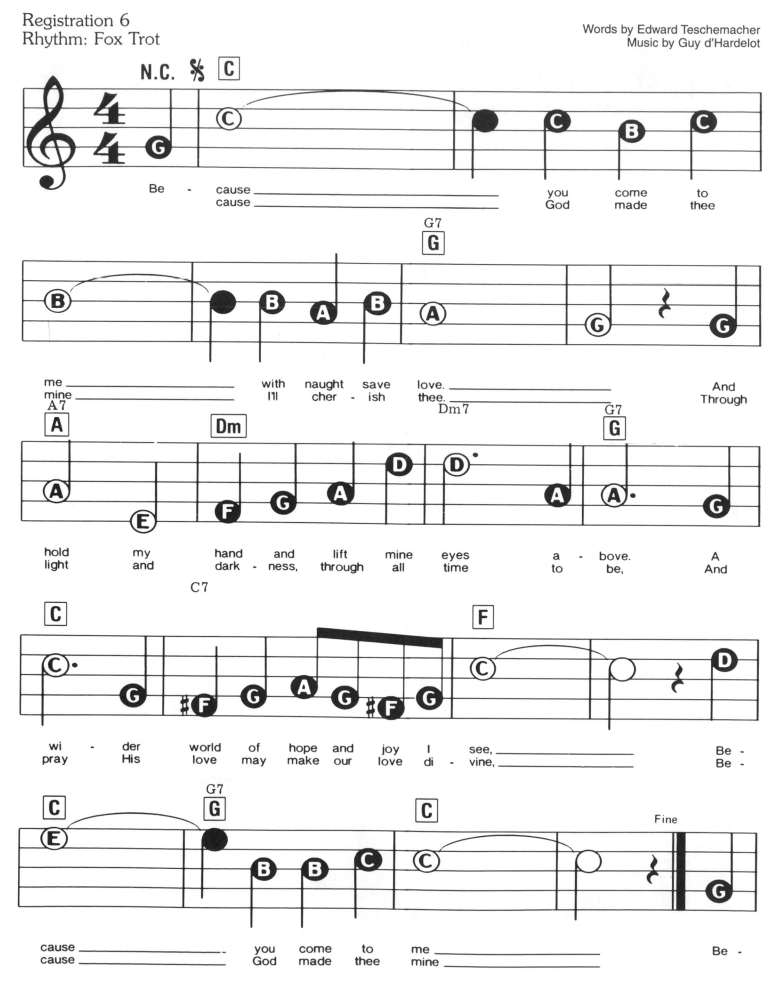

Copyright © 1994 by HAL LEONARD CORPORATION
International Copyright Secured   All Rights Reserved

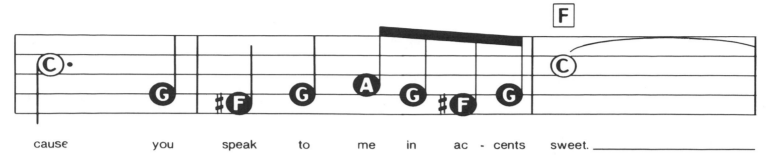

cause   you   speak   to   me   in   ac - cents   sweet._____

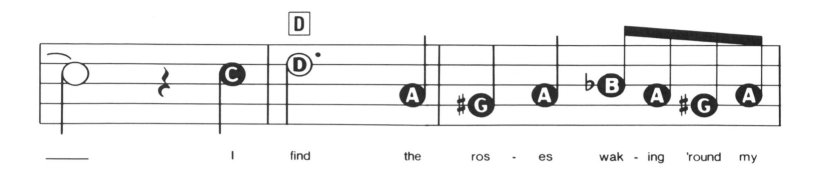

_____   I   find   the   ros - es   wak - ing   'round   my

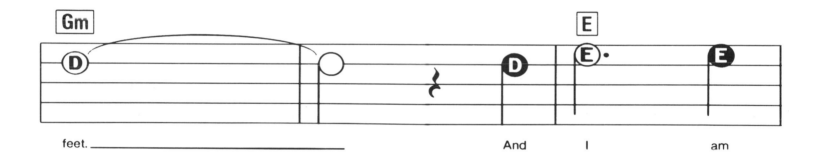

feet._____   And   I   am

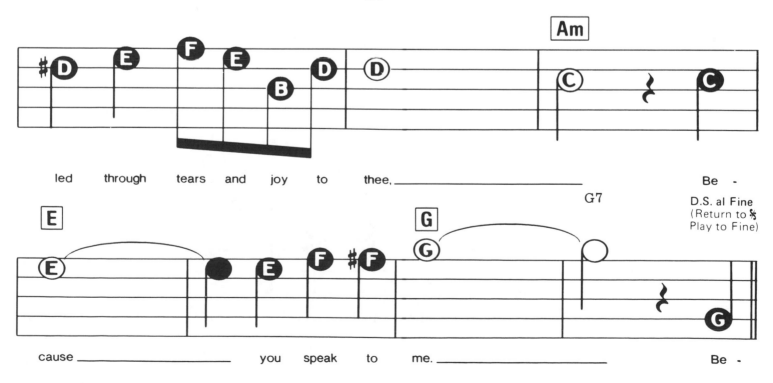

led   through   tears   and   joy   to   thee,_____   Be -

cause_____   you   speak   to   me._____   Be -

D.S. al Fine
(Return to ٪
Play to Fine)

The Bells of St. Mary's

Registration 4
Rhythm: Fox Trot or Swing

Words by Douglas Furber
Music by A. Emmett Adams

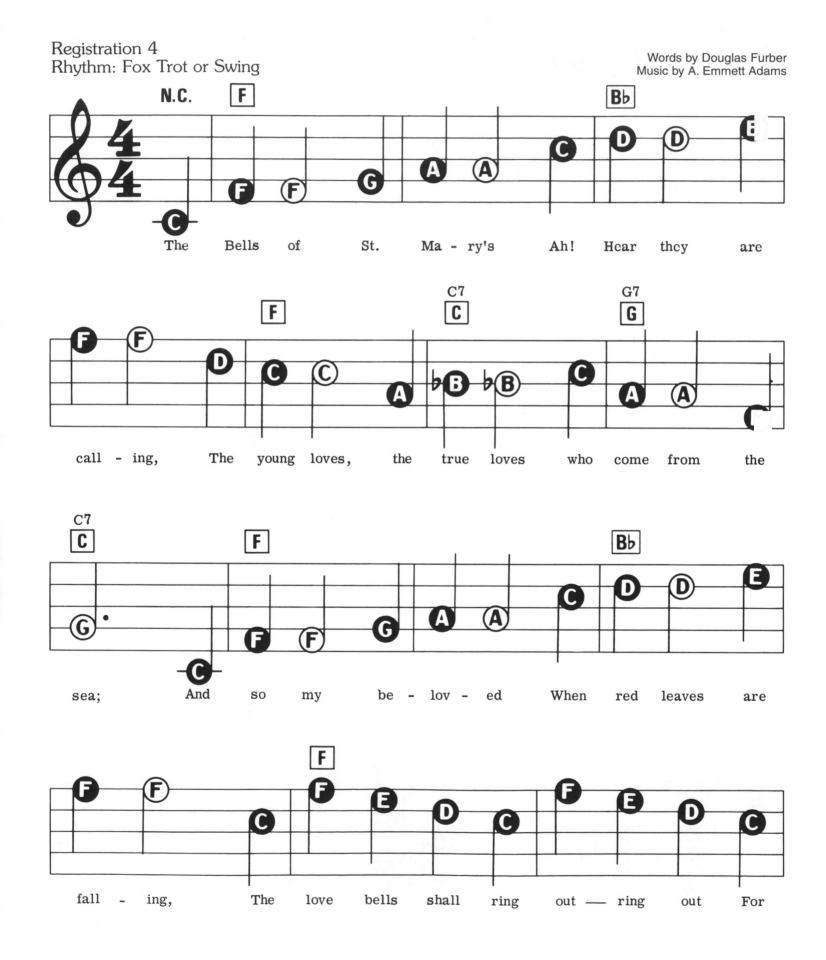

Copyright © 1994 by HAL LEONARD CORPORATION
International Copyright Secured   All Rights Reserved

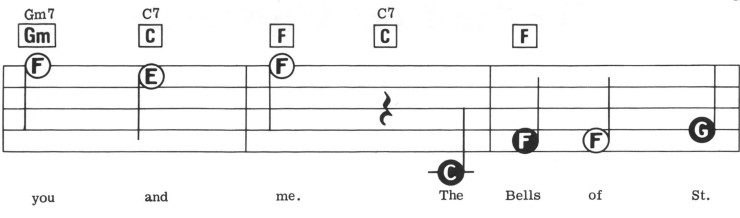

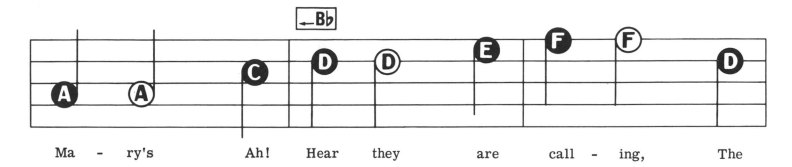

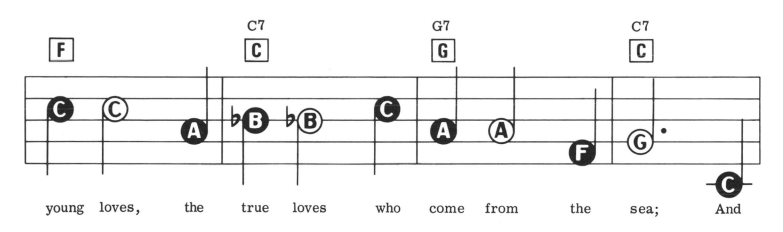

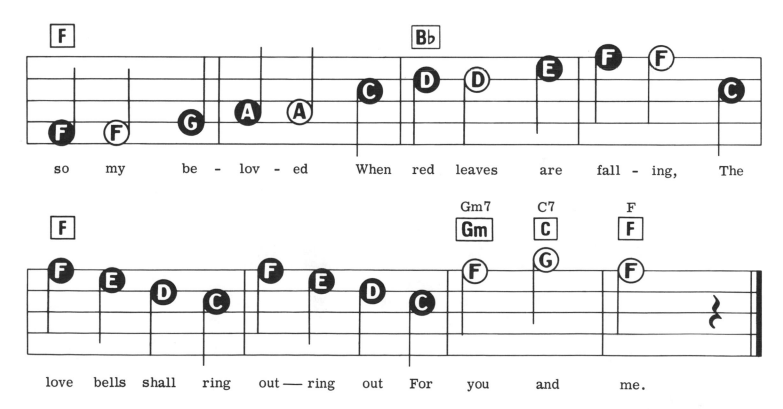

By the Beautiful Sea

Registration 2
Rhythm: Ballad

Words by Harold R. Atteridge
Music by Harry Carroll

Copyright © 1994 by HAL LEONARD CORPORATION
International Copyright Secured   All Rights Reserved

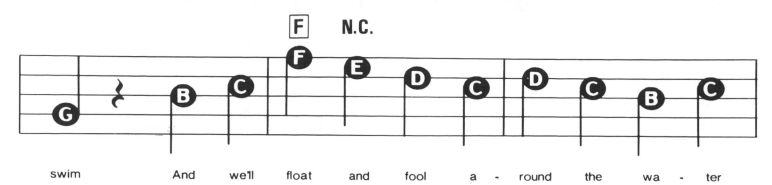

swim   And   we'll   float   and   fool   a - round   the   wa - ter

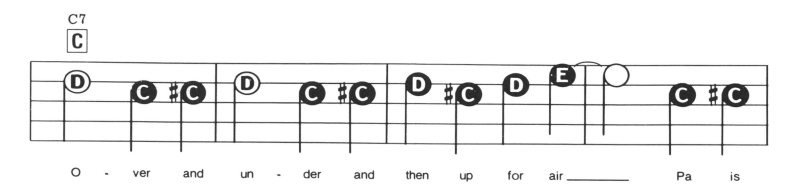

O - ver   and   un - der   and   then   up   for   air _____   Pa   is

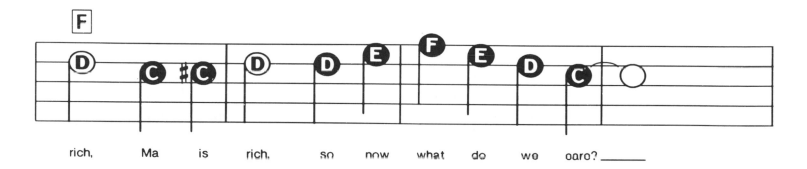

rich,   Ma   is   rich,   so   now   what   do   we   care? _____

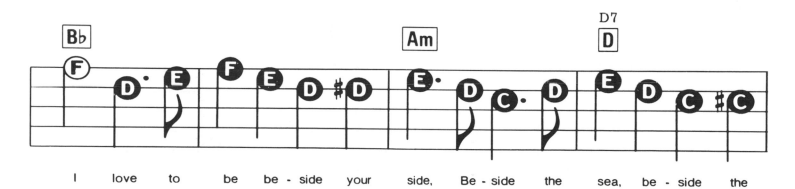

I   love   to   be   be - side   your   side,   Be - side   the   sea,   be - side   the

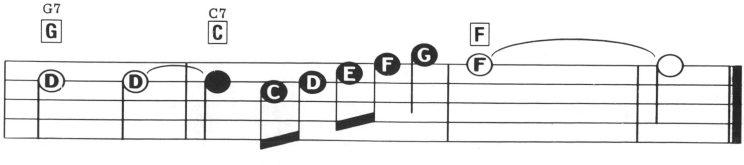

sea - side _____   by   the   beau - ti - ful   sea. _____

By the Light of the Silvery Moon

Registration 2
Rhythm: Swing

Lyrics by Ed Madden
Music by Gus Edwards

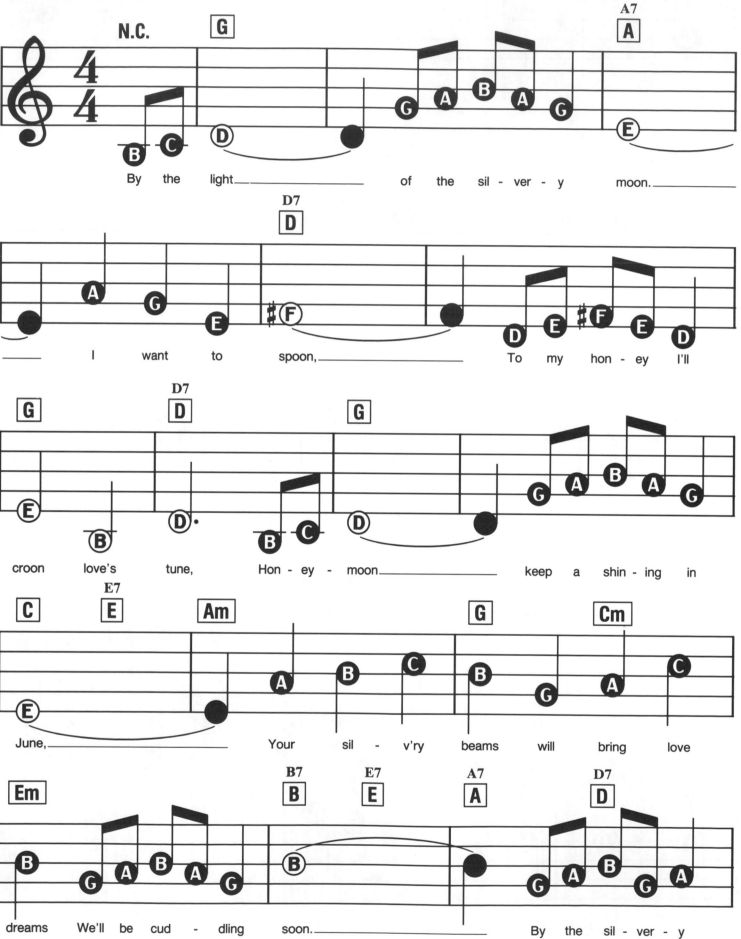

Copyright © 1990 by HAL LEONARD CORPORATION
International Copyright Secured   All Rights Reserved

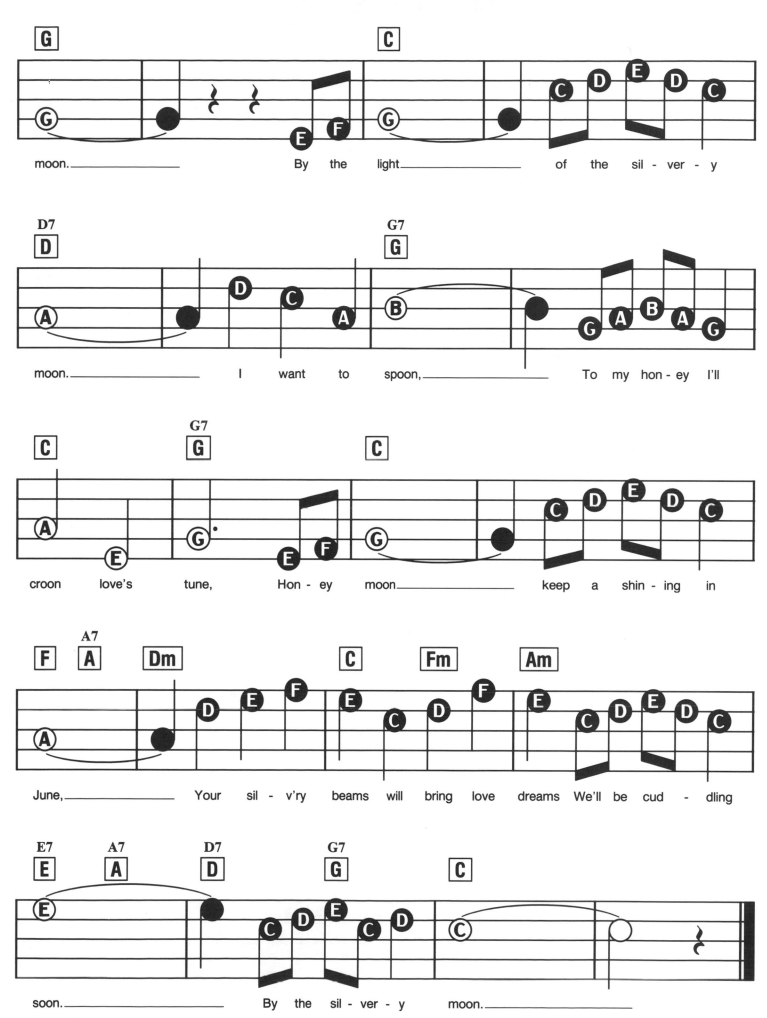

Careless Love

Registration 8
Rhythm: Fox Trot or Swing

Anonymous

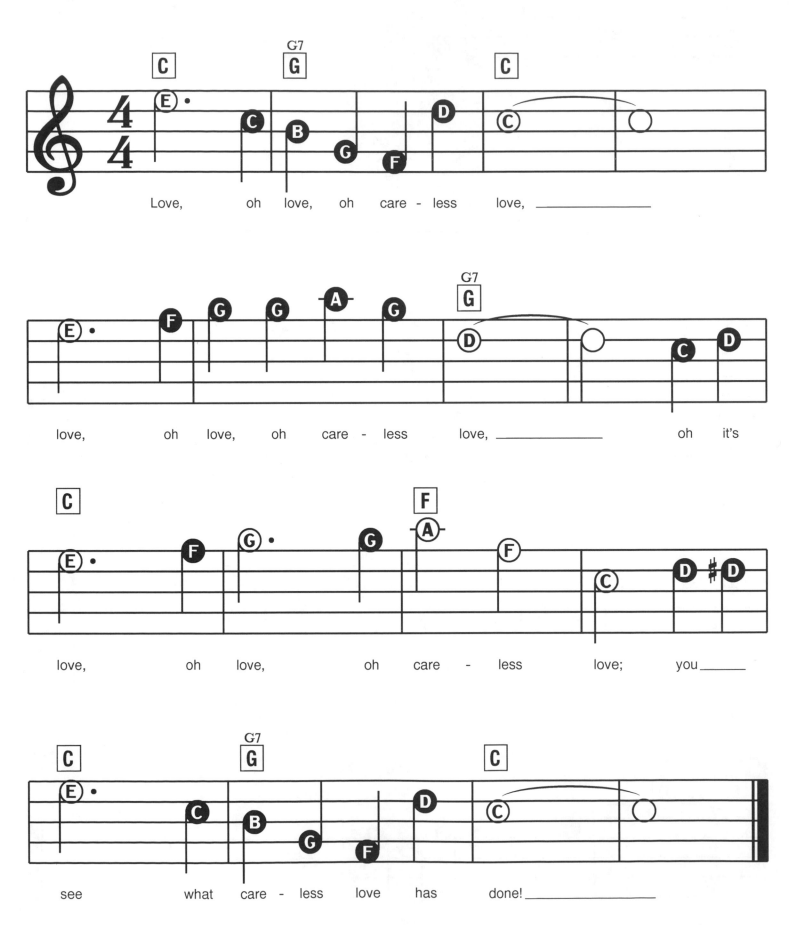

Copyright © 1974 by HAL LEONARD CORPORATION
International Copyright Secured   All Rights Reserved

Come, Josephine in My Flying Machine
(Up She Goes!)

Registration 7
Rhythm: Waltz

Music by Fred Fischer
Words by Alfred Bryan

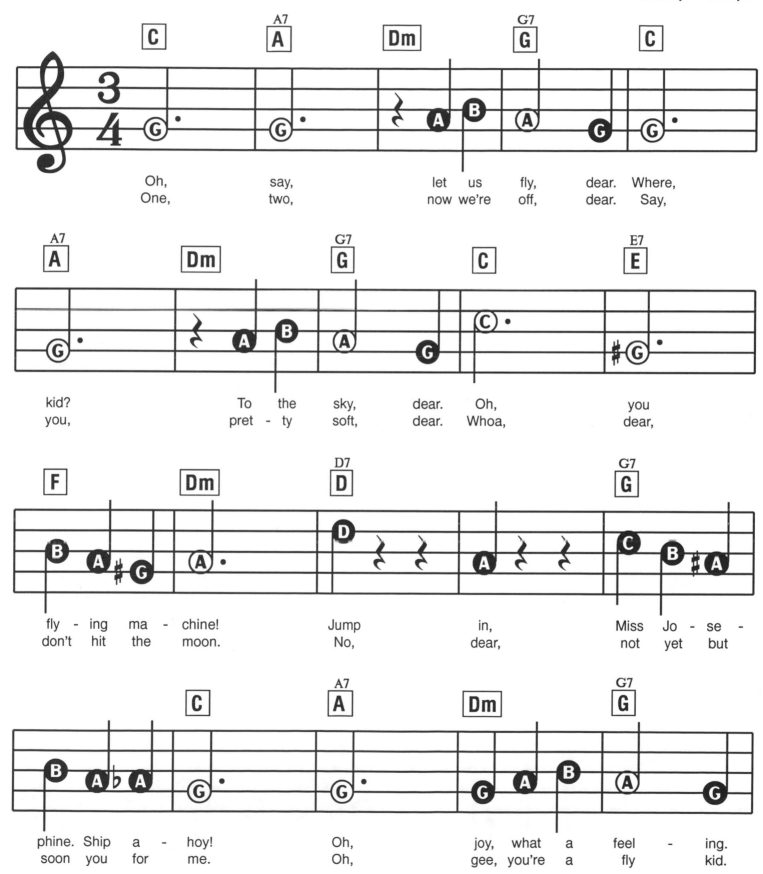

Copyright © 1994 by HAL LEONARD CORPORATION
International Copyright Secured   All Rights Reserved

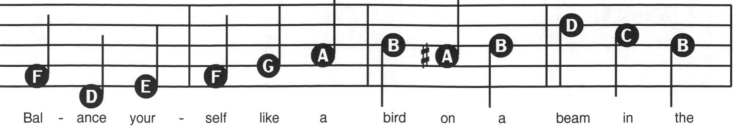

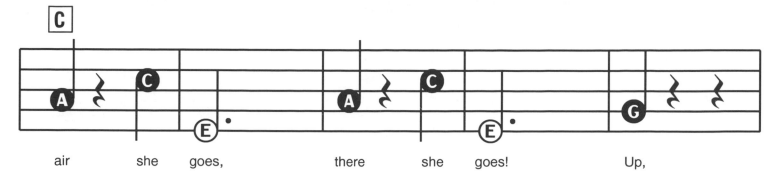

air she goes, there she goes! Up,

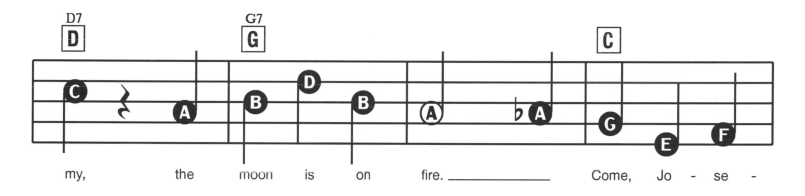

up, up, a lit - tle bit high - er. Oh,

my, the moon is on fire. _____ Come, Jo - se -

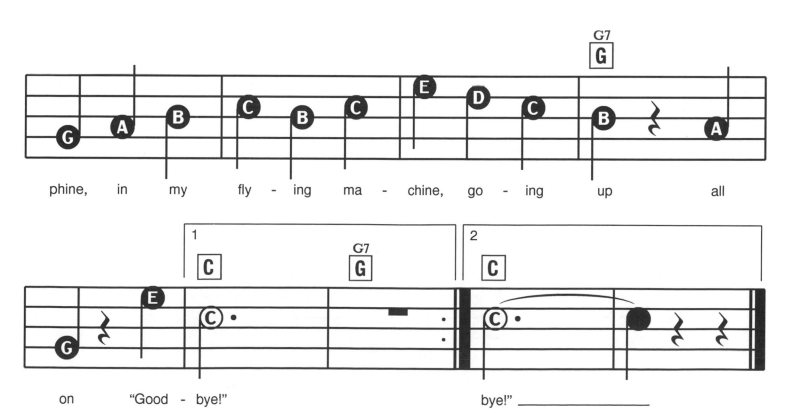

phine, in my fly - ing ma - chine, go - ing up all

on "Good - bye!" bye!" _____

Chinatown, My Chinatown

Registration 4
Rhythm: Swing

Words by William Jerome
Music by Jean Schwartz

Copyright © 1994 by HAL LEONARD CORPORATION
International Copyright Secured   All Rights Reserved

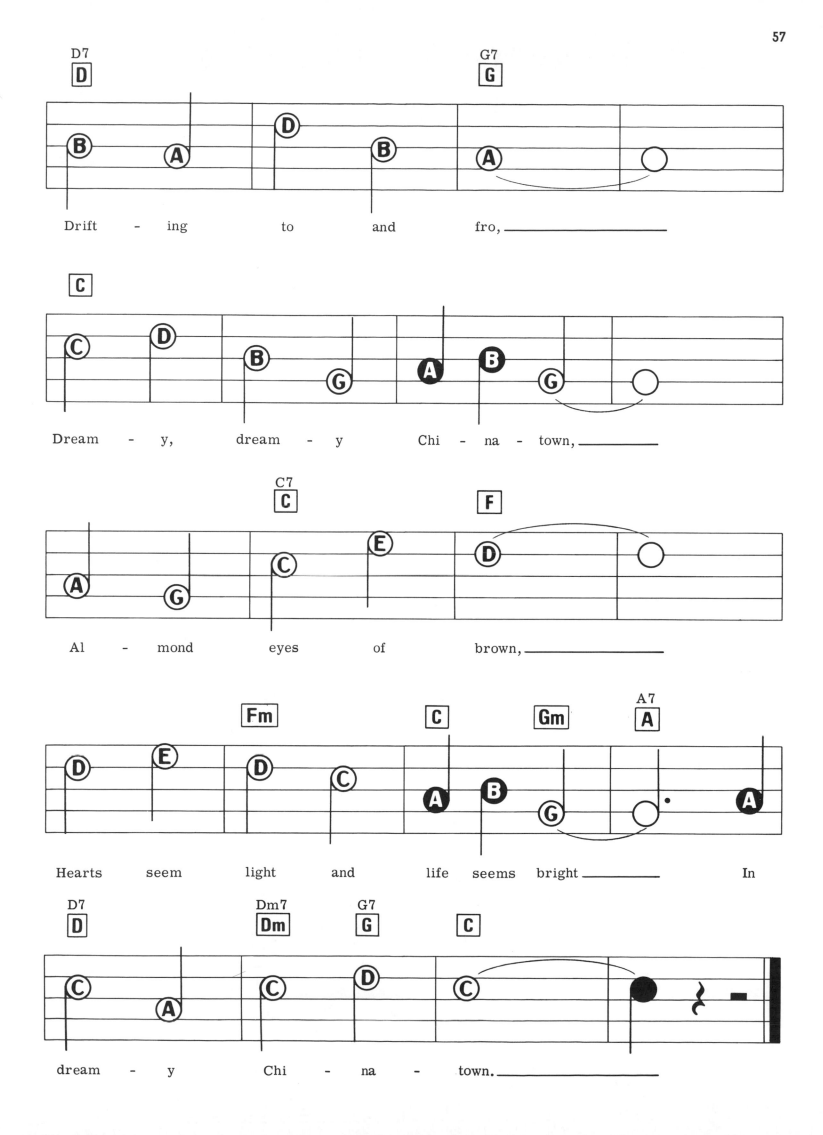

Cuddle Up a Little Closer, Lovey Mine

Registration 3
Rhythm: Swing

Words by Otto Harbach
Music by Karl Hoschna

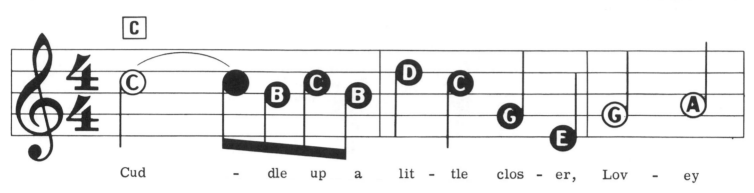

Cud - dle up a lit - tle clos - er, Lov - ey

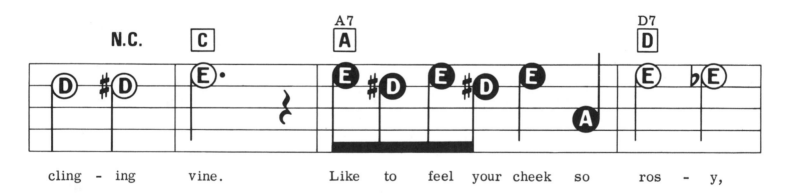

mine, Cud - dle up and be my lit - tle

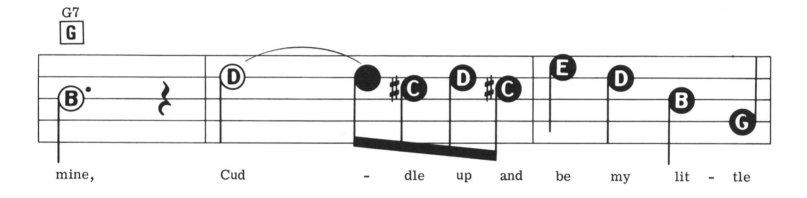

cling - ing vine. Like to feel your cheek so ros - y,

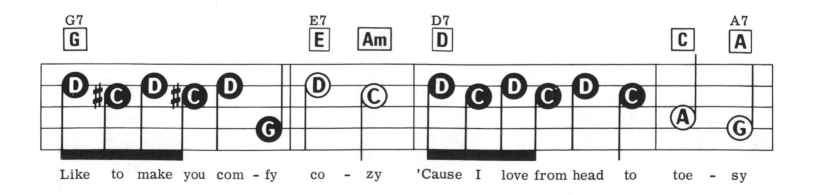

Like to make you com - fy co - zy 'Cause I love from head to toe - sy

Copyright © 1994 by HAL LEONARD CORPORATION
International Copyright Secured All Rights Reserved

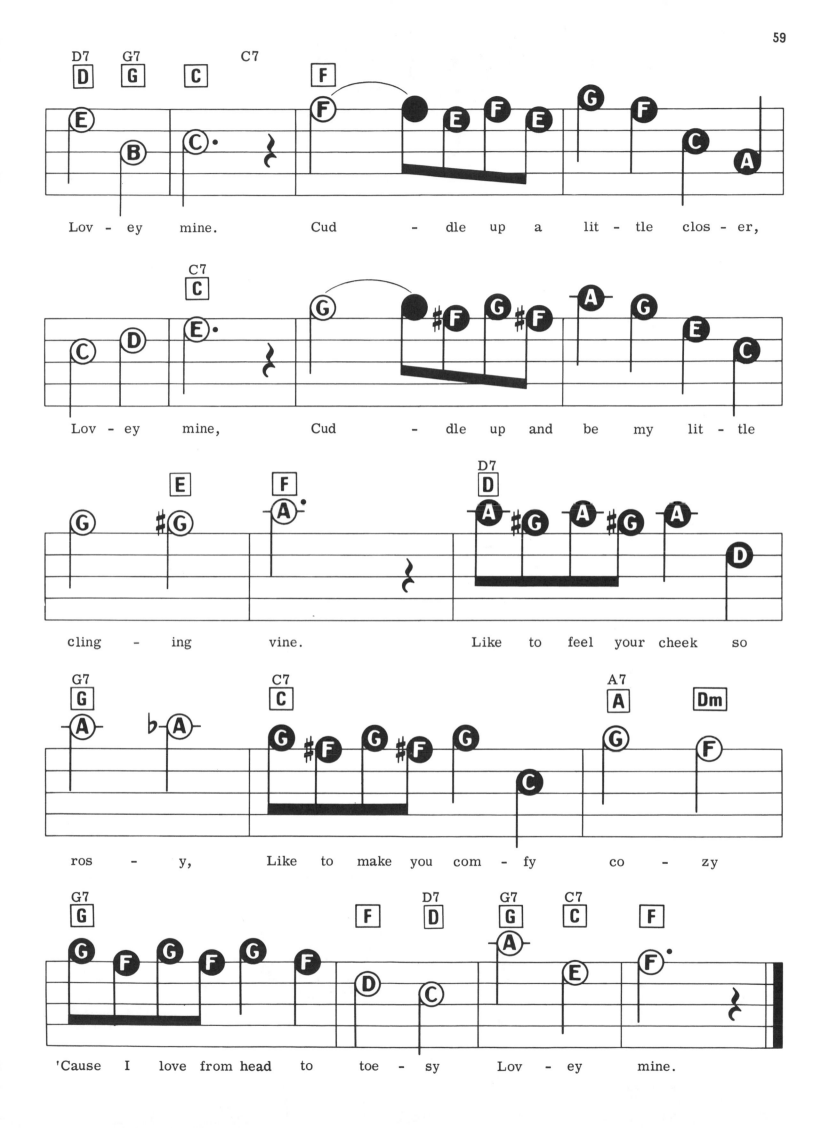

Danny Boy
(Londonderry Air)
featured in the Television Series THE DANNY THOMAS SHOW

Registration 10
Rhythm: 8 Beat or Pops

Words by Frederick Edward Weatherly
Music is Irish Traditional

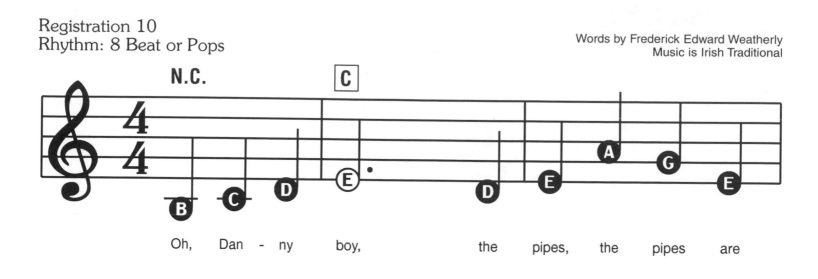

Oh, Dan - ny boy, the pipes, the pipes are

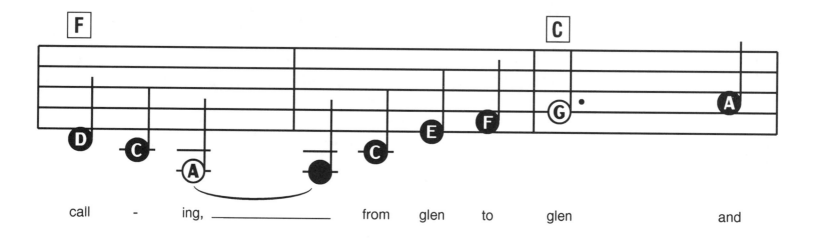

call - ing, _____ from glen to glen and

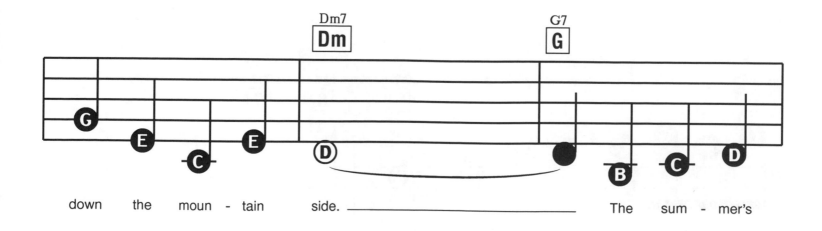

down the moun - tain side. _____ The sum - mer's

Copyright © 1994 by HAL LEONARD CORPORATION
International Copyright Secured   All Rights Reserved

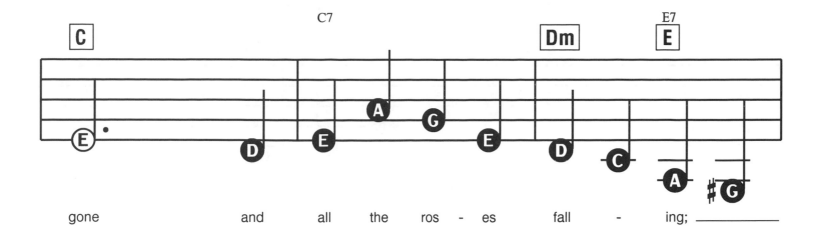

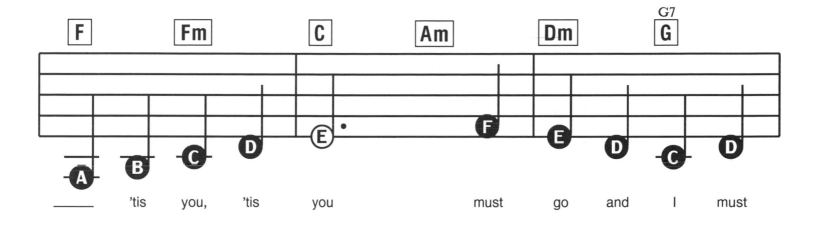

gone   and   all   the   ros - es   fall - ing; _____

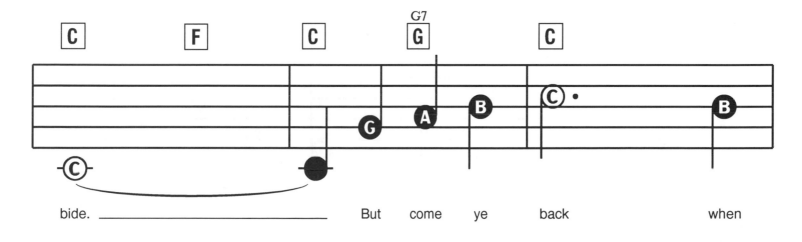

_____ 'tis you,   'tis   you   must   go   and   I   must

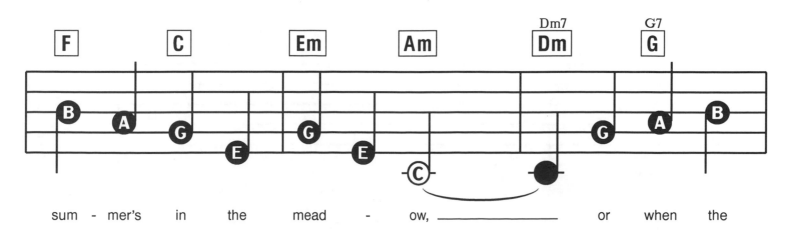

bide. _____   But   come   ye   back   when

sum - mer's   in   the   mead - ow, _____   or   when   the

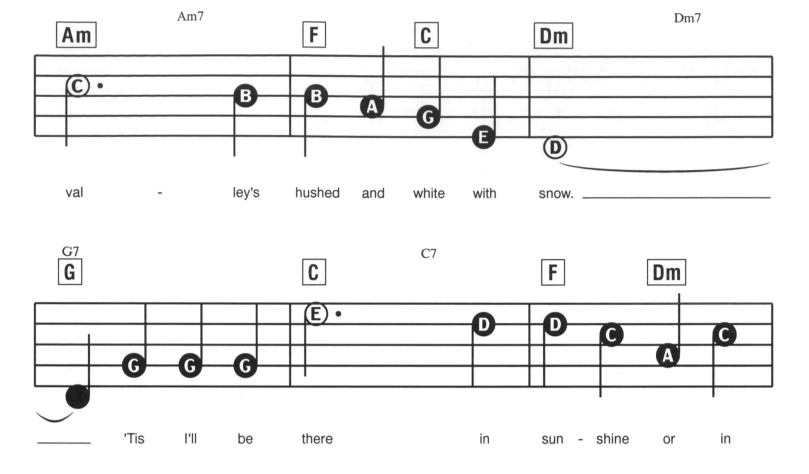

val - ley's hushed and white with snow. _____

_____ 'Tis I'll be there in sun - shine or in

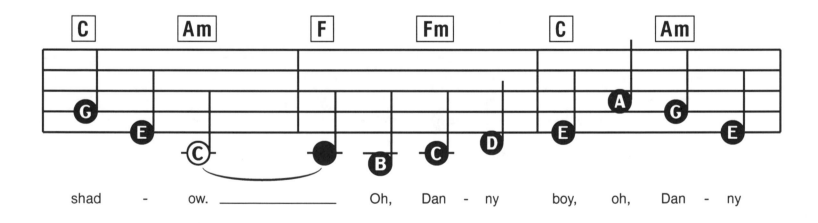

shad - ow. _____ Oh, Dan - ny boy, oh, Dan - ny

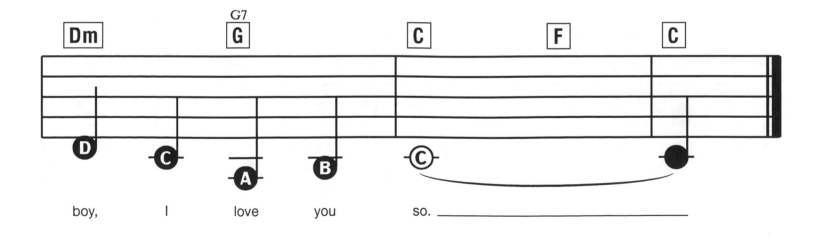

boy, I love you so. _____

Dardanella

Registration 10
Rhythm: Ragtime or Fox Trot

Words by Fred Fisher
Music by Felix Bernard and Johnny S. Black

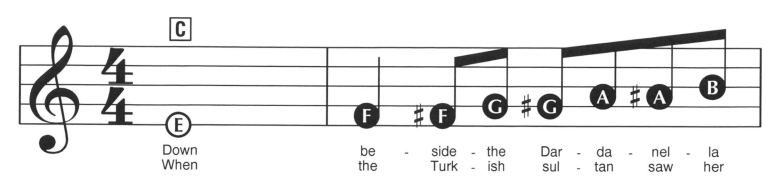

Down .... be - side - the Dar - da - nel - la
When .... the Turk - ish sul - tan saw her

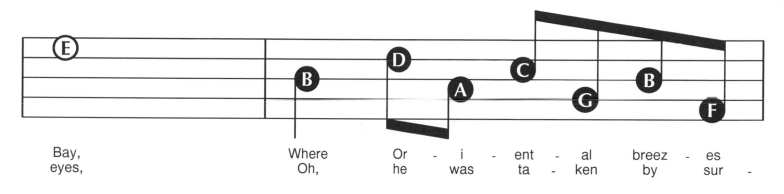

Bay, ... Where Or - i - ent - al breez - es
eyes, ... Oh, he was ta - ken by sur -

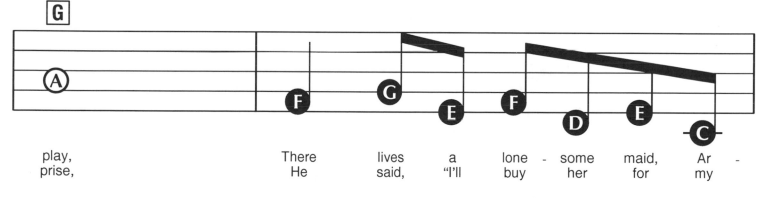

play, ... There lives a lone - some maid, Ar -
prise, ... He said, "I'll buy her for my

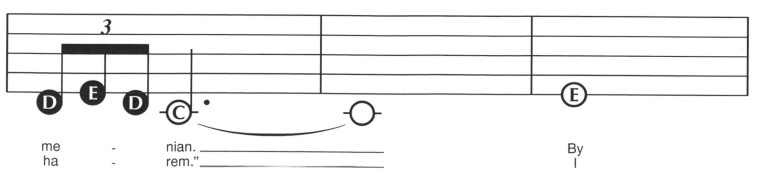

me - nian. _____ By
ha - rem." _____ I

Copyright © 1996 by HAL LEONARD CORPORATION
International Copyright Secured   All Rights Reserved

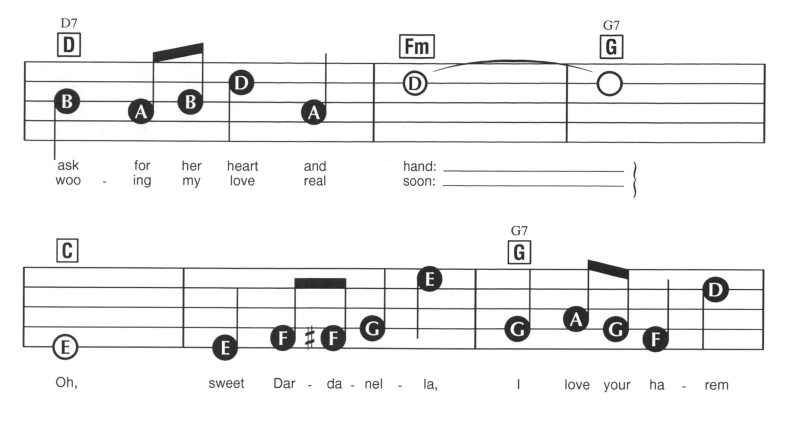

ask   for   her   heart   and   hand: _____

woo - ing my love   and   real   soon: _____

Oh,   sweet   Dar - da - nel - la,   I   love your ha - rem

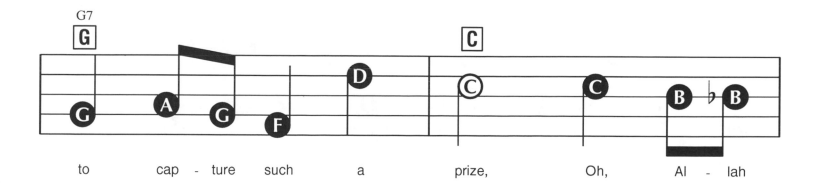

eyes,   I'm   a   luck - y fel - low

to   cap - ture such   a   prize,   Oh,   Al - lah

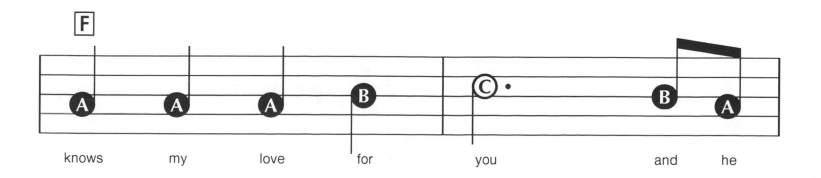

knows   my   love   for   you   and   he

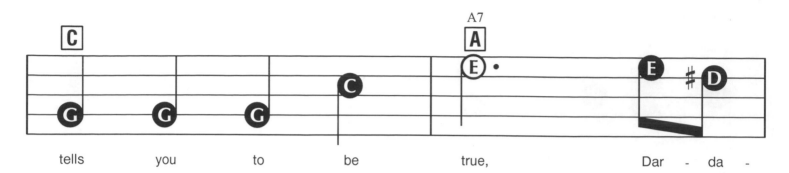

tells   you   to   be   true,   Dar - da -

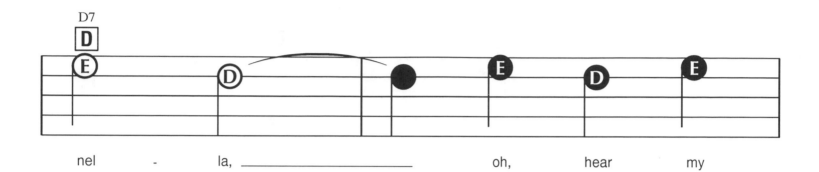

nel - la, _____ oh,   hear   my

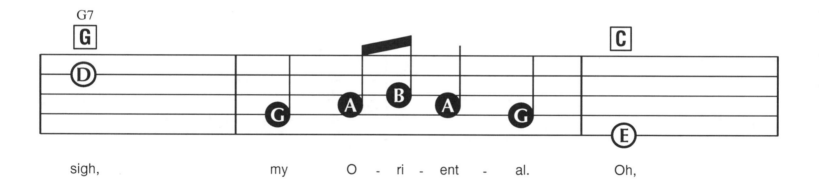

sigh,   my   O - ri - ent - al.   Oh,

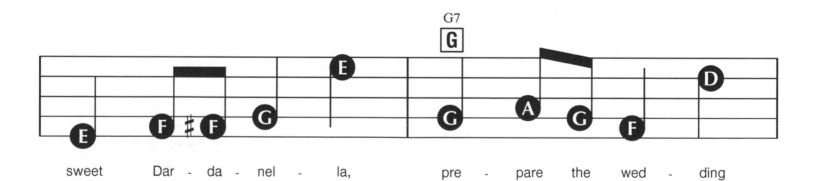

sweet   Dar - da - nel - la,   pre - pare   the   wed - ding

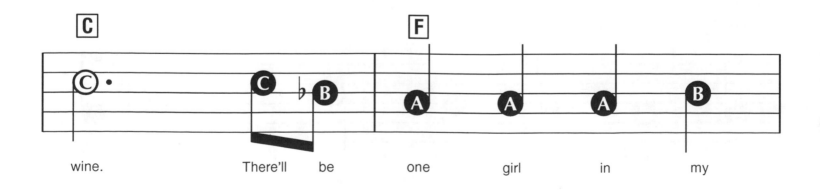

wine.   There'll   be   one   girl   in   my

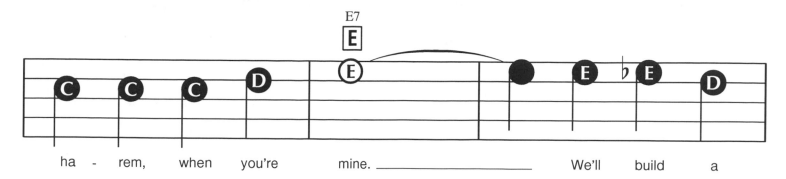

ha - rem, when you're   mine. _____ We'll build a

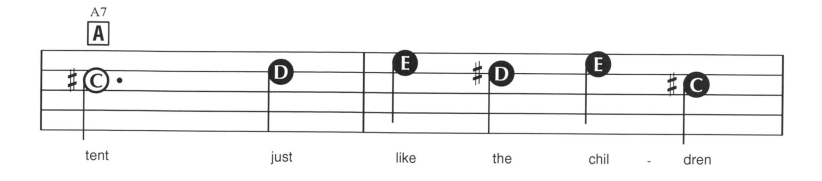

tent   just   like   the   chil - dren

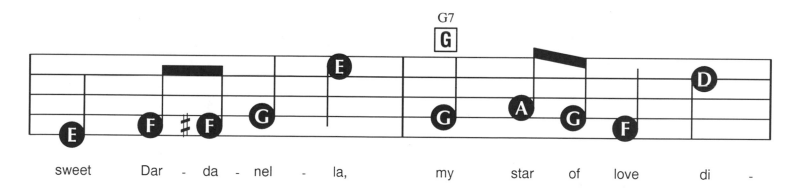

of   the   O - ri - ent.   Oh,

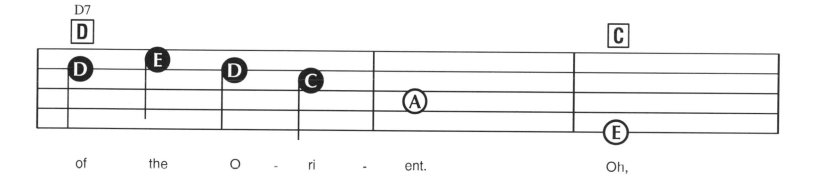

sweet   Dar - da - nel - la,   my   star of love di -

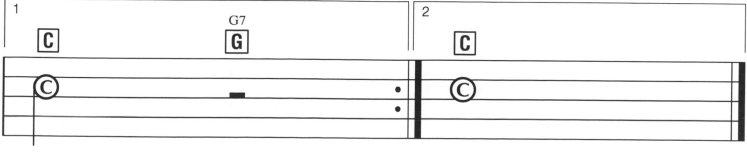

vine.   vine.

The Darktown Strutters' Ball
from THE STORY OF VERNON AND IRENE CASTLE

Registration 8
Rhythm: Polka, Fox-Trot, or Dixie

Words and Music by
Shelton Brooks

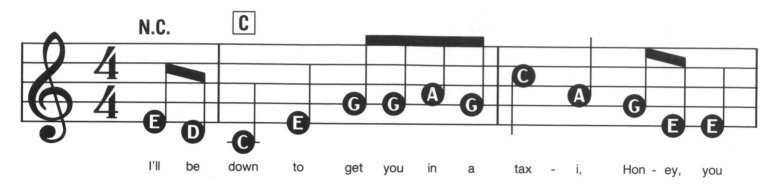

I'll be down to get you in a tax - i, Hon - ey, you

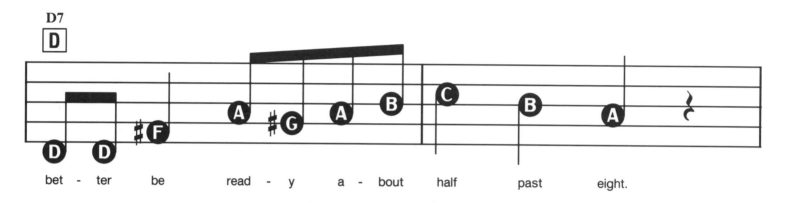

bet - ter be read - y a - bout half past eight.

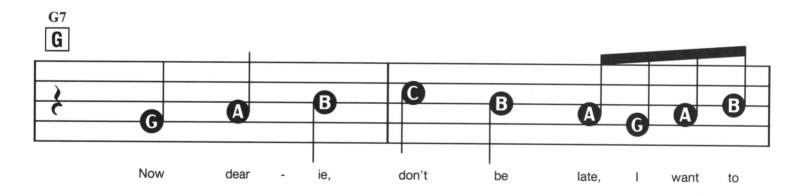

Now dear - ie, don't be late, I want to

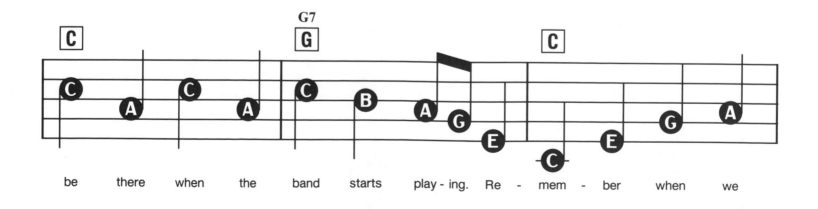

be there when the band starts play - ing. Re - mem - ber when we

Copyright © 1996 by HAL LEONARD CORPORATION
International Copyright Secured   All Rights Reserved

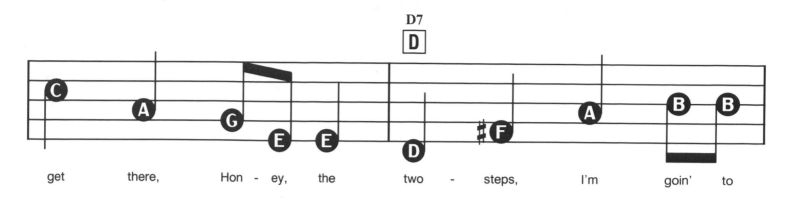

get there, Hon - ey, the two - steps, I'm goin' to

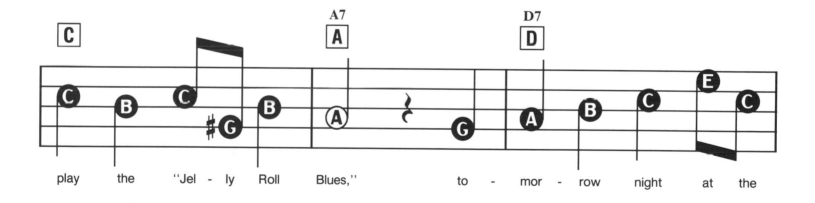

have 'em all. Goin' to dance out both my shoes when they

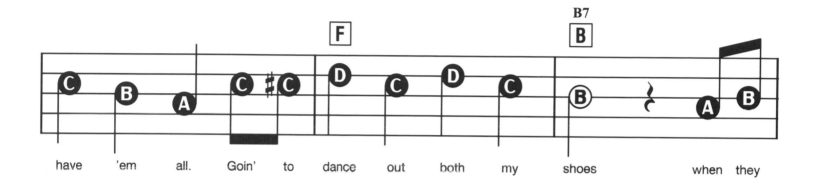

play the "Jel - ly Roll Blues," to - mor - row night at the

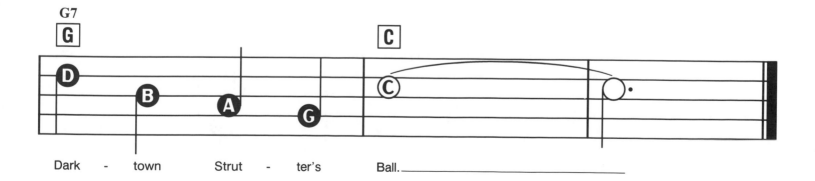

Dark - town Strut - ter's Ball.

Down by the Old Mill Stream

Registration 3
Rhythm: Waltz

Words and Music by
Tell Taylor

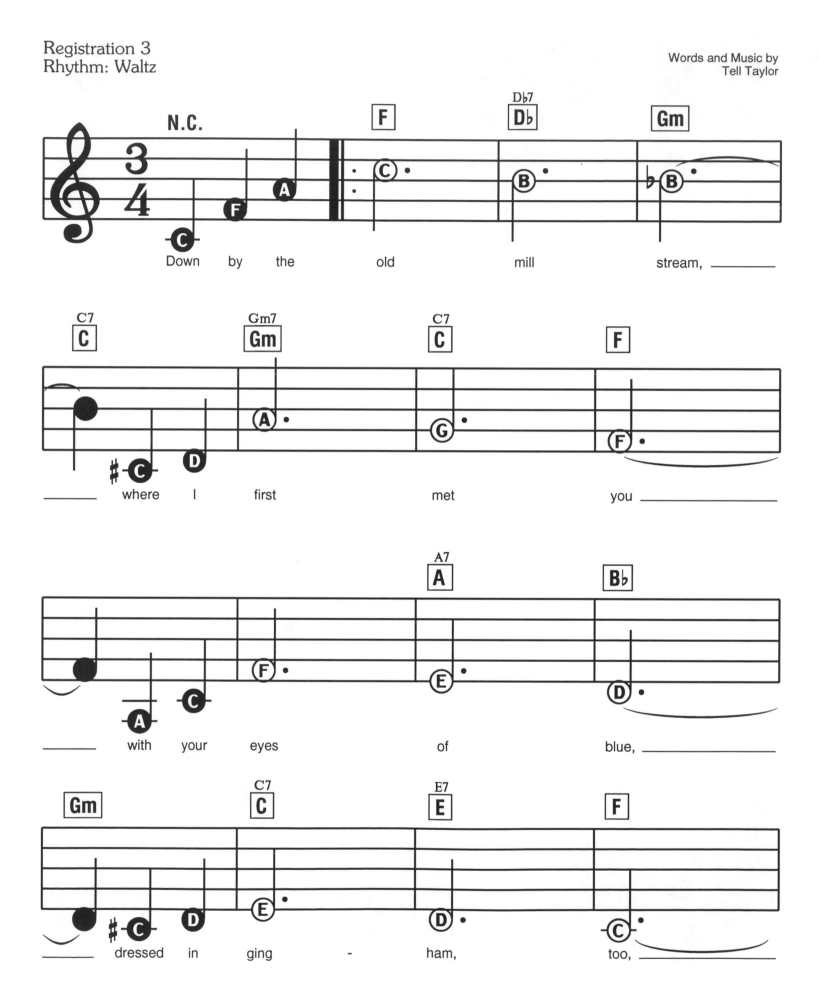

Copyright © 1994 by HAL LEONARD CORPORATION
International Copyright Secured   All Rights Reserved

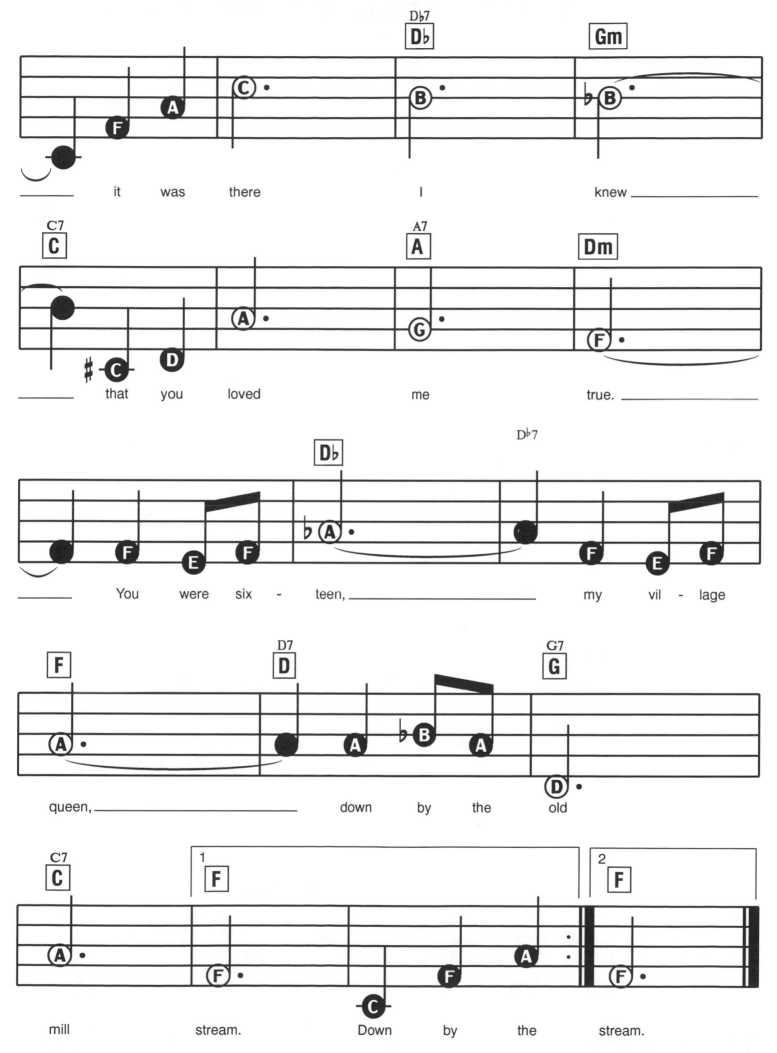

The Entertainer
featured in the Motion Picture THE STING

Registration 8
Rhythm: March or Polka

By Scott Joplin

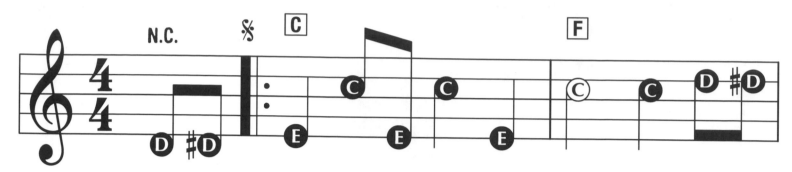

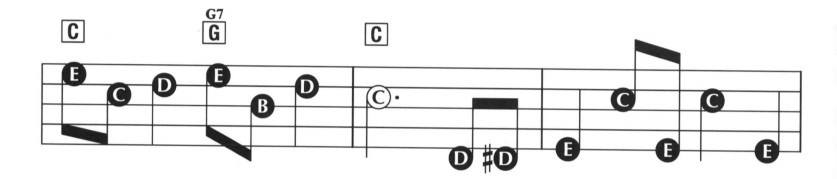

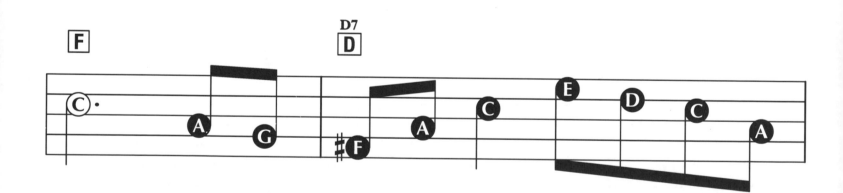

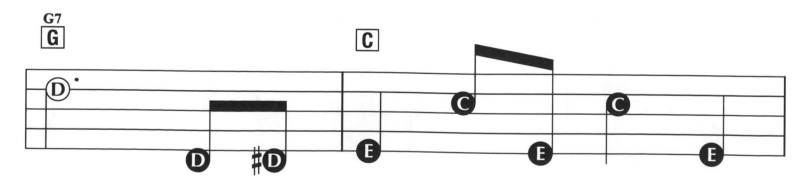

Copyright © 1994 by HAL LEONARD CORPORATION
International Copyright Secured   All Rights Reserved

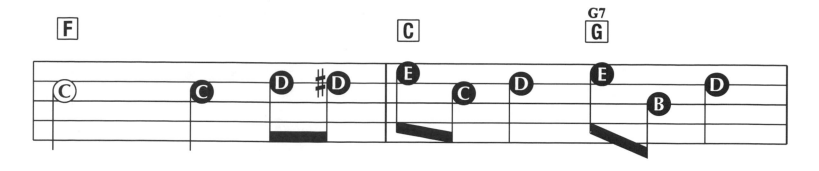

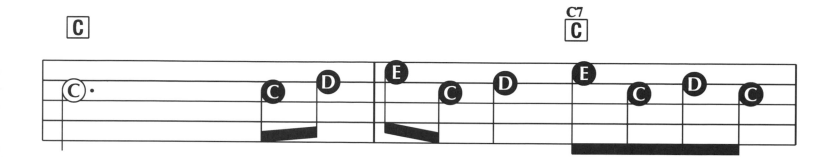

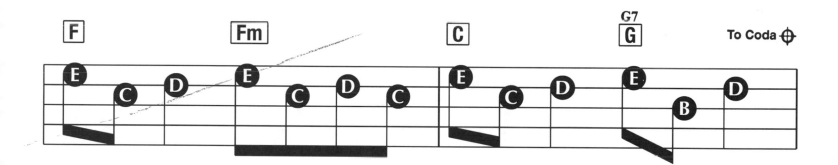

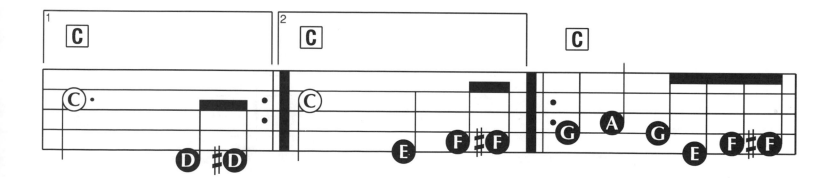

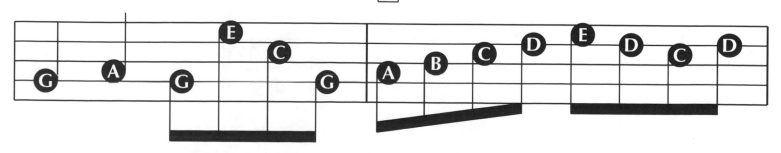

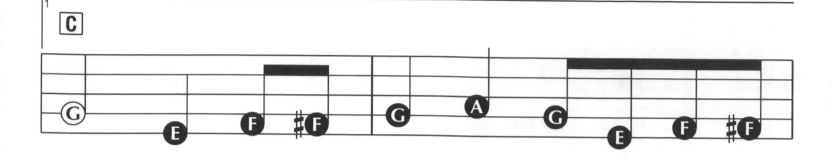

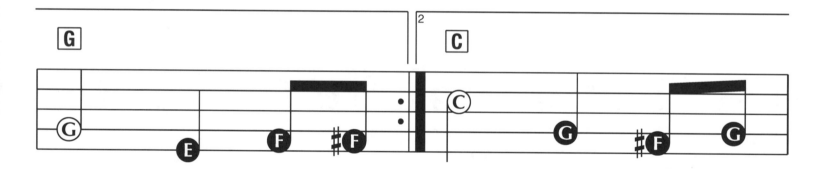

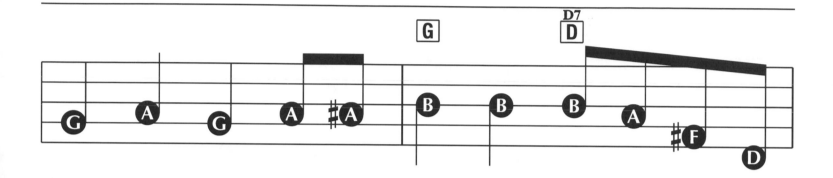

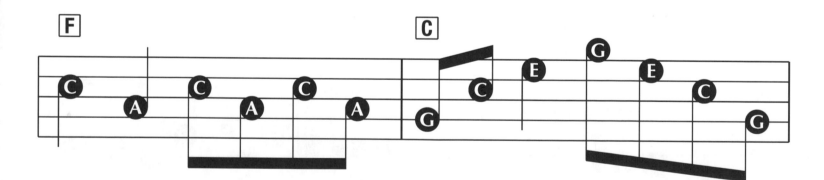

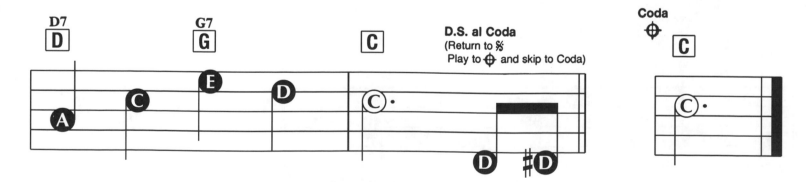

Every Little Movement
(Has a Meaning All Its Own)

Registration 2
Rhythm: Fox Trot or Swing

Words by Otto Harbach
Music by Karl Hoschna

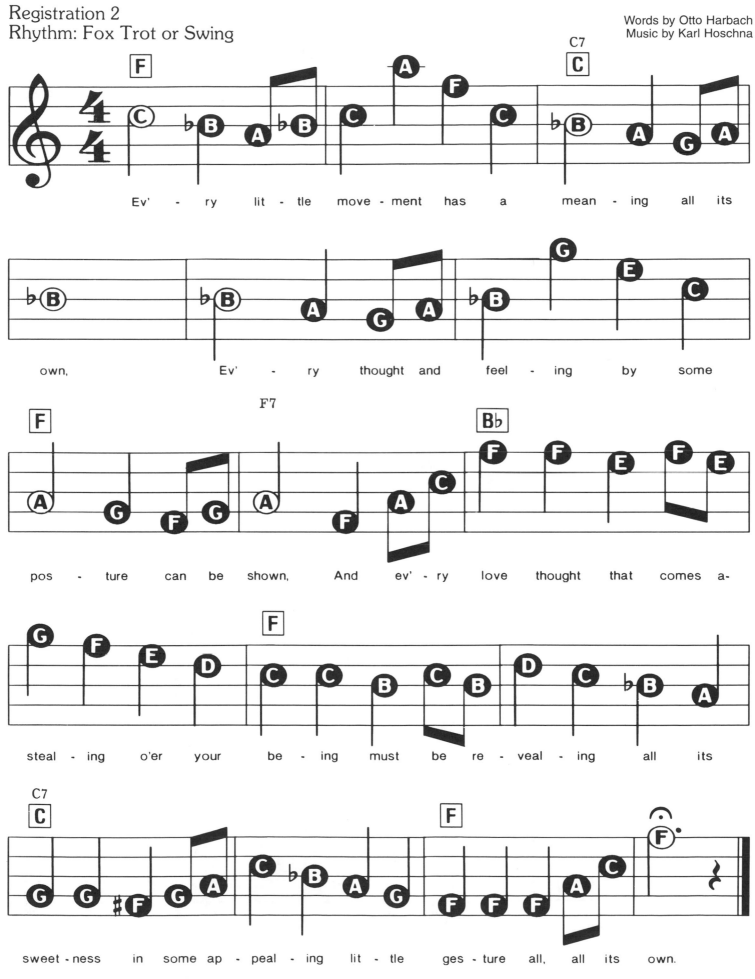

Copyright © 1991 by HAL LEONARD CORPORATION
International Copyright Secured   All Rights Reserved

Fascination
(Valse Tzigane)

Registration 10
Rhythm: Waltz

By F. D. Marchetti

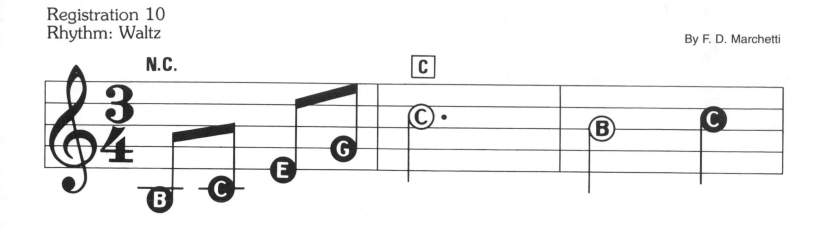

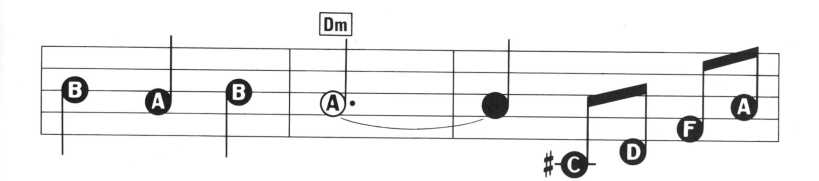

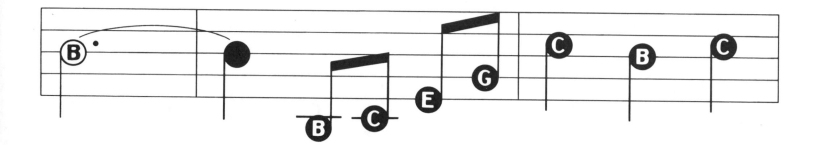

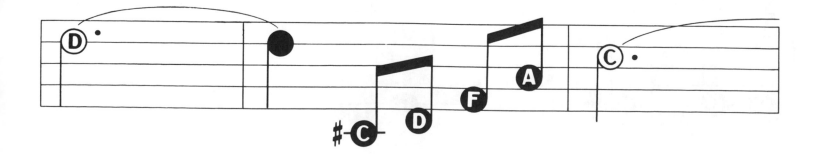

Copyright © 1994 by HAL LEONARD CORPORATION
International Copyright Secured   All Rights Reserved

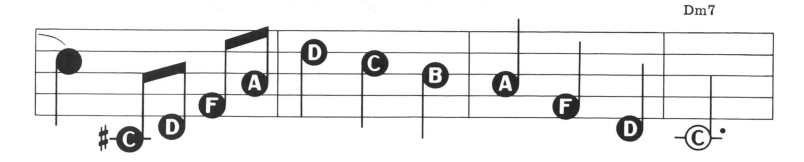

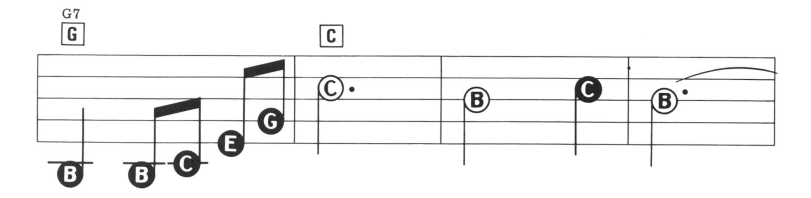

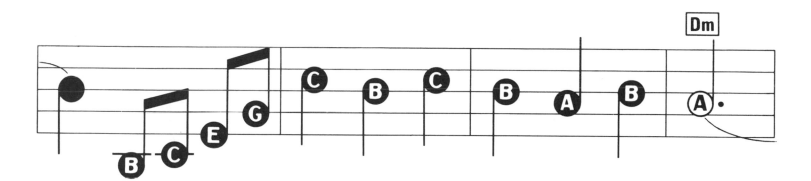

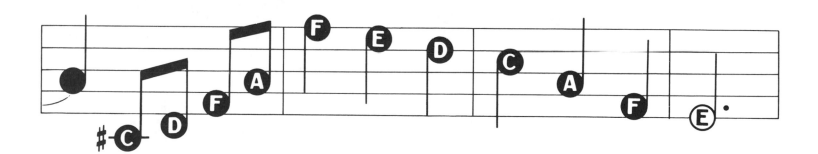

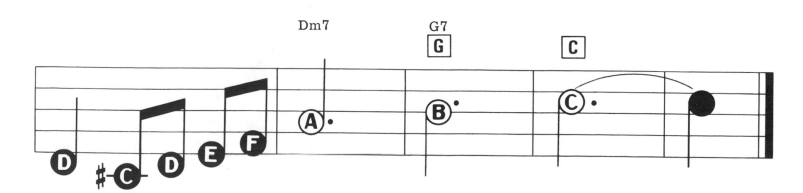

For Me and My Gal

from FOR ME AND MY GAL

Registration 3
Rhythm: Swing

Words by Edgar Leslie and E. Ray Goetz
Music by George W. Meyer

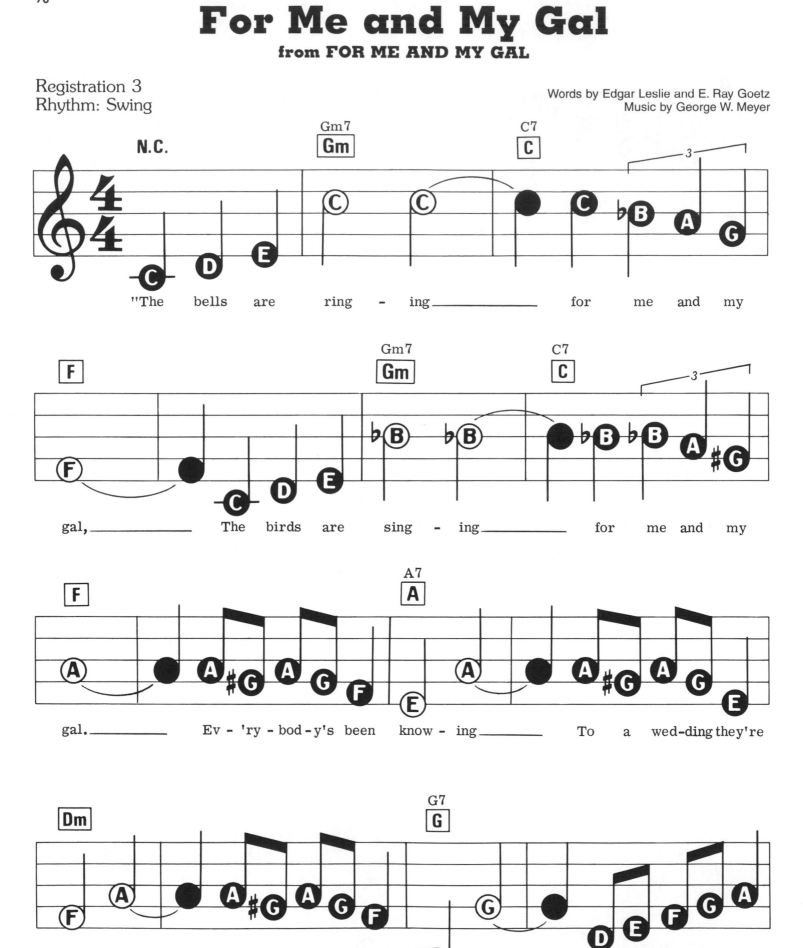

Copyright © 1994 by HAL LEONARD CORPORATION
International Copyright Secured   All Rights Reserved

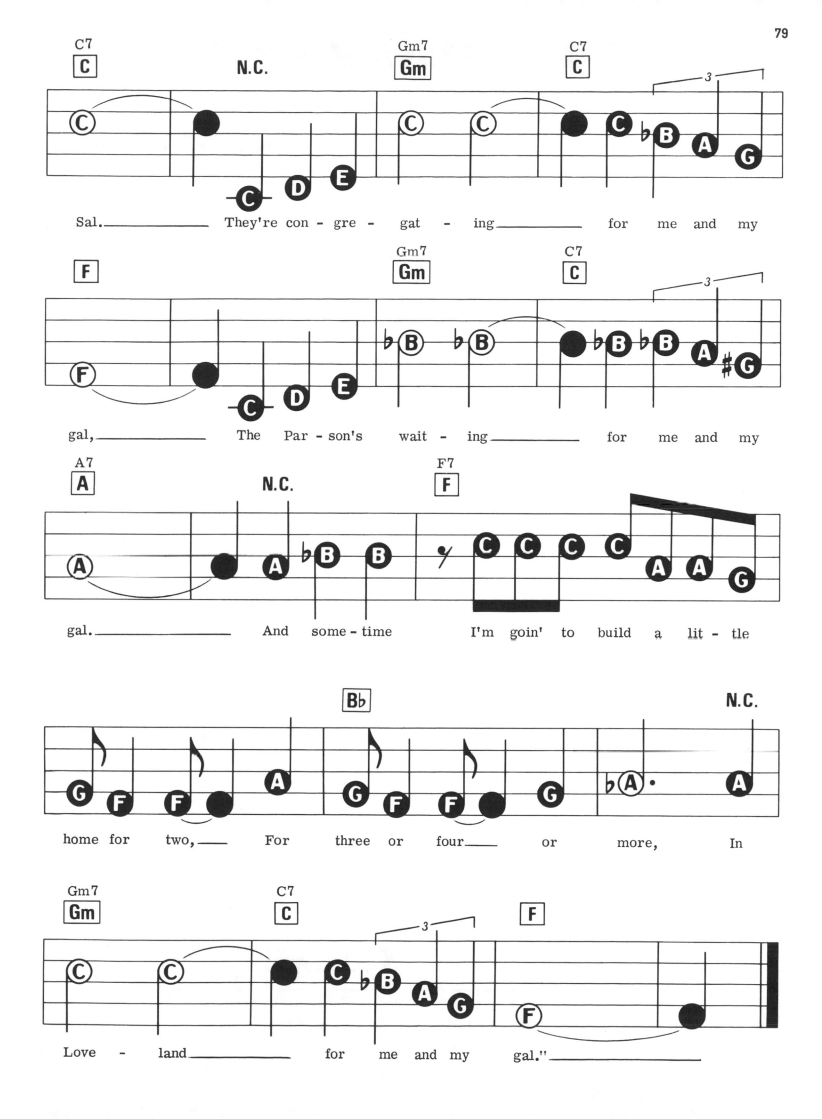

The Glow Worm

Registration 4
Rhythm: Fox Trot or Cha-Cha

English Words by Lilla Cayley Robinson
German Words and Music by Paul Lincke

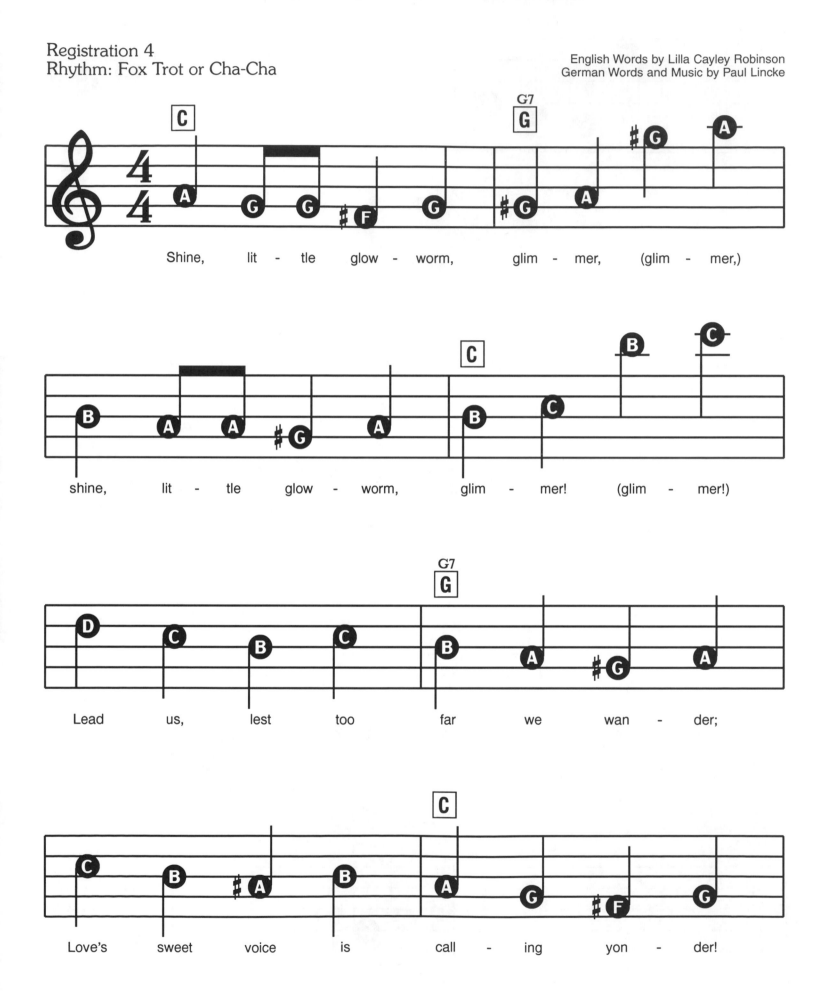

Copyright © 1994 by HAL LEONARD CORPORATION
International Copyright Secured   All Rights Reserved

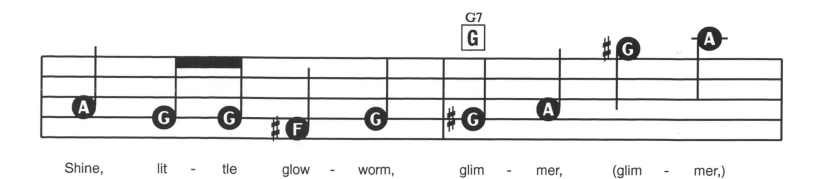

Shine, lit - tle glow - worm, glim - mer, (glim - mer,)

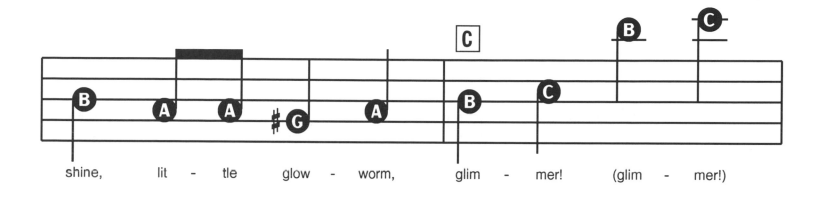

shine, lit - tle glow - worm, glim - mer! (glim - mer!)

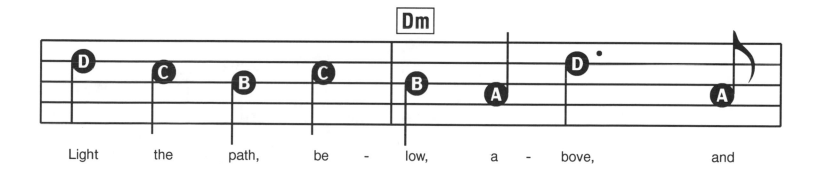

Light the path, be - low, a - bove, and

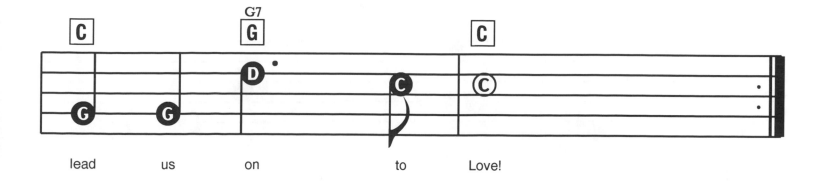

lead us on to Love!

A Good Man Is Hard to Find

Registration 5
Rhythm: 2-Beat, Swing, or Shuffle

Words and Music by
Eddie Green

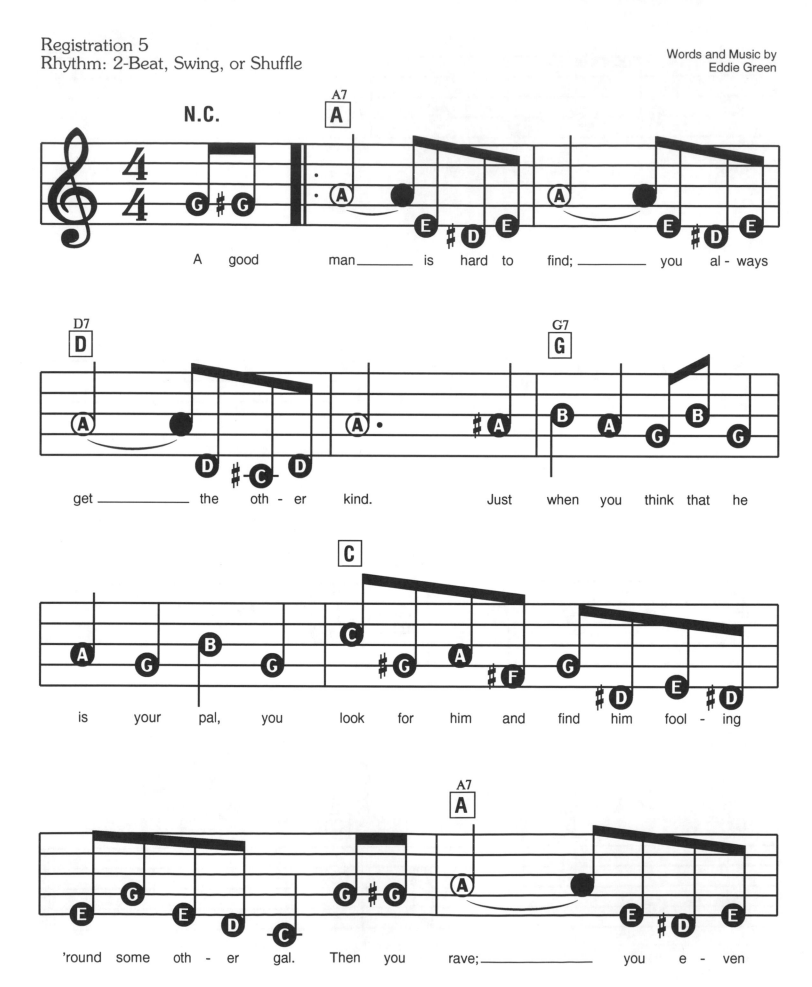

Copyright © 1993 by HAL LEONARD CORPORATION
International Copyright Secured   All Rights Reserved

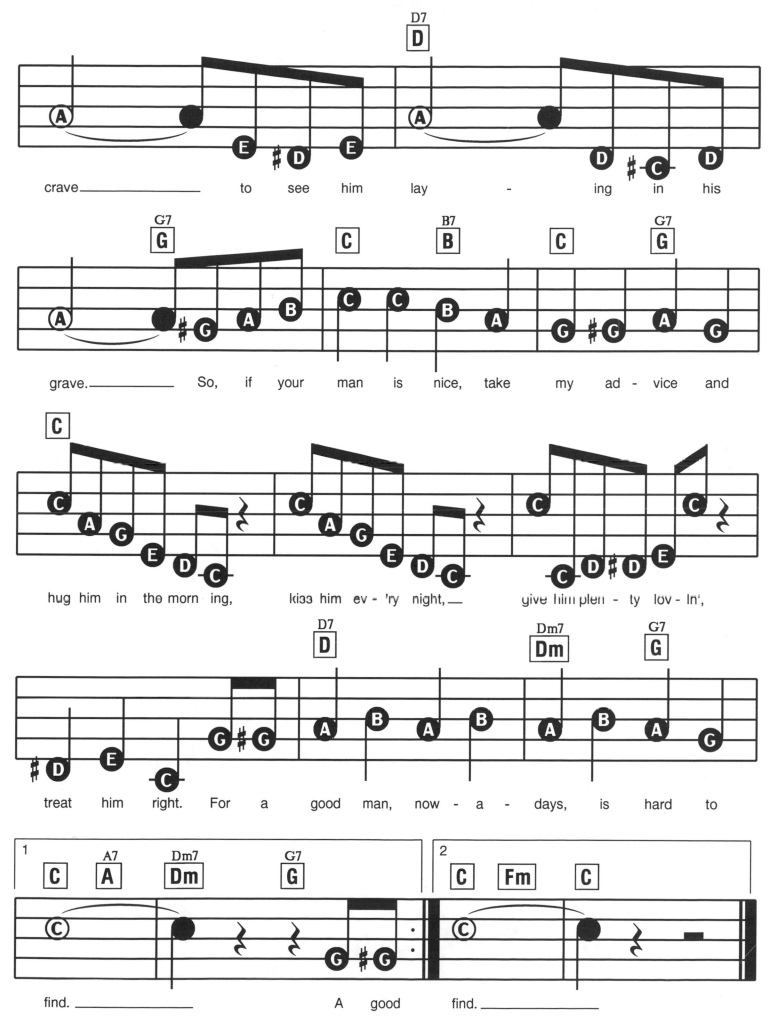

Goodbye, My Lady Love

Registration 2
Rhythm: March or Fox Trot

Words and Music by
Joseph E. Howard

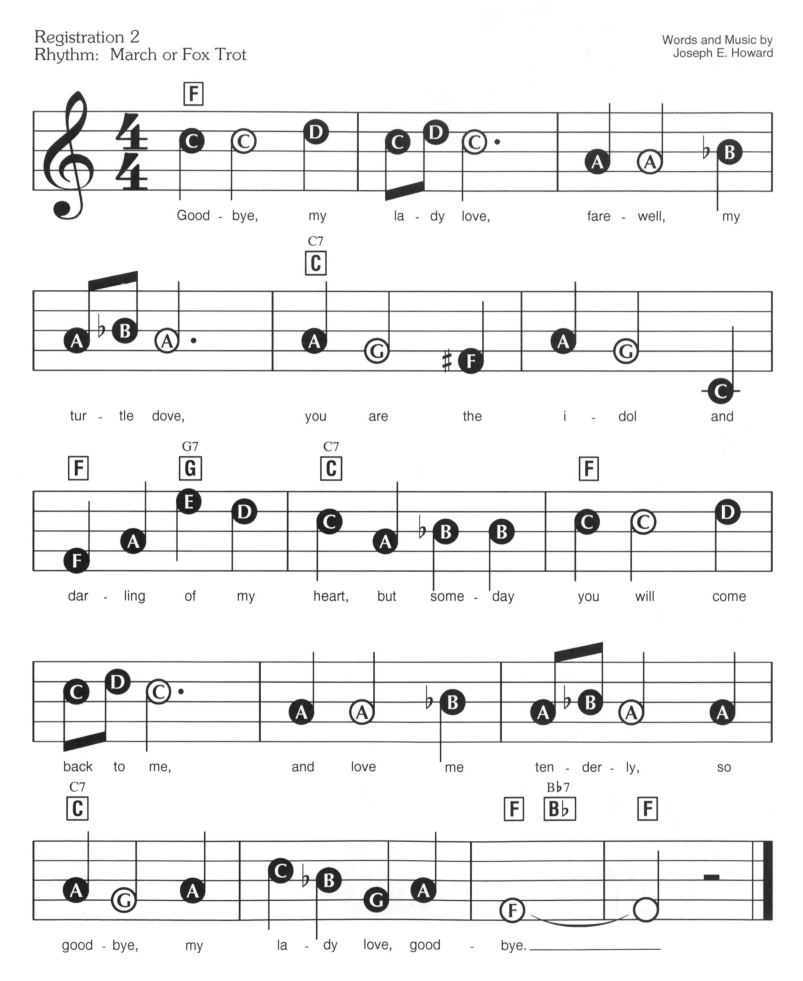

Copyright © 1996 by HAL LEONARD CORPORATION
International Copyright Secured   All Rights Reserved

(There'll Be)
A Hot Time in the Old Town Tonight

Registration 7
Rhythm: March

Words by Joe Hayden
Music by Theodore M. Metz

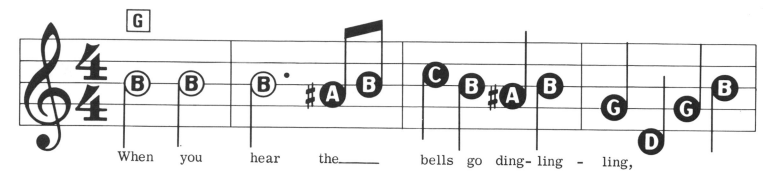

When you hear the ___ bells go ding- ling - ling,

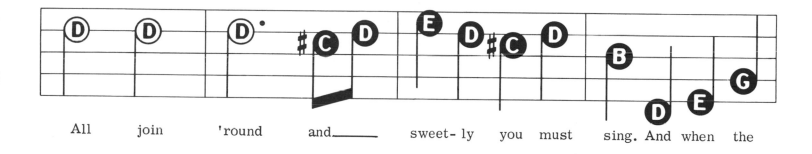

All join 'round and ___ sweet- ly you must sing. And when the

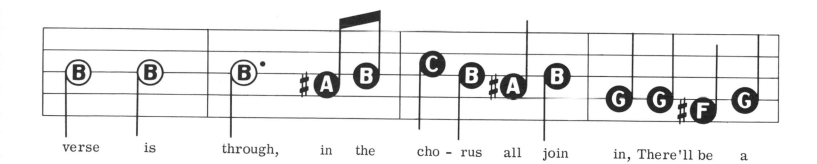

verse is through, in the cho - rus all join in, There'll be a

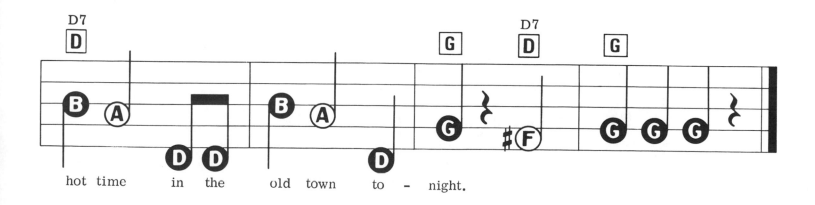

hot time in the old town to - night.

Copyright © 1994 by HAL LEONARD CORPORATION
International Copyright Secured   All Rights Reserved

Gypsy Love Song

from THE FORTUNE TELLER

Registration 5
Rhythm: Pops or 8 Beat

Words by Harry B. Smith
Music by Victor Herbert

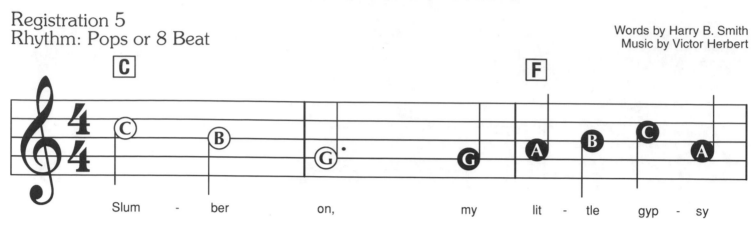

Slum - ber on, my lit - tle gyp - sy

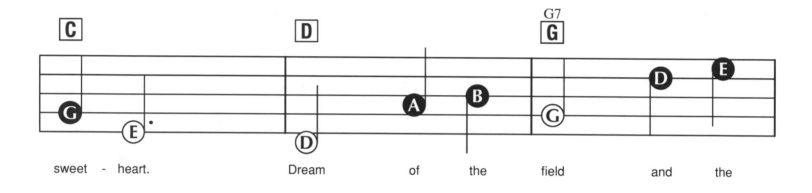

sweet - heart. Dream of the field and the

grove. _____ Can you hear me,

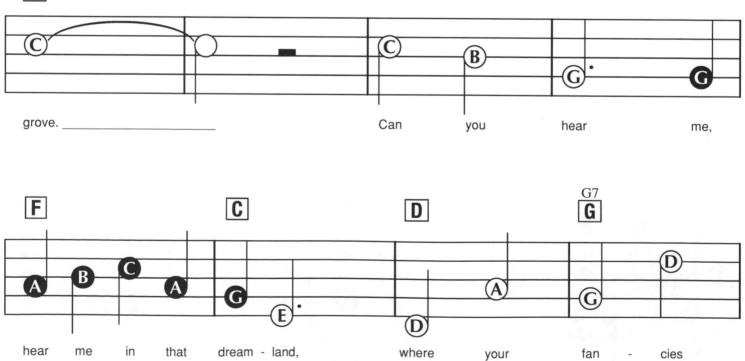

hear me in that dream - land, where your fan - cies

Copyright © 1994 by HAL LEONARD CORPORATION
International Copyright Secured   All Rights Reserved

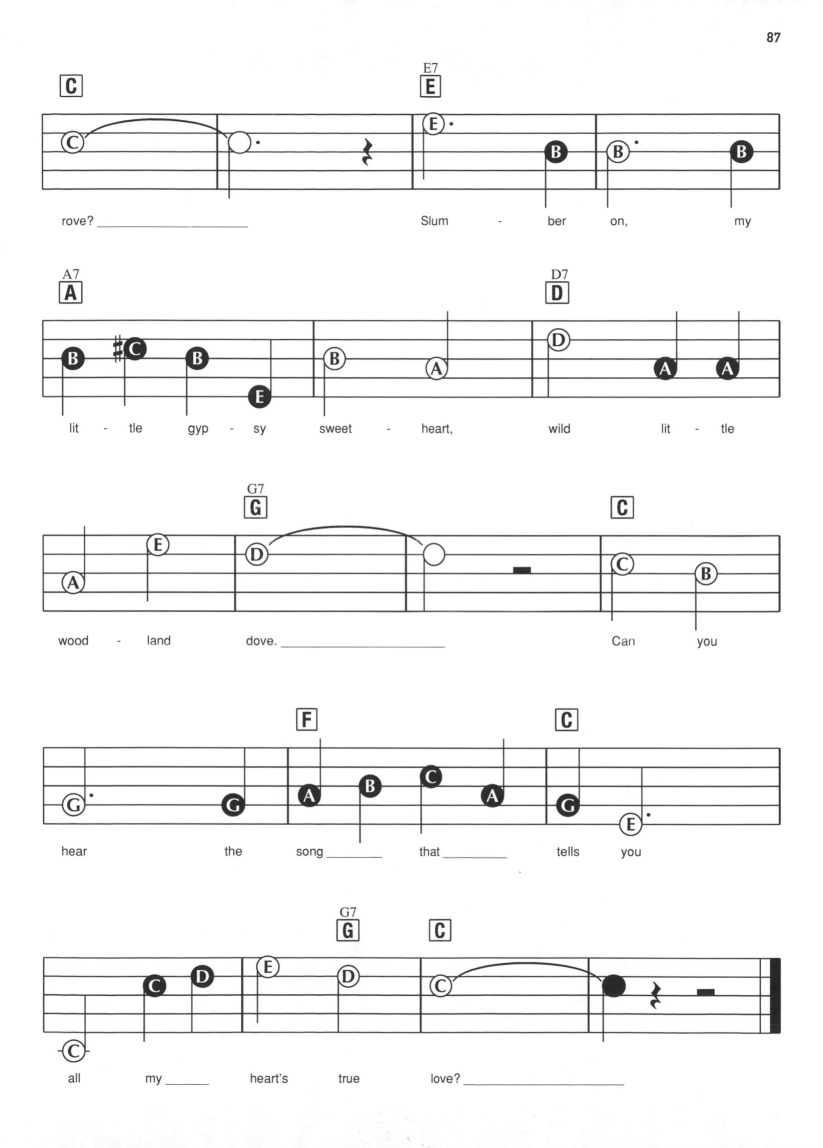

Hearts and Flowers

Registration 1
Rhythm: Fox Trot

Words by Mary D. Brine
Music by Theodore Moses Tobani

Copyright © 1994 by HAL LEONARD CORPORATION
International Copyright Secured   All Rights Reserved

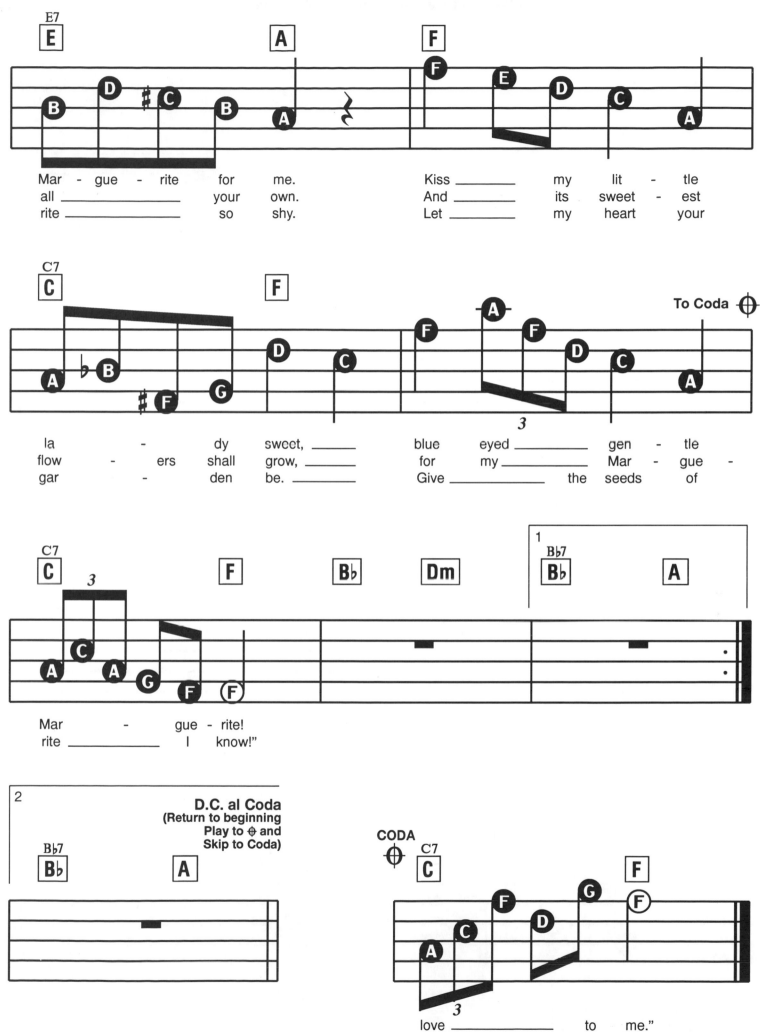

Hello! Ma Baby

Registration 7
Rhythm: Swing

Words by Ida Emerson
Music by Joseph E. Howard

Copyright © 1994 by HAL LEONARD CORPORATION
International Copyright Secured   All Rights Reserved

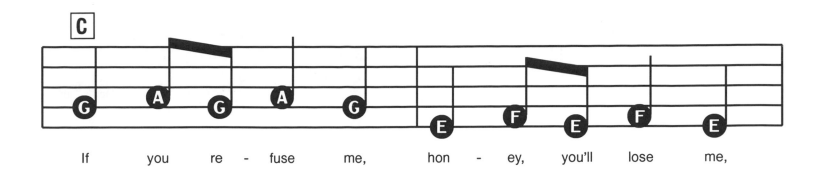

C

If you re - fuse me, hon - ey, you'll lose me,

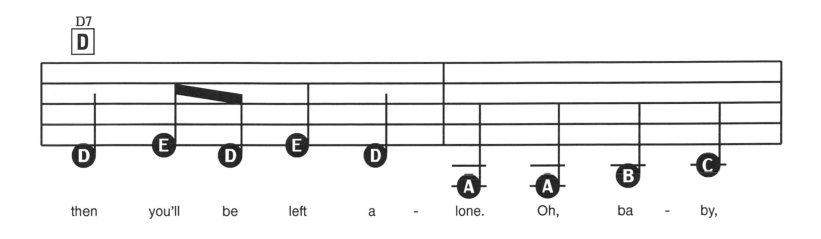

D7
D

then you'll be left a - lone. Oh, ba - by,

G7
G

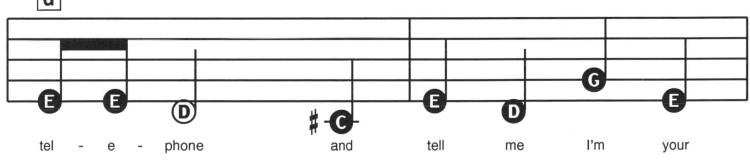

tel - e - phone and tell me I'm your

C   **F7** **F**   **C**

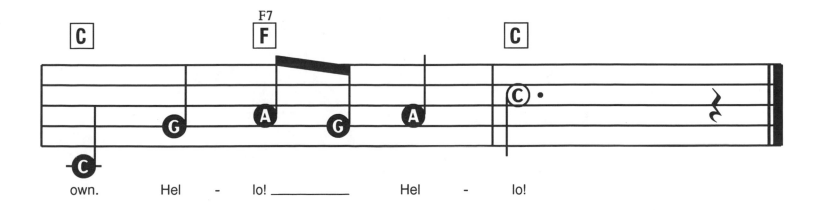

own. Hel - lo! _____ Hel - lo!

How 'Ya Gonna Keep 'Em Down on the Farm?

(After They've Seen Paree)

Registration 8
Rhythm: March

Words by Sam M. Lewis and Joe Young
Music by Walter Donaldson

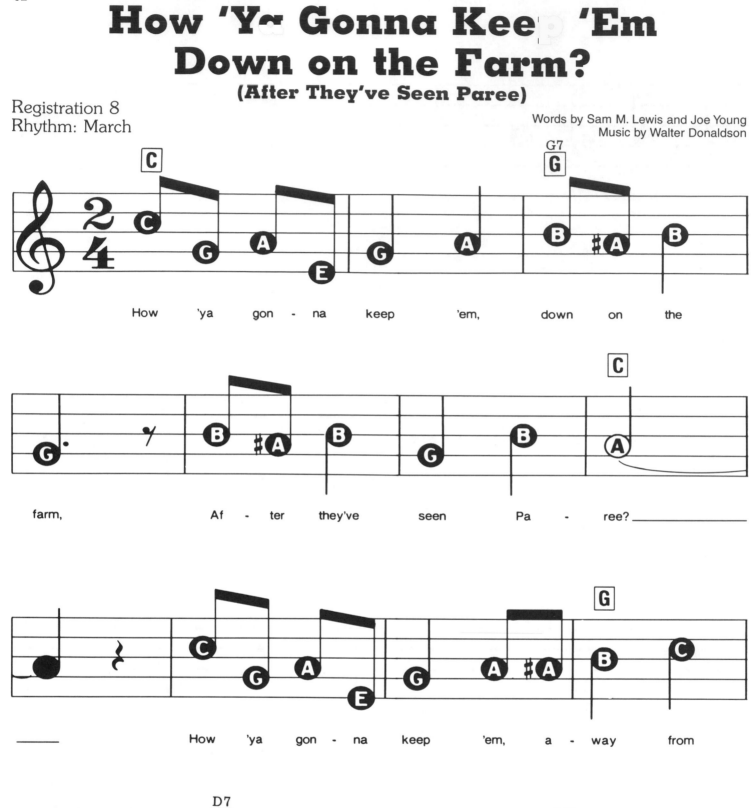

How 'ya gon - na keep 'em, down on the farm, Af - ter they've seen Pa - ree? _____

_____ How 'ya gon - na keep 'em, a - way from Broad - way; Jazz - in' a - roun', And paint - in' the

Copyright © 1996 by HAL LEONARD CORPORATION
International Copyright Secured   All Rights Reserved

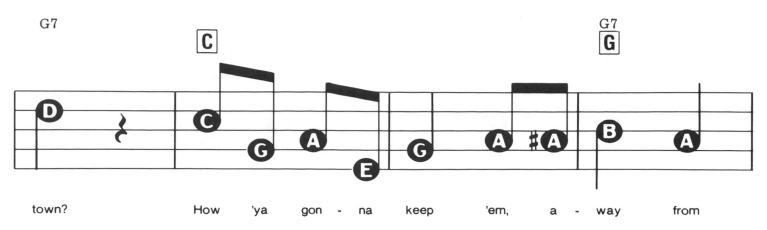

town?   How 'ya   gon - na   keep   'em,   a - way   from

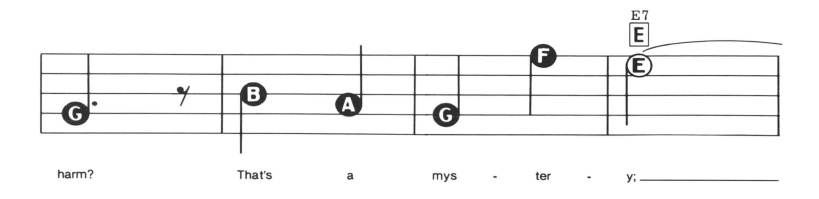

harm?   That's   a   mys - ter - y; _____

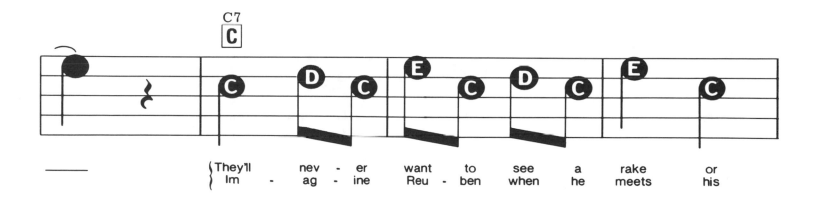

____   {They'll   nev - er   want   to   see   a   rake   or
       Im - ag - ine   Reu - ben   when   he   meets   his

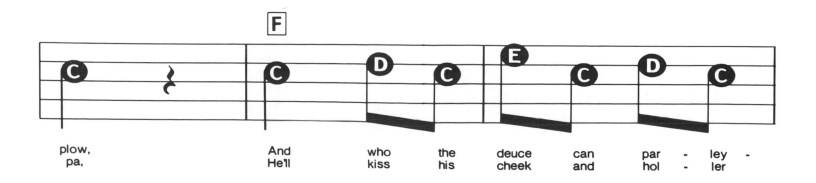

plow,   And   who   the   deuce   can   par - ley -
pa,   He'll   kiss   his   cheek   and   hol - ler

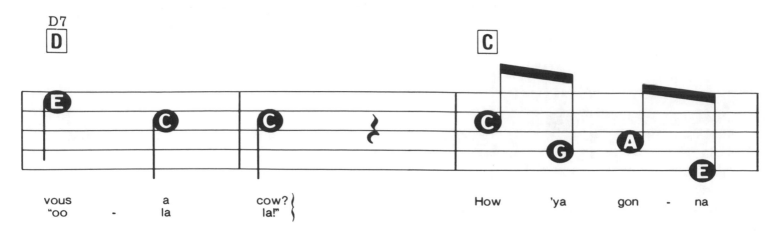

vous   a   cow?   How   'ya   gon -   na
"oo -   la   la!"

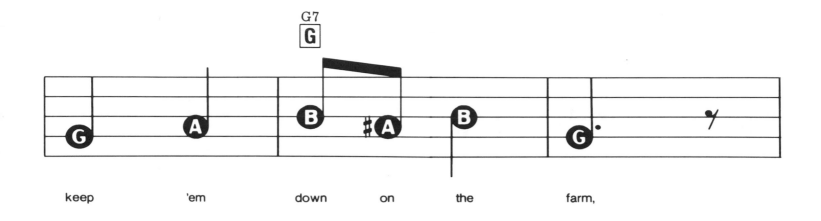

keep   'em   down   on   the   farm,

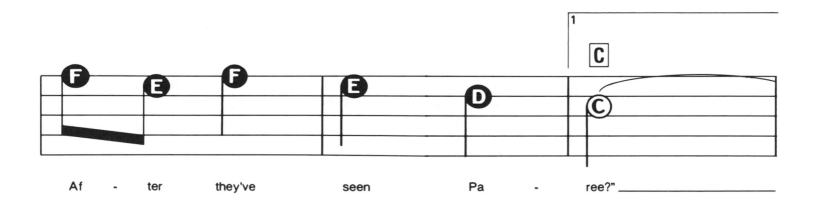

Af - ter   they've   seen   Pa -   ree?"

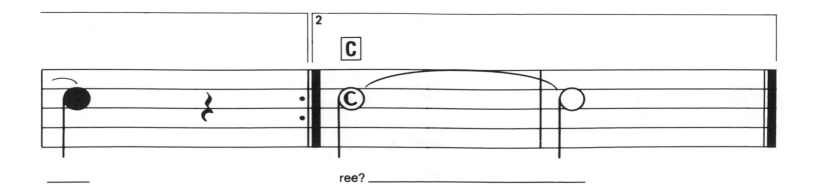

ree?

I Didn't Raise My Boy to Be a Soldier

Words by Alfred Bryan
Music by Al Piantadosi

Registration 4
Rhythm: Pops

Ten mil - lion sol - diers to the war have gone, who may
vic - to - ry can cheer a moth - er's heart, when she

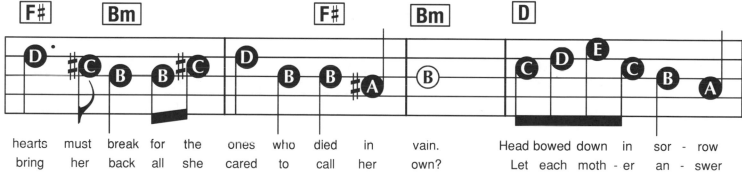

nev - er re - turn a gain. Ten mil - lion moth - ers'
looks at her blight - ed home? What vic - to - ry can

hearts must break for the ones who died in vain. Head bowed down in sor - row
bring her back all she cared to call her own? Let each moth - er an - swer

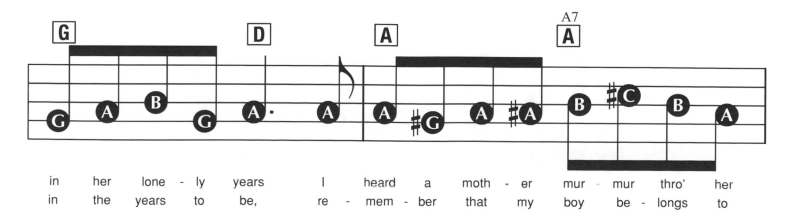

in her lone - ly years I heard a moth - er mur - mur thro' her
in the years to be, re - mem - ber that my boy be - longs to

Copyright © 1991 by HAL LEONARD CORPORATION
International Copyright Secured   All Rights Reserved

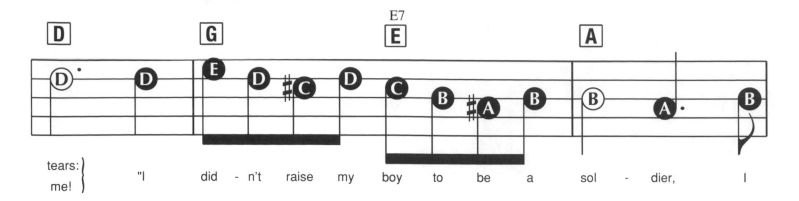

tears: } "I did-n't raise my boy to be a sol - dier, I
me! }

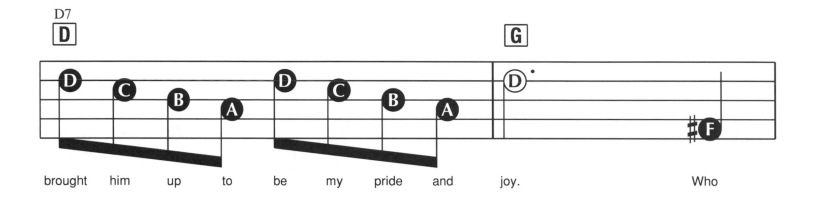

brought him up to be my pride and joy. Who

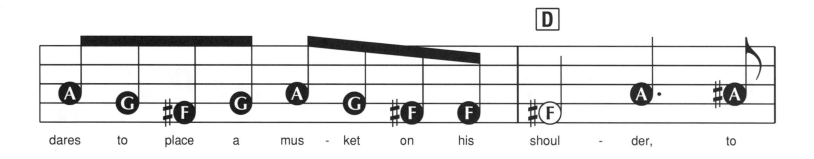

dares to place a mus - ket on his shoul - der, to

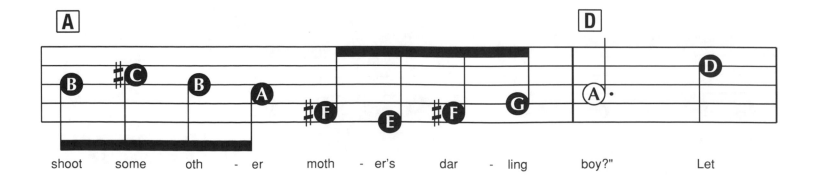

shoot some oth - er moth - er's dar - ling boy?" Let

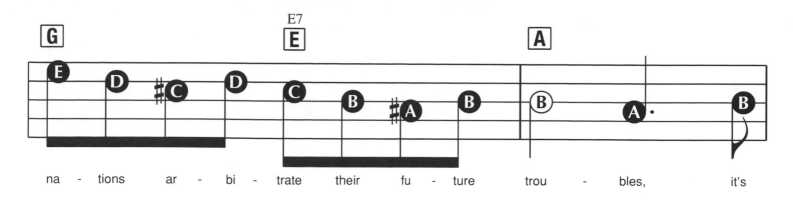

na - tions ar - bi - trate their fu - ture trou - bles, it's

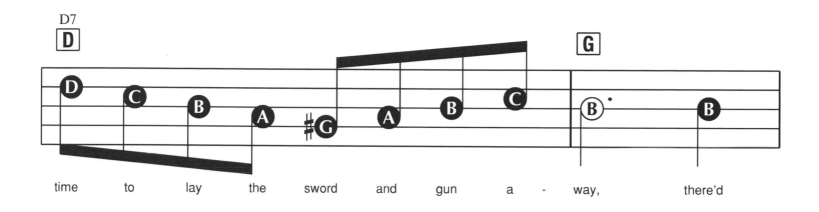

time to lay the sword and gun a - way, there'd

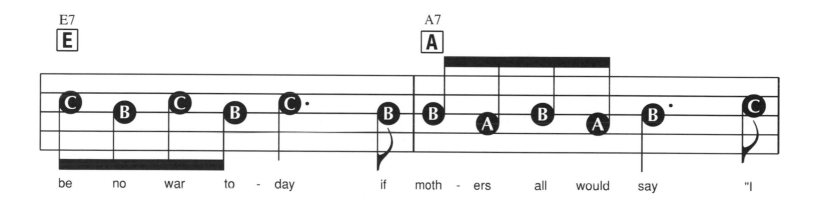

be no war to - day if moth - ers all would say "I

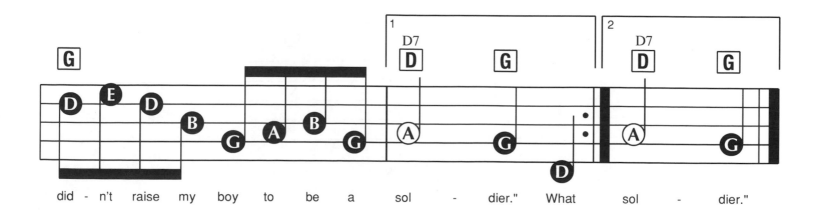

did - n't raise my boy to be a sol - dier." What sol - dier."

I Love a Piano
from the Stage Production STOP! LOOK! LISTEN!

Registration 8
Rhythm: Swing

Words and Music by
Irving Berlin

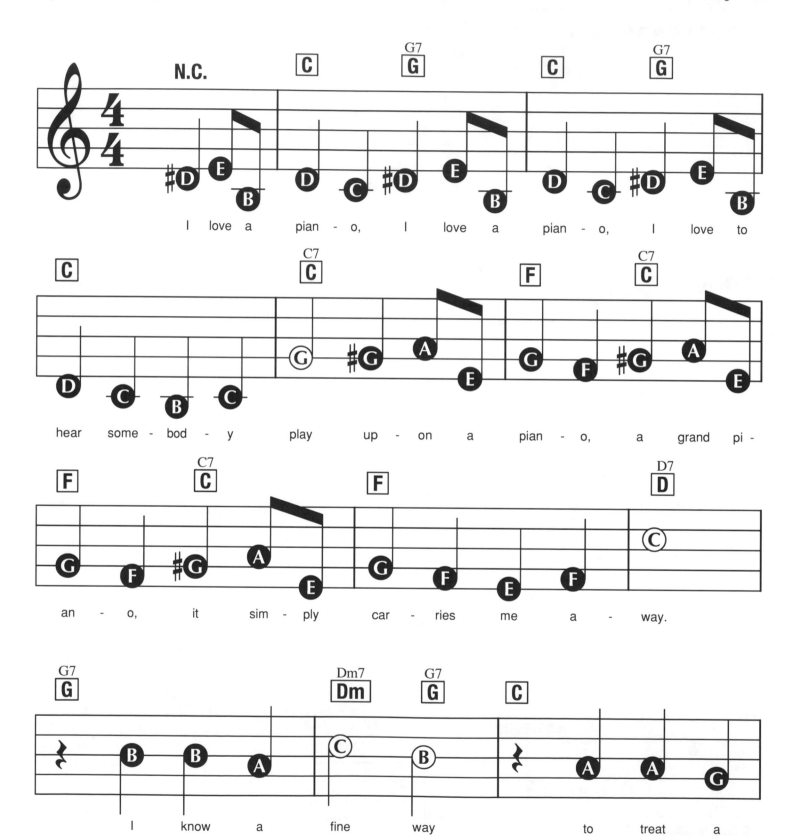

© Copyright 1915 by Irving Berlin
Copyright Renewed
International Copyright Secured   All Rights Reserved

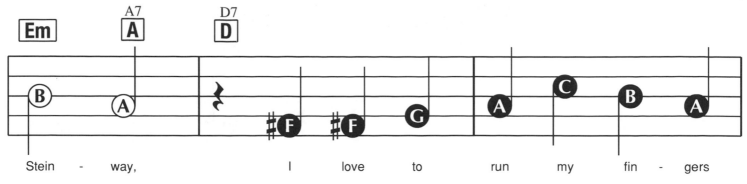

Stein - way, I love to run my fin - gers

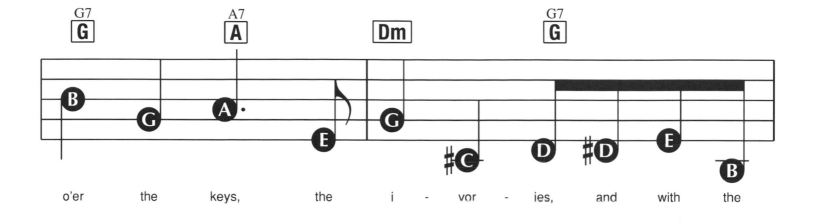

o'er the keys, the i - vor - ies, and with the

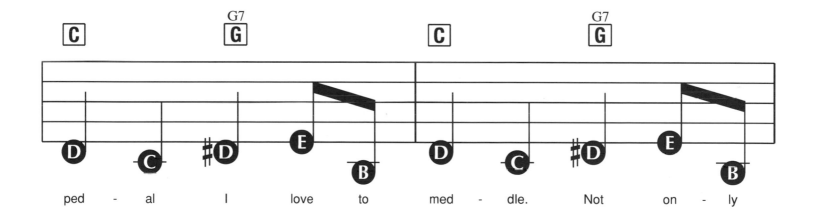

ped - al I love to med - dle. Not on - ly

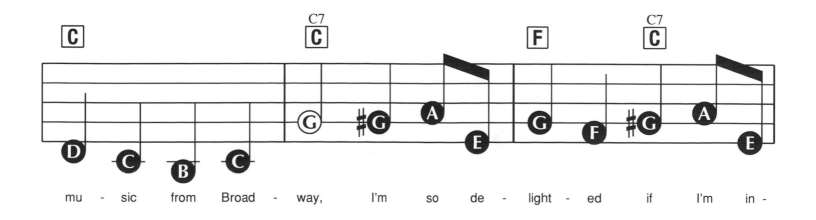

mu - sic from Broad - way, I'm so de - light - ed if I'm in -

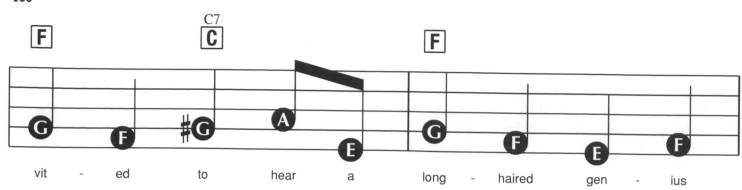

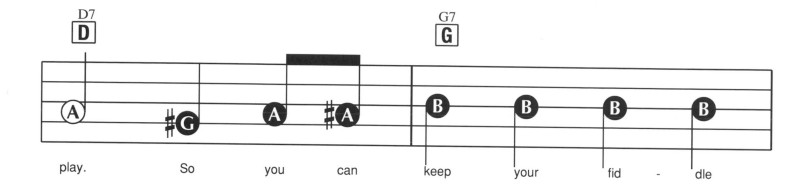

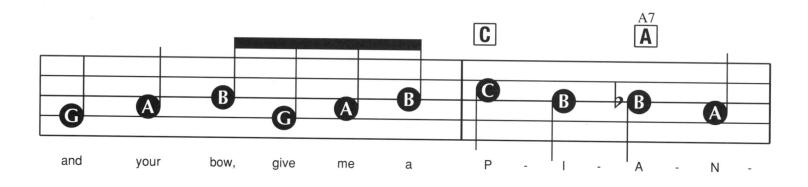

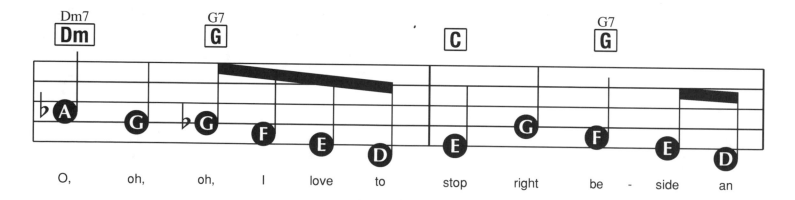

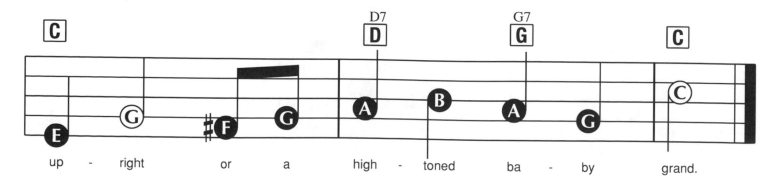

I Wonder Who's Kissing Her Now

Registration 1
Rhythm: Waltz

Lyrics by Will M. Hough and Frank R. Adams
Music by Joseph E. Howard and Harold Orlob

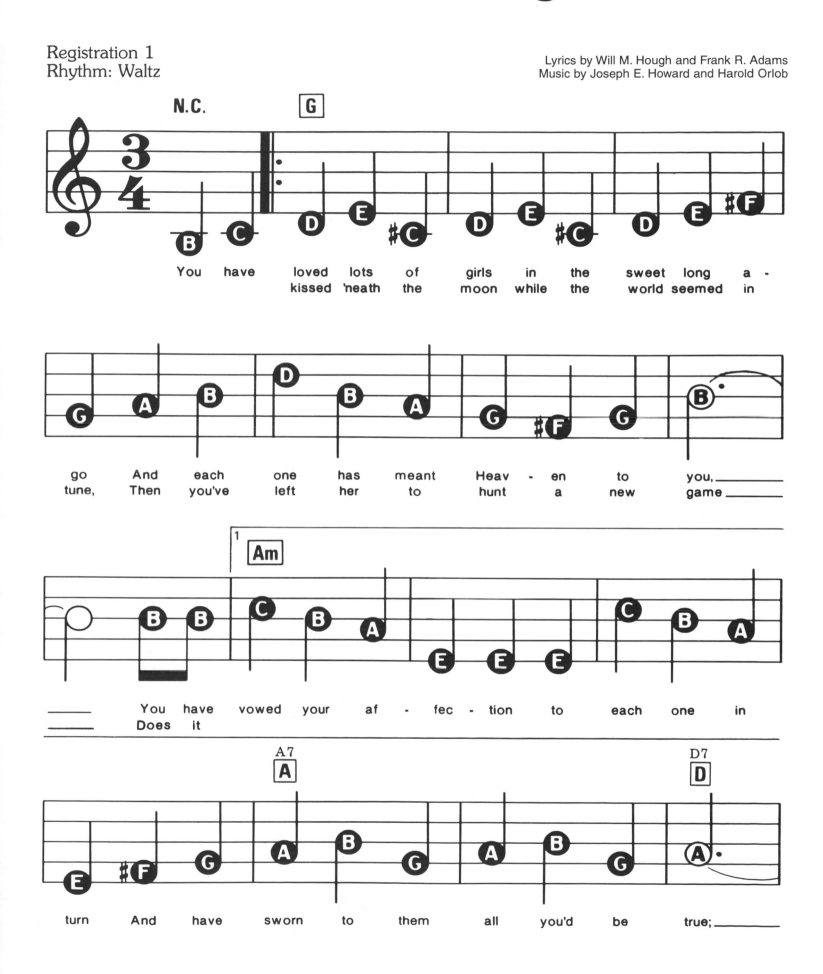

Copyright © 1994 by HAL LEONARD CORPORATION
International Copyright Secured   All Rights Reserved

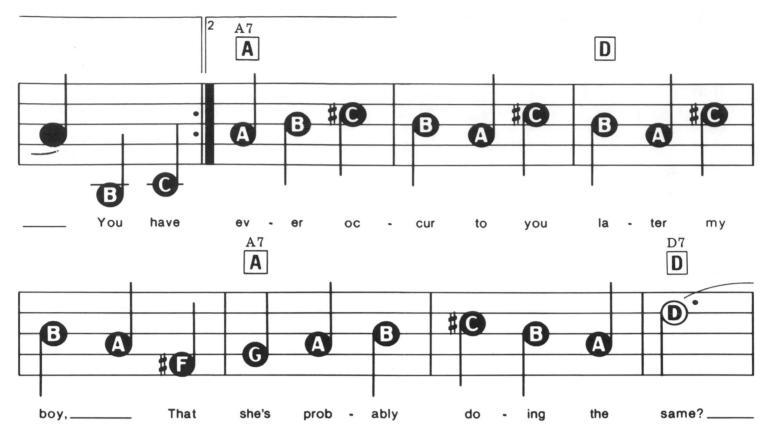

You have ev - er oc - cur to you la - ter my

boy, ____ That she's prob - ably do - ing the same? ____

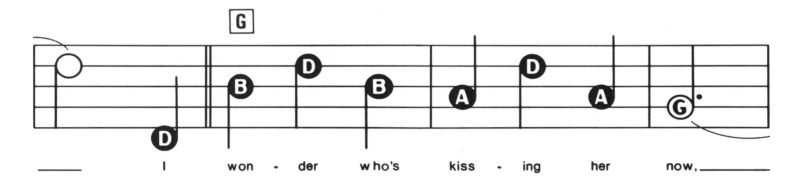

____ I won - der who's kiss - ing her now, ____

Won - der who's teach - ing her how, ____

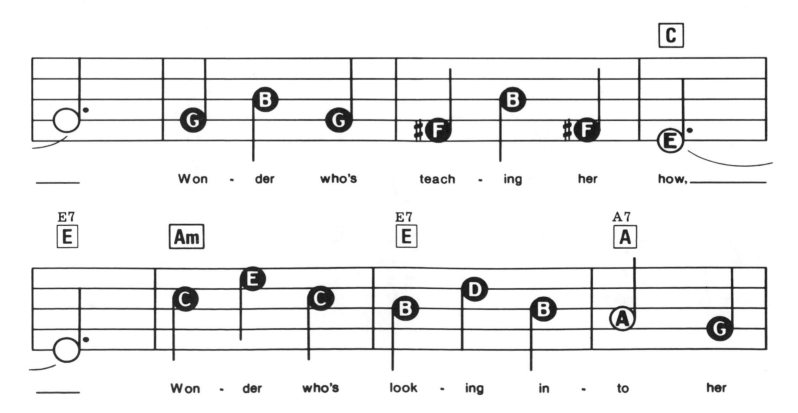

____ Won - der who's look - ing in - to her

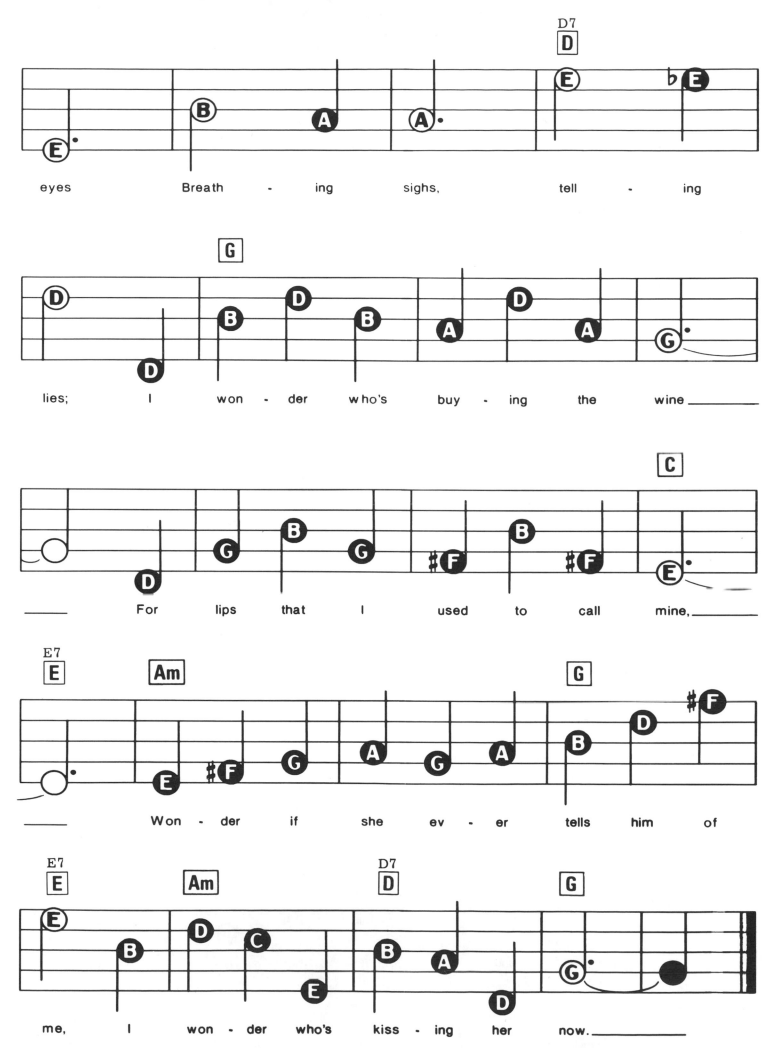

I Want a Girl
(Just Like the Girl That Married Dear Old Dad)

Registration 2
Rhythm: Swing or Jazz

Words by William Dillon
Music by Harry von Tilzer

Copyright © 1990 by HAL LEONARD CORPORATION
International Copyright Secured   All Rights Reserved

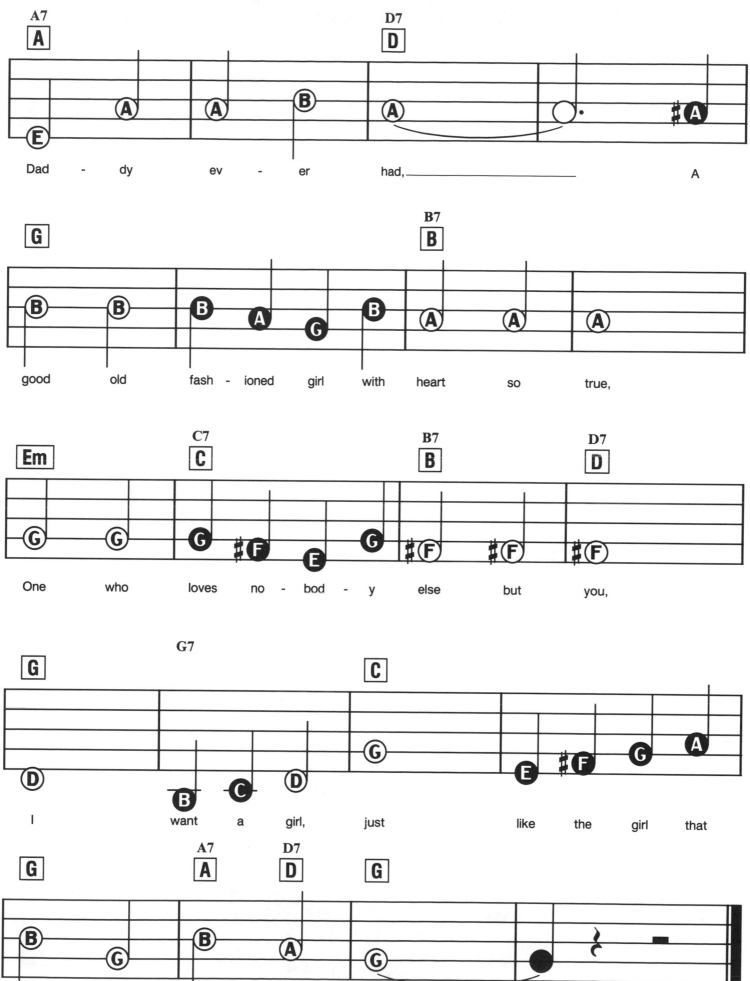

I'm Always Chasing Rainbows

Registration 1
Rhythm: Swing

Words by Joseph McCarthy
Music by Harry Carroll

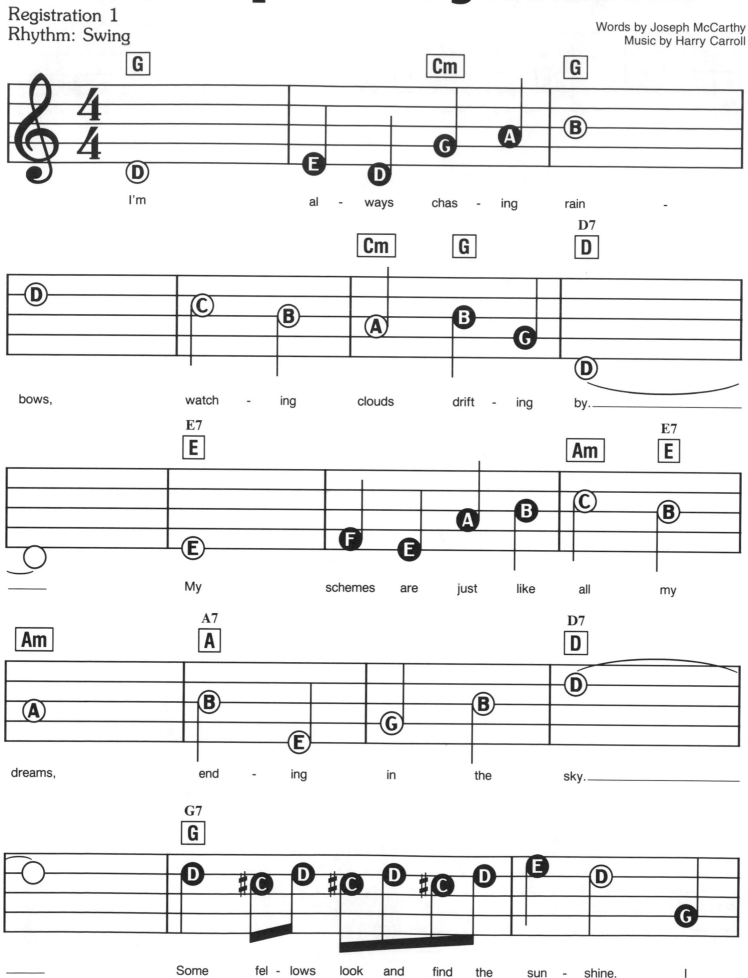

Copyright © 1996 by HAL LEONARD CORPORATION
International Copyright Secured   All Rights Reserved

al - ways look and find the rain.   Some fel - lows make a win - ning

some - time.   I nev - er e - ven make a gain. Be - lieve me,

I'm al - ways chas - ing rain -

bows, wait - ing to find a lit - tle blue - bird in

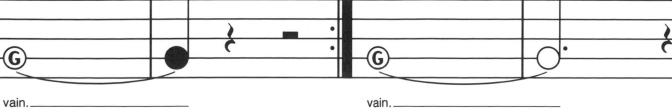

vain. _____ vain. _____

I'm Falling in Love with Someone

Registration 5
Rhythm: Waltz

Words by Rida Johnson Young
Music by Victor Herbert

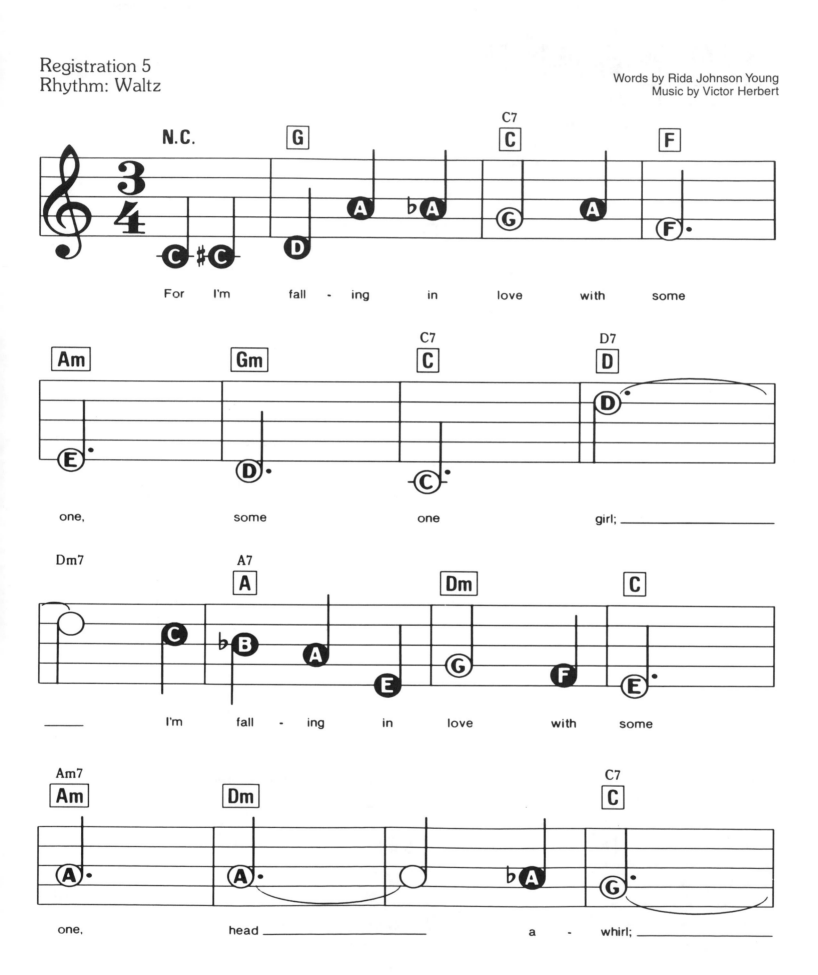

Copyright © 1994 by HAL LEONARD CORPORATION
International Copyright Secured   All Rights Reserved

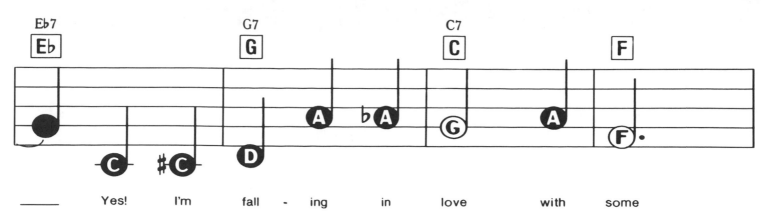

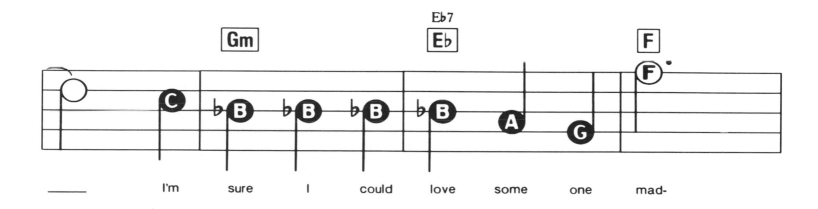

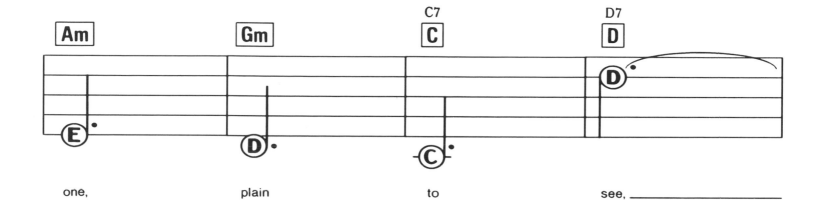

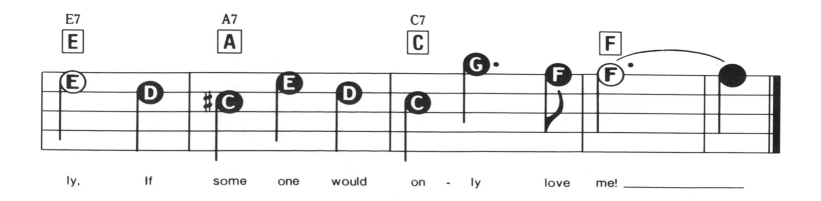

If I Had My Way

Registration 2
Rhythm: Waltz

Words by Lou Klein
Music by James Kendis

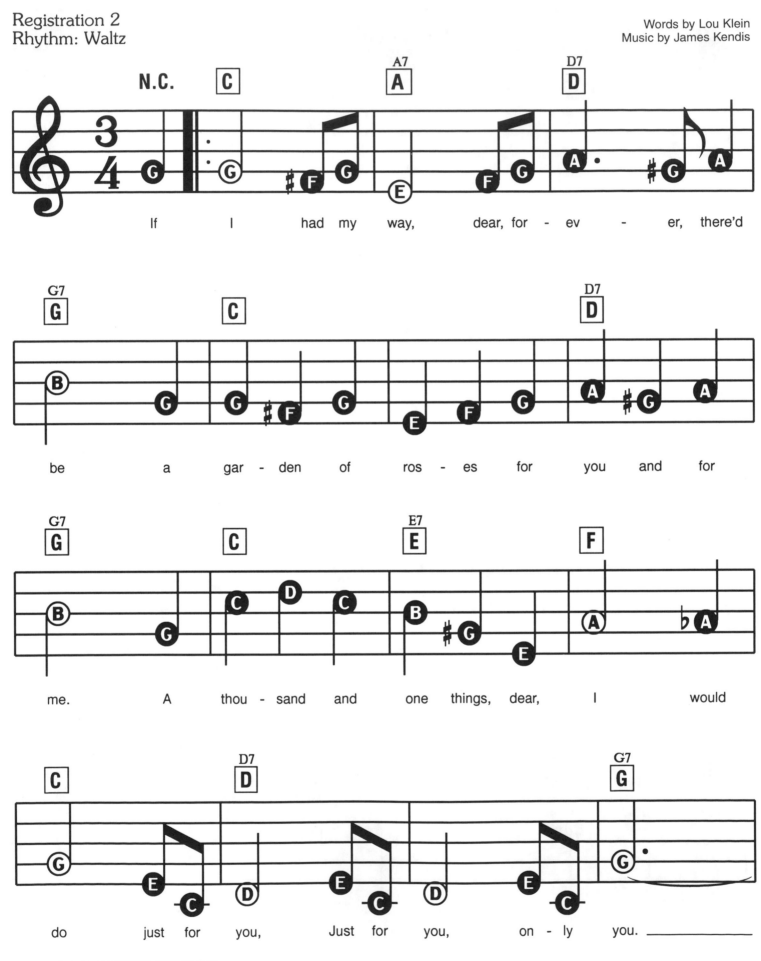

If I had my way, dear, for - ev - er, there'd be a gar - den of ros - es for you and for me. A thou - sand and one things, dear, I would do just for you, Just for you, on - ly you. _____

Copyright © 1994 by HAL LEONARD CORPORATION
International Copyright Secured   All Rights Reserved

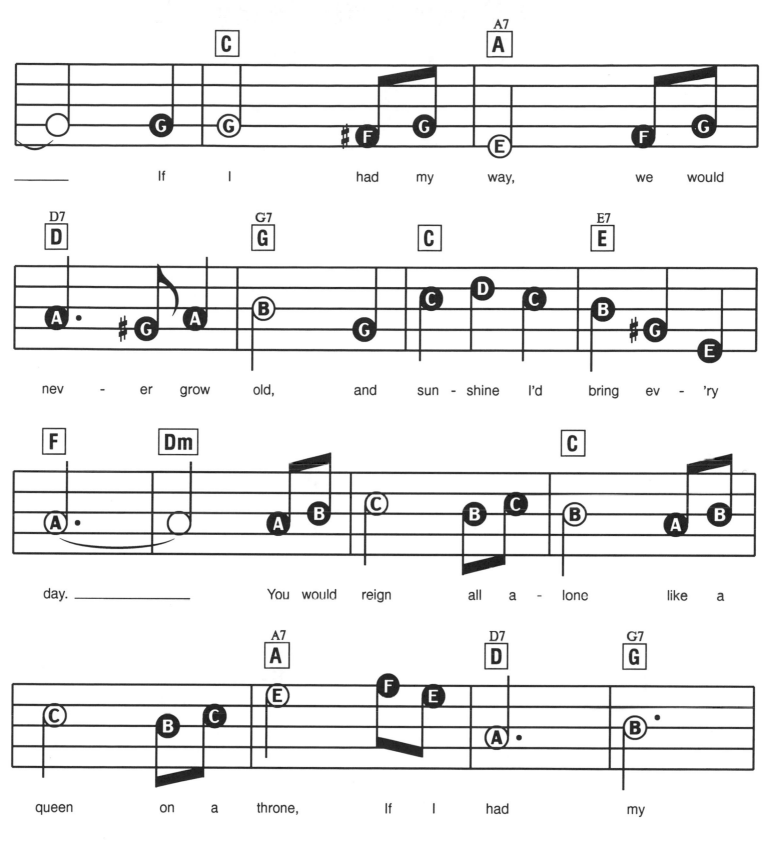

If I had my way, we would nev - er grow old, and sun - shine I'd bring ev - 'ry day. _____ You would reign all a - lone like a queen on a throne, If I had my

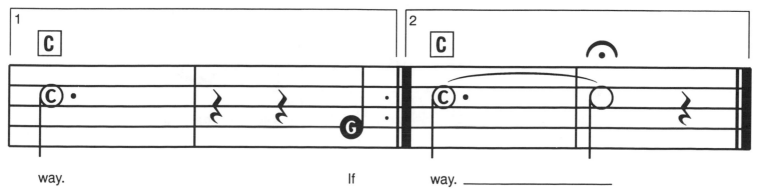

way.   If way. _____

If You Were the Only Girl in the World

Registration 10
Rhythm: Waltz

Words by Clifford Grey
Music by Nat D. Ayer

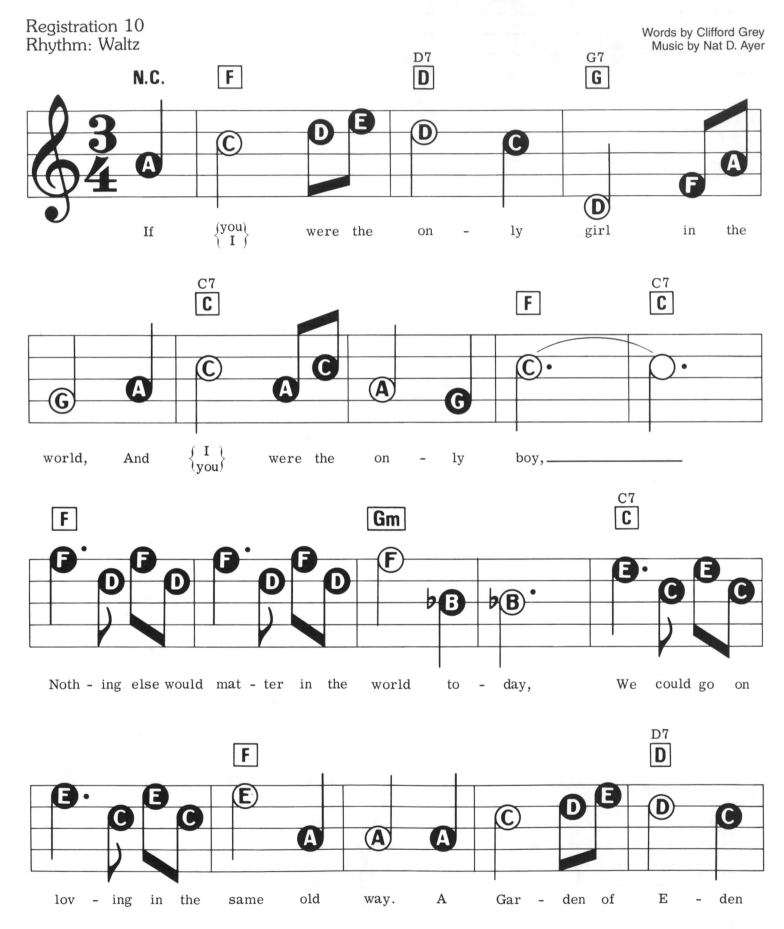

Copyright © 1996 by HAL LEONARD CORPORATION
International Copyright Secured   All Rights Reserved

113

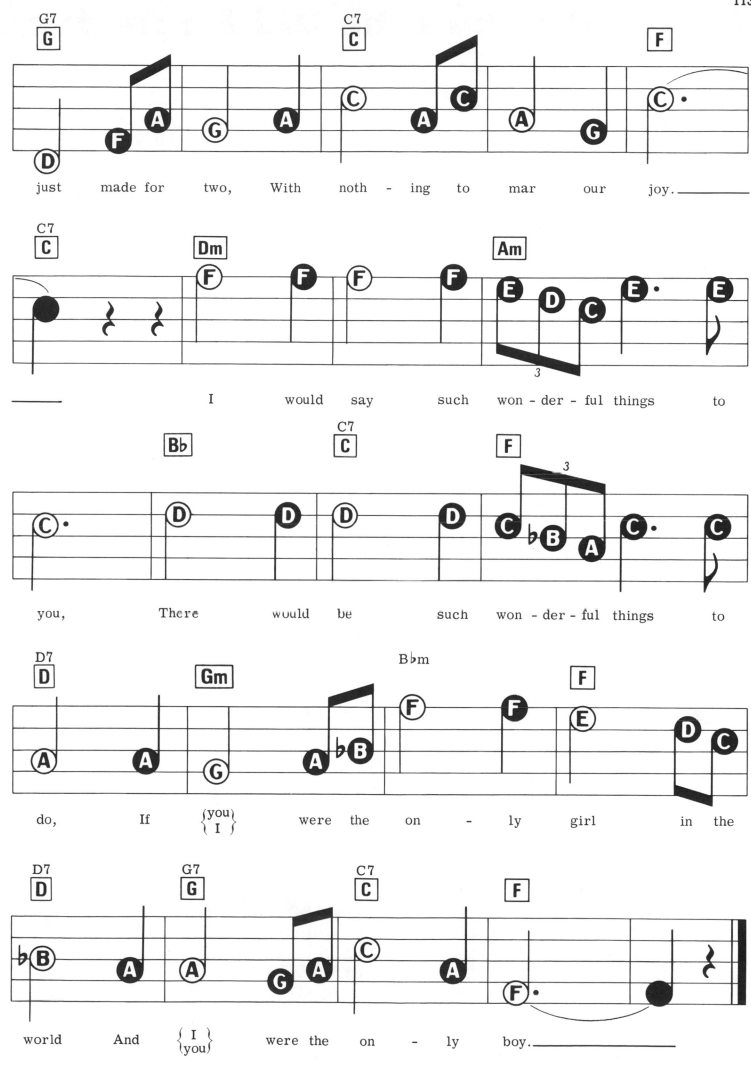

In the Shade of the Old Apple Tree

Registration 3
Rhythm: Waltz

Words by Harry H. Williams
Music by Egbert Van Alstyne

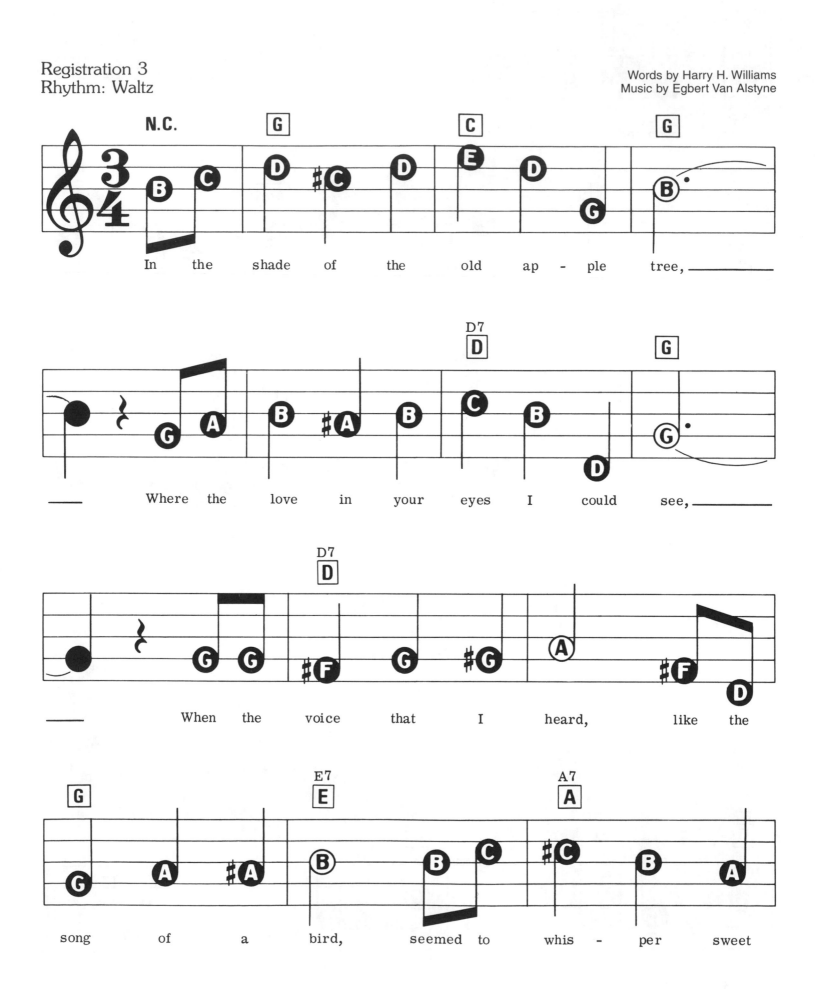

Copyright © 1994 by HAL LEONARD CORPORATION
International Copyright Secured   All Rights Reserved

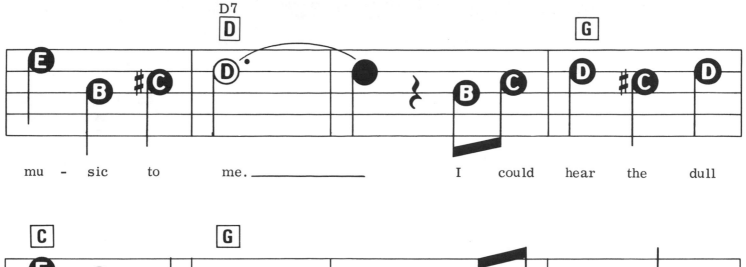

mu - sic to me. _____ I could hear the dull

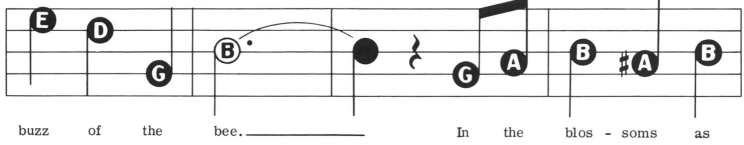

buzz of the bee. _____ In the blos - soms as

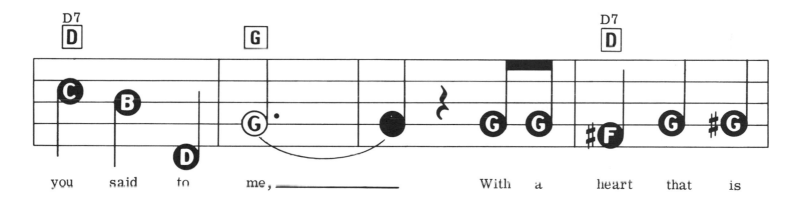

you said to me, _____ With a heart that is

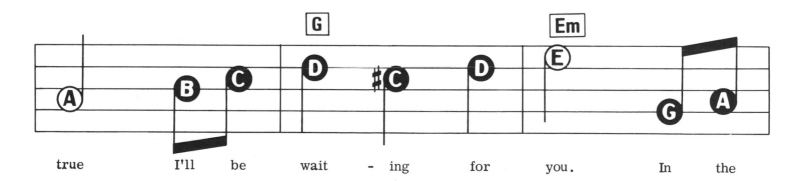

true I'll be wait - ing for you. In the

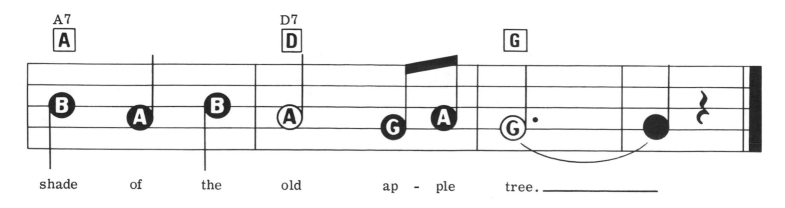

shade of the old ap - ple tree. _____

Indiana
(Back Home Again in Indiana)

Registration 3
Rhythm: Swing

Words by Ballard MacDonald
Music by James F. Hanley

Copyright © 1994 by HAL LEONARD CORPORATION
International Copyright Secured   All Rights Reserved

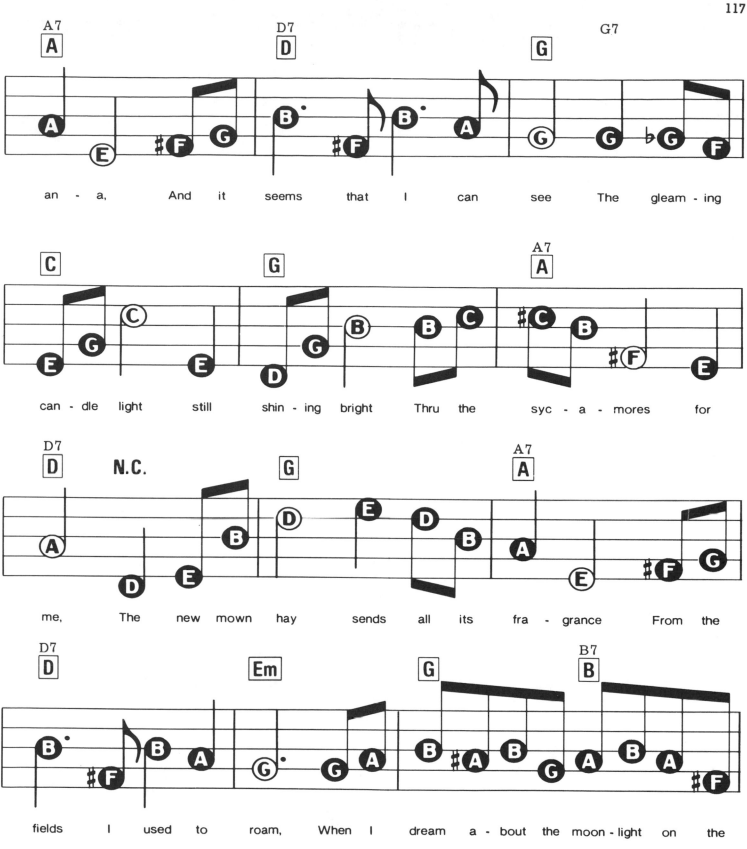

an - a, And it seems that I can see The gleam - ing

can - dle light still shin - ing bright Thru the syc - a - mores for

me, The new mown hay sends all its fra - grance From the

fields I used to roam, When I dream a - bout the moon - light on the

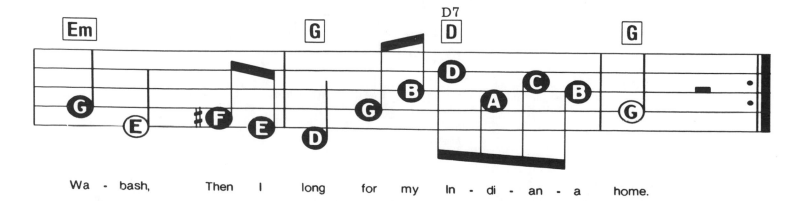

Wa - bash, Then I long for my In - di - an - a home.

It's a Long, Long Way to Tipperary

Registration 8
Rhythm: March

Words and Music by Jack Judge
and Harry Williams

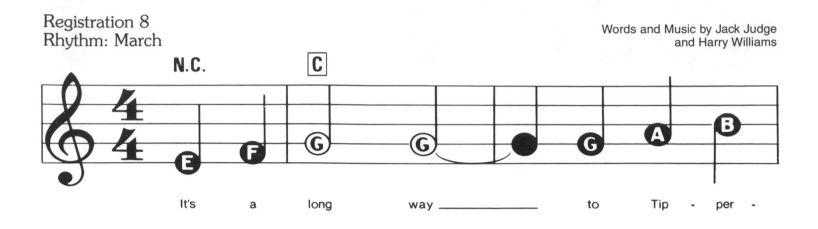

It's a long way _____ to Tip - per -

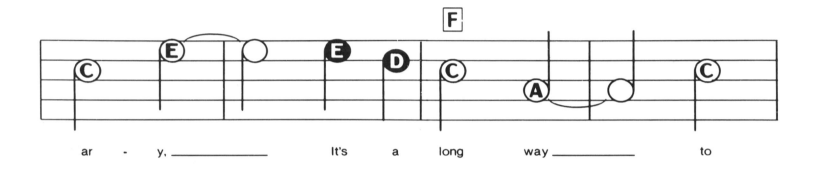

ar - y, _____ It's a long way _____ to

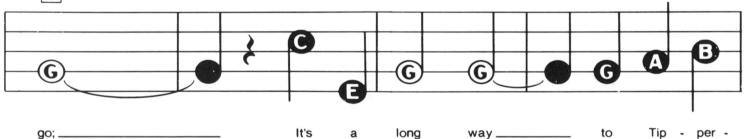

go; _____ It's a long way _____ to Tip - per -

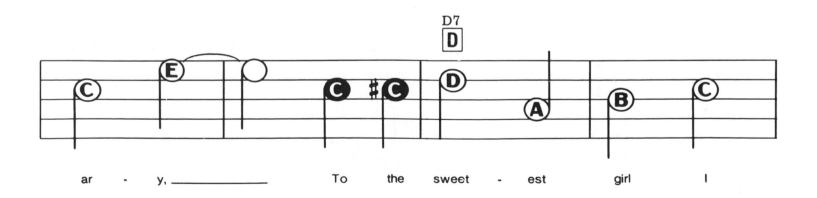

ar - y, _____ To the sweet - est girl I

Copyright © 1994 by HAL LEONARD CORPORATION
International Copyright Secured   All Rights Reserved

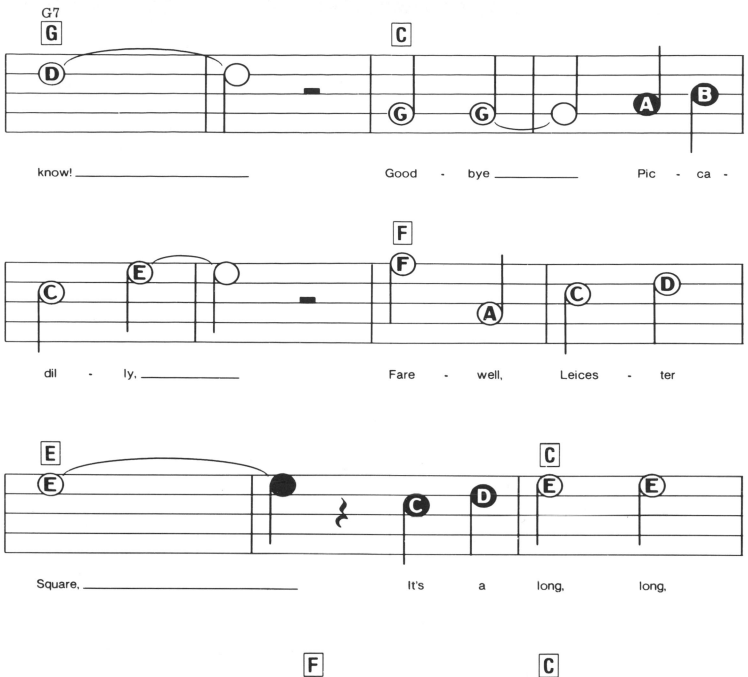

know! _____ Good - bye _____ Pic - ca -

dil - ly, _____ Fare - well, Leices - ter

Square, _____ It's a long, long,

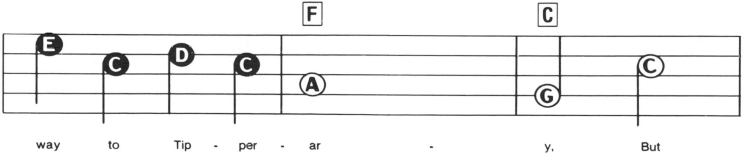

way to Tip - per - ar - y, But

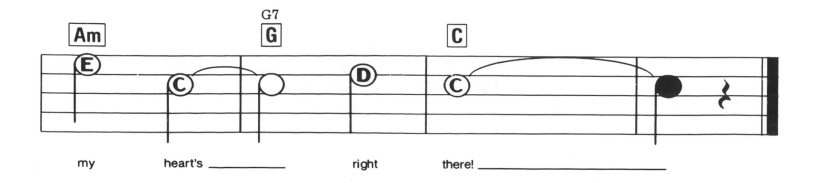

my heart's _____ right there! _____

K-K-K-Katy

Registration 1
Rhythm: 6/8 March

Words and Music by
Geoffrey O'Hara

Copyright © 1995 by HAL LEONARD CORPORATION
International Copyright Secured   All Rights Reserved

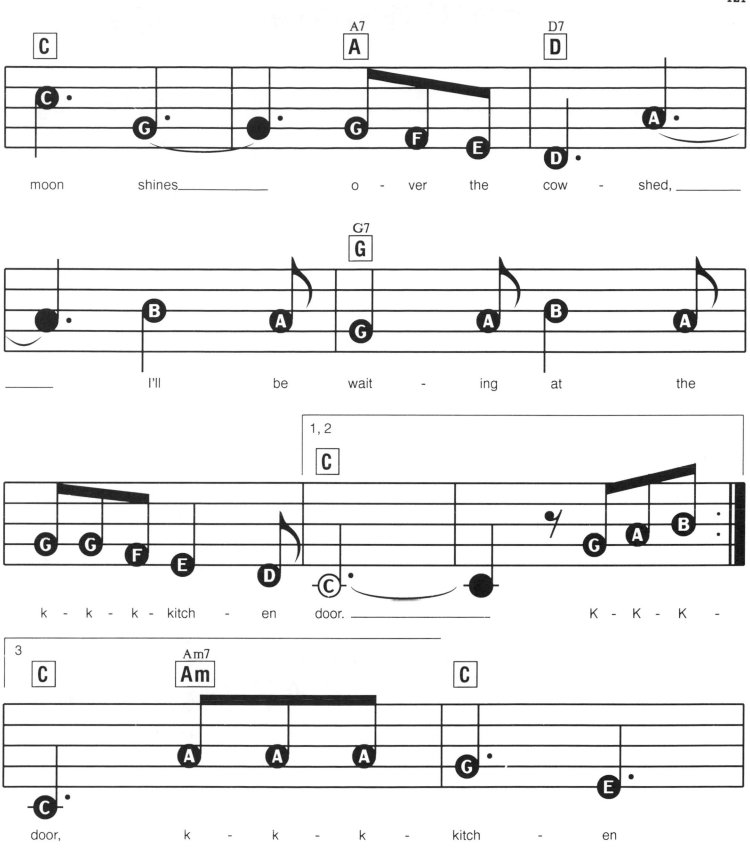

moon shines_____ o - ver the cow - shed, _____

_____ I'll be wait - ing at the

k - k - k - kitch - en door. _____ K - K - K -

door, k - k - k - kitch - en

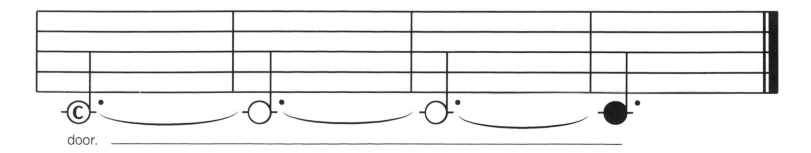

door. _____

Let Me Call You Sweetheart

Registration 3
Rhythm: Waltz

Words by Beth Slater Whitson
Music by Leo Friedman

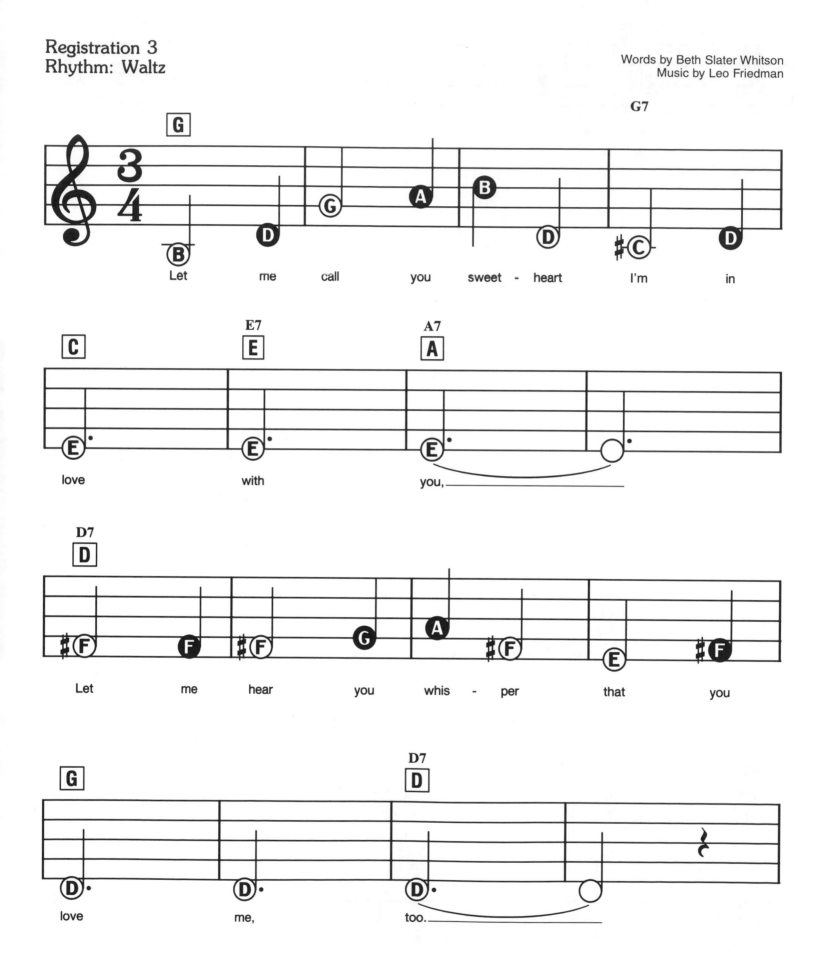

Copyright © 1990 by HAL LEONARD CORPORATION
International Copyright Secured   All Rights Reserved

123

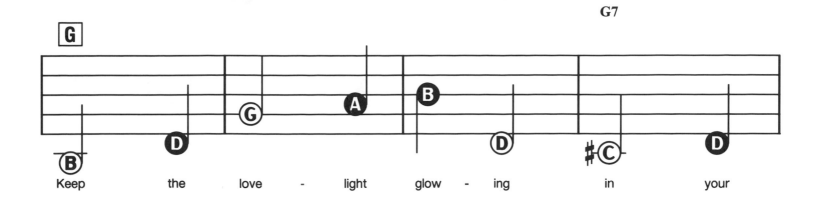

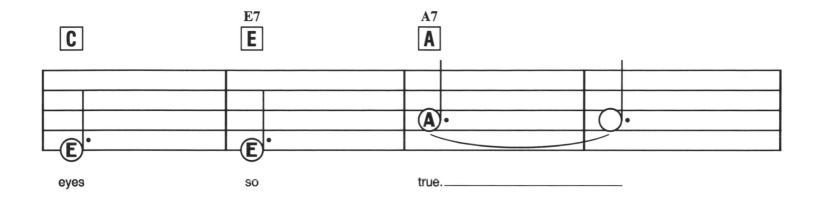

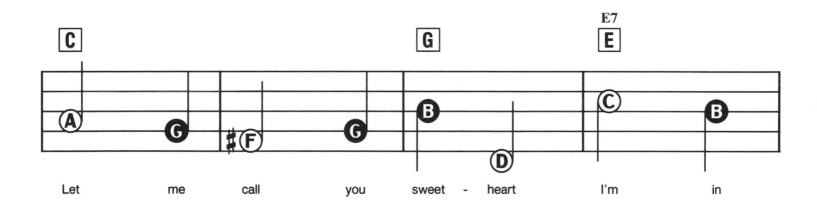

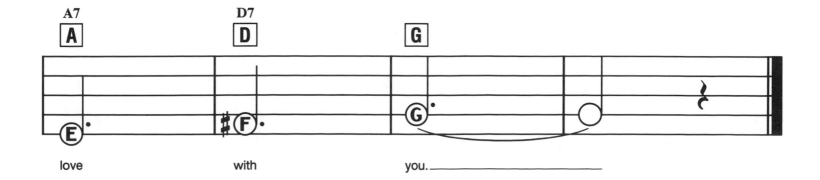

Let the Rest of the World Go By

Registration 5
Rhythm: Waltz

Words by J. Keirn Brennan
Music by Ernest R. Ball

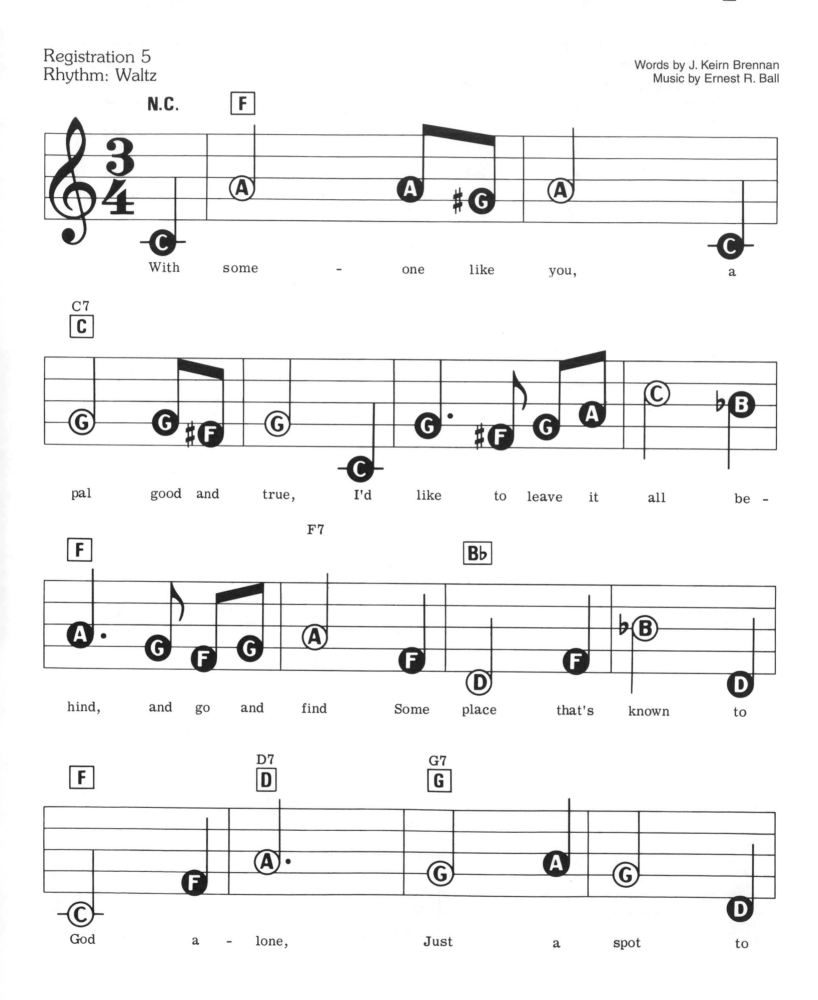

Copyright © 1996 by HAL LEONARD CORPORATION
International Copyright Secured   All Rights Reserved

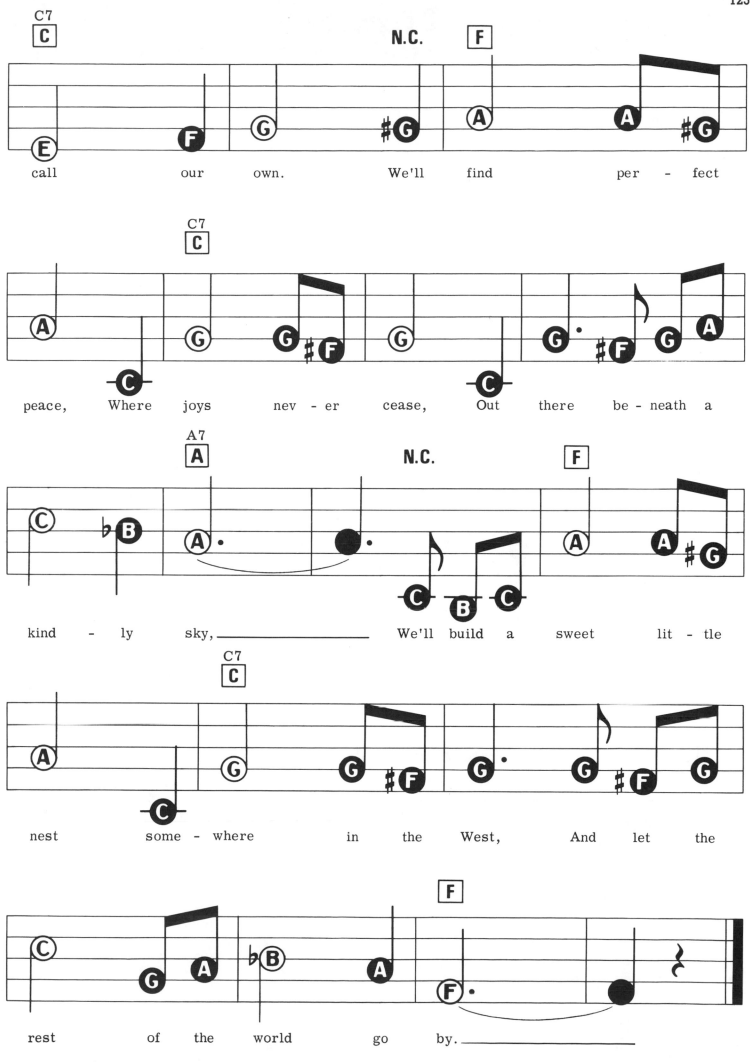

Mandy
from YIP, YIP, YAPHANK and ZIEGFELD FOLLIES

Registration 5
Rhythm: Swing

Words and Music by
Irving Berlin

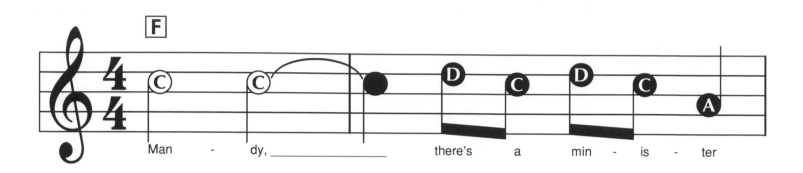

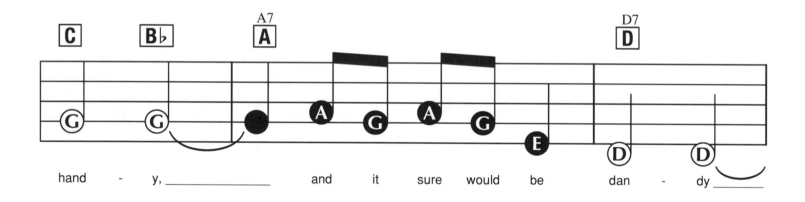

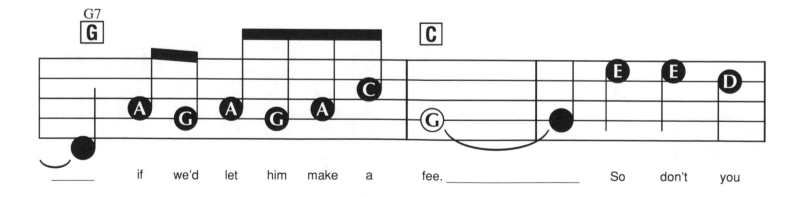

© Copyright 1919 by Irving Berlin
Copyright Renewed
© Copyright Assigned to Winthrop Rutherfurd, Jr., Anne Phipps Sidamon-Eristoff and Theodore R. Jackson as Trustees of God Bless America Fund
International Copyright Secured   All Rights Reserved

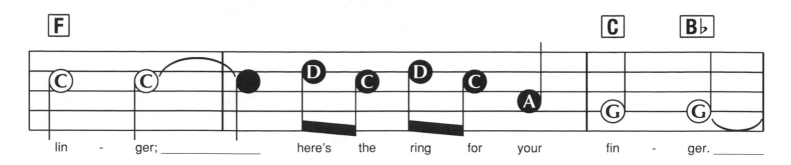

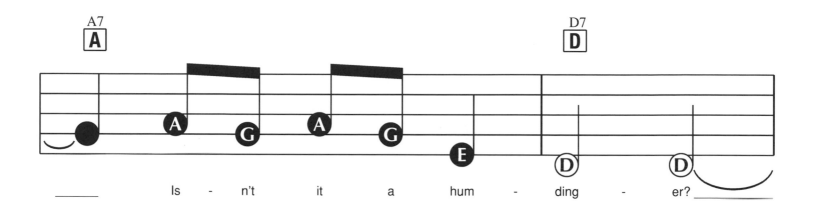

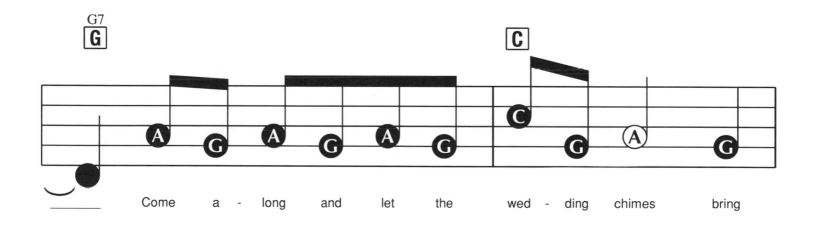

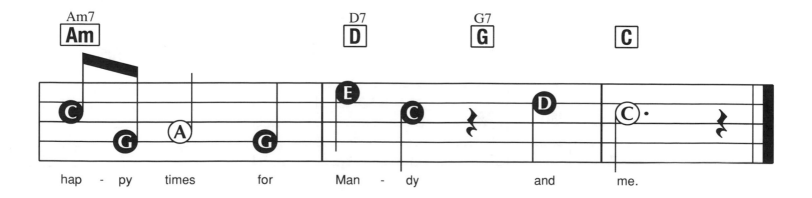

Maple Leaf Rag

Registration 8
Rhythm: March or Polka

Music by Scott Joplin

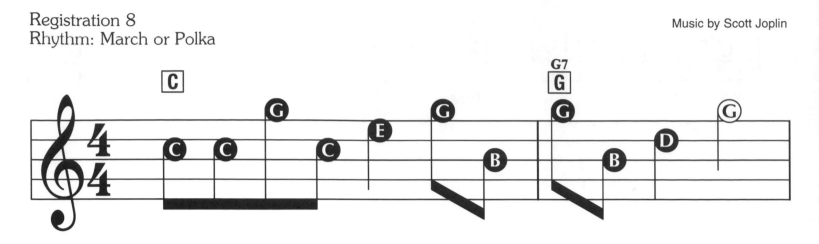

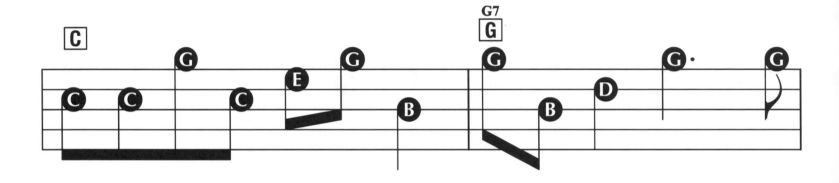

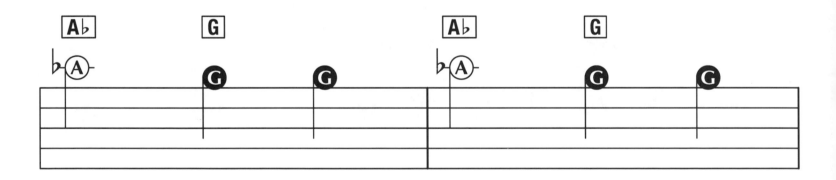

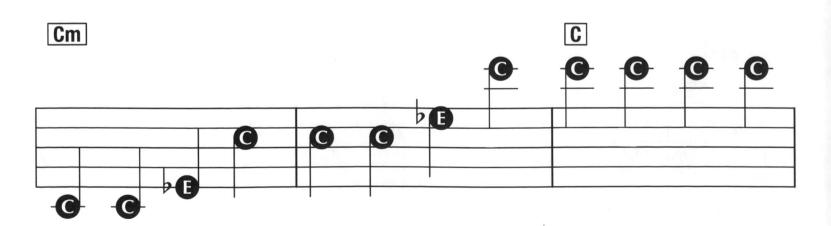

Copyright © 1994 by HAL LEONARD CORPORATION
International Copyright Secured   All Rights Reserved

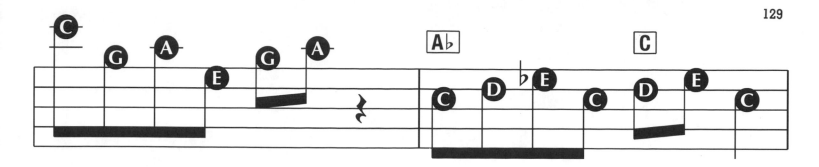

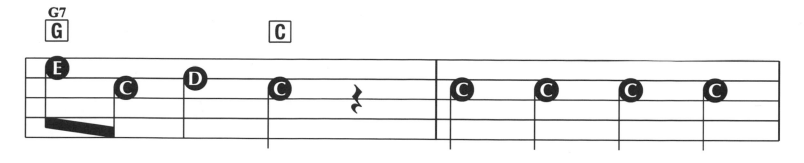

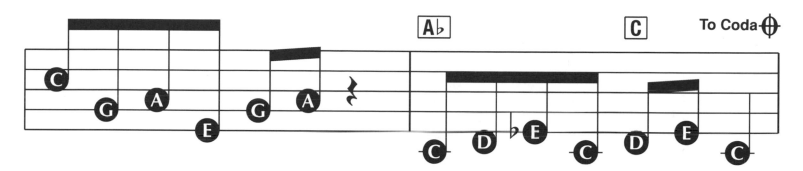

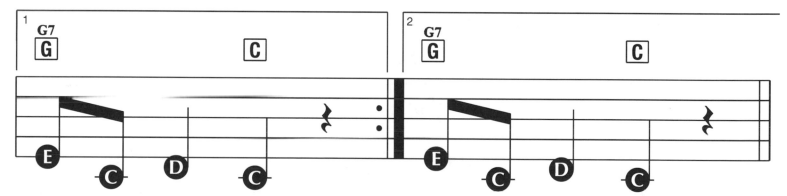

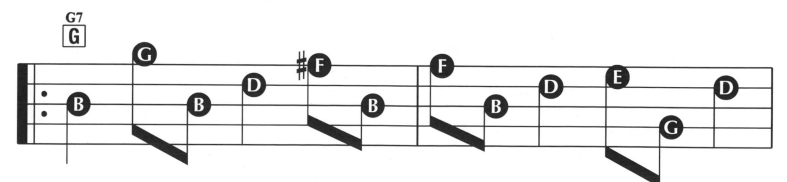

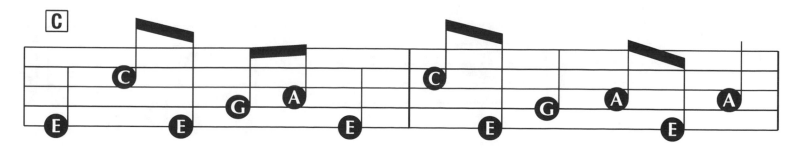

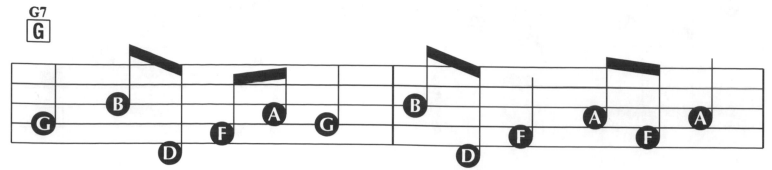

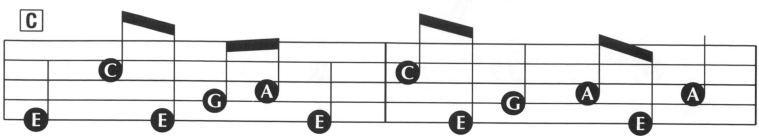

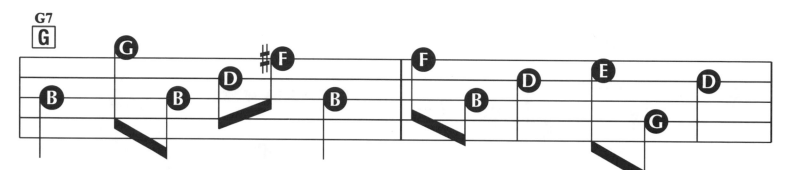

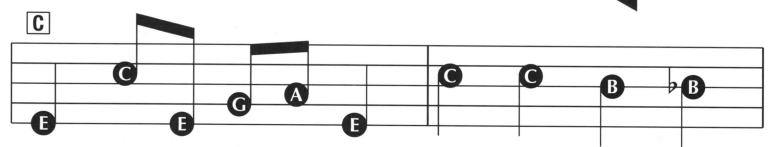

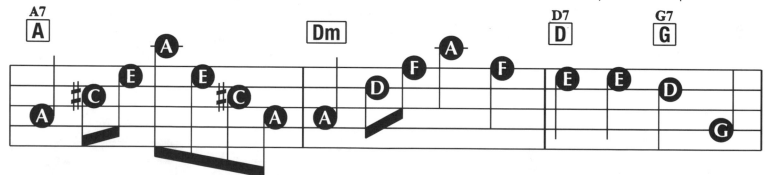

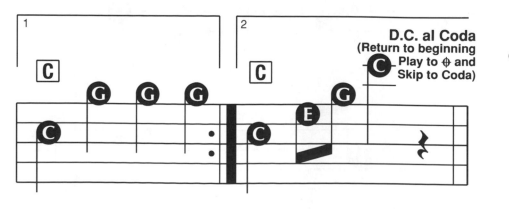

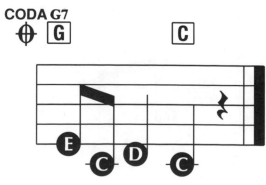

March of the Toys

Registration 5
Rhythm: 6/8 March

By Victor Herbert

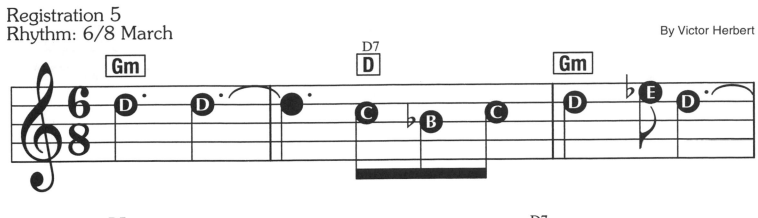

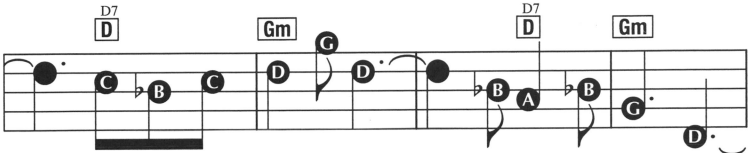

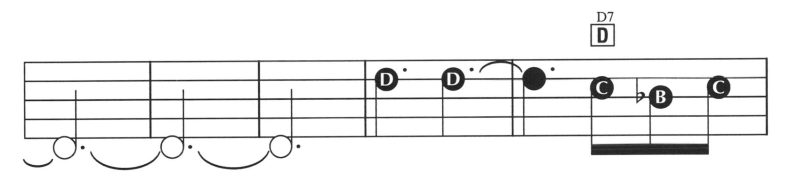

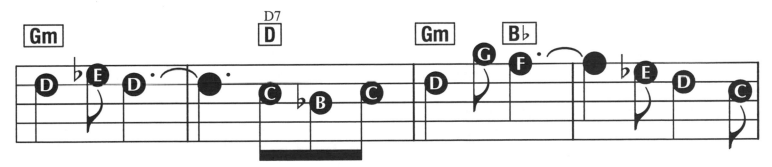

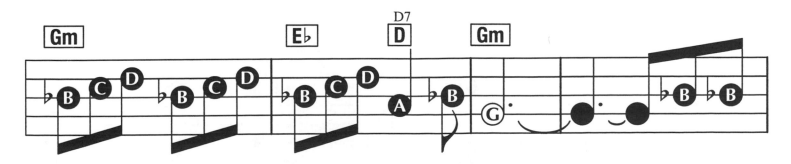

Copyright © 1994 by HAL LEONARD CORPORATION
International Copyright Secured   All Rights Reserved

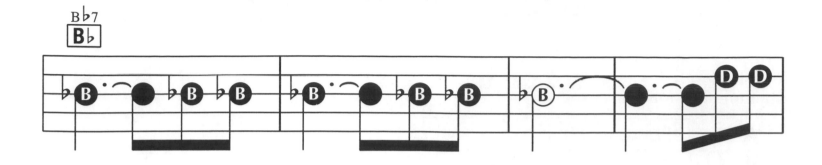

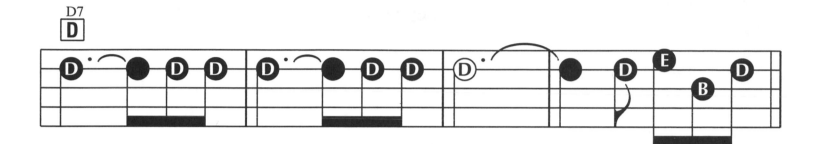

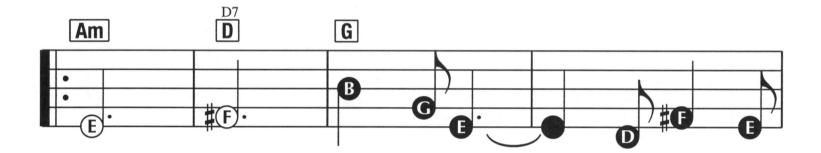

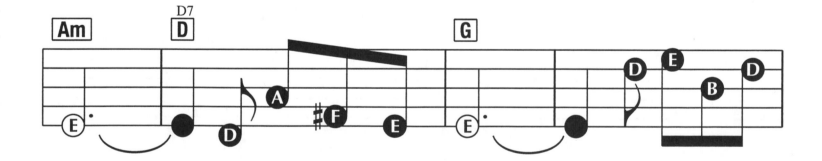

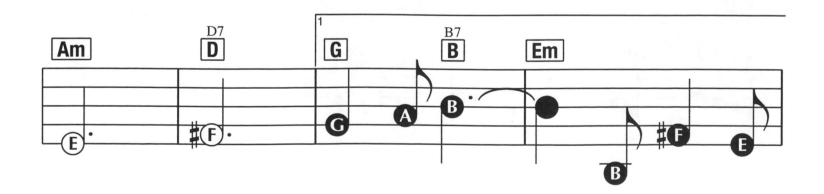

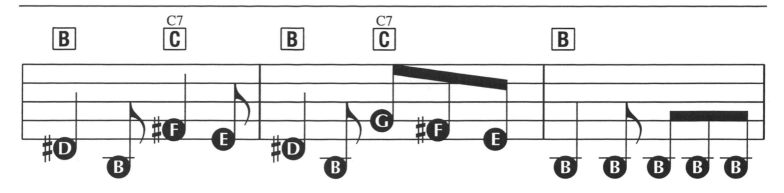

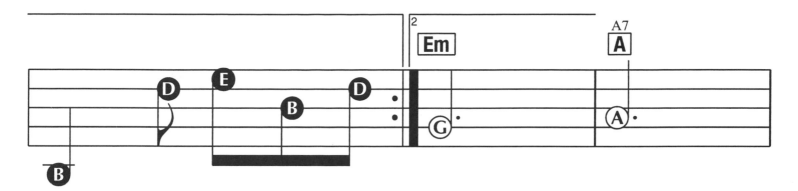

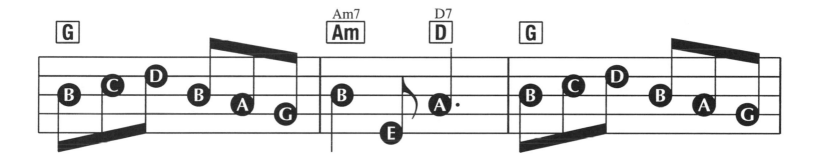

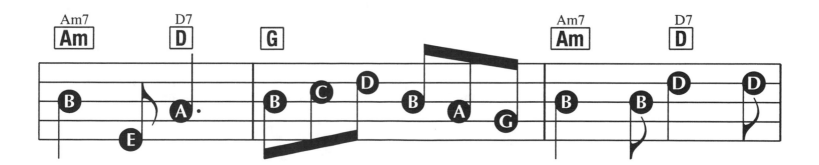

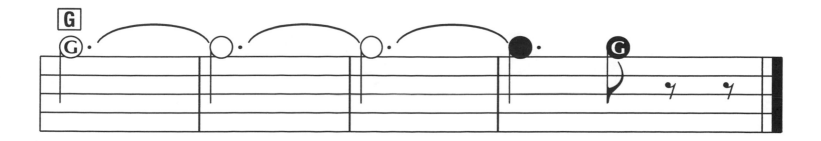

Marcheta
(A Love Song of Old Mexico)

Registration 2
Rhythm: Waltz

Words and Music by
Victor L. Schertzinger

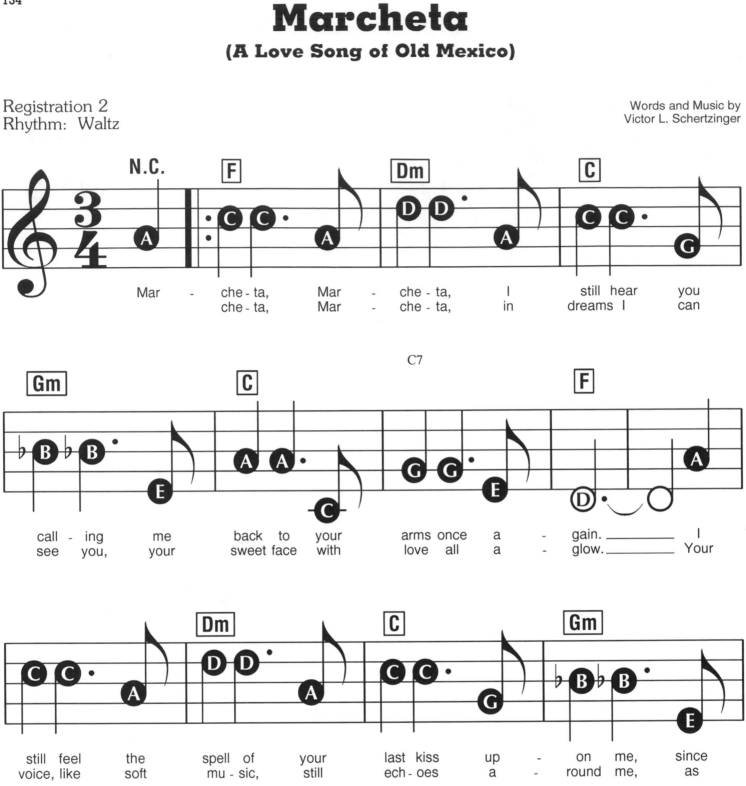

Mar - che - ta, Mar - che - ta, I still hear you
che - ta, Mar - che - ta, in dreams I can

call - ing me back to your arms once a - gain. _____ I
see you, your sweet face with love all a - glow. _____ Your

still feel the spell of your last kiss up - on me, since
voice, like the soft mu - sic, your still ech - oes a - round me, as

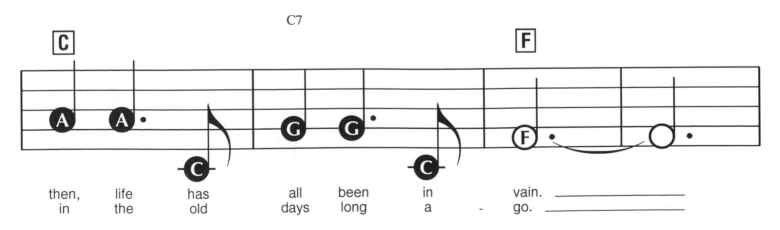

then, life has all been in vain. _____
in the old days long a - go. _____

Copyright © 1996 by HAL LEONARD CORPORATION
International Copyright Secured   All Rights Reserved

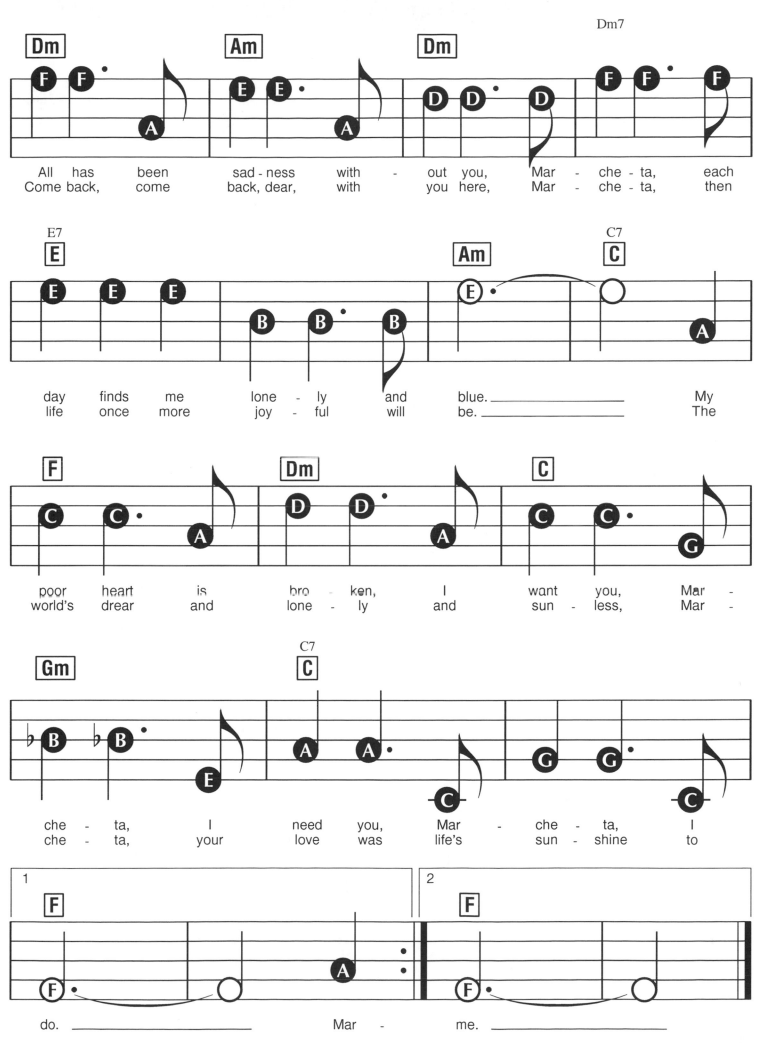

Meet Me Tonight in Dreamland

Registration 5
Rhythm: Waltz

Words by Beth Slater Whitson
Music by Leo Friedman

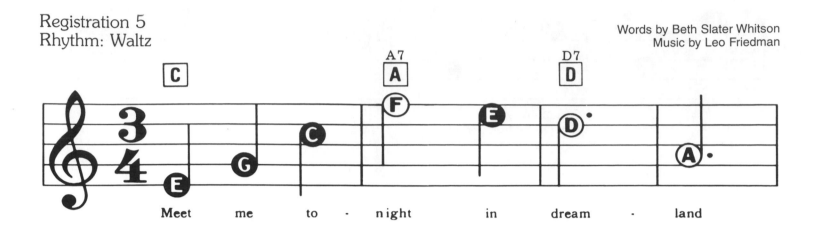

Meet me to - night in dream - land

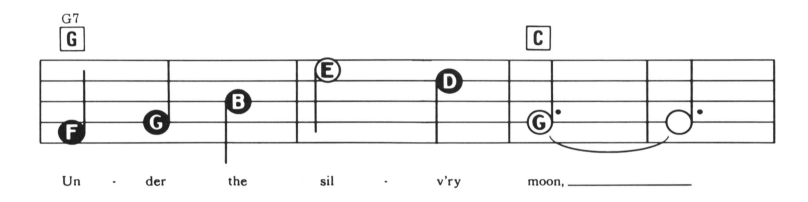

Un - der the sil - v'ry moon,

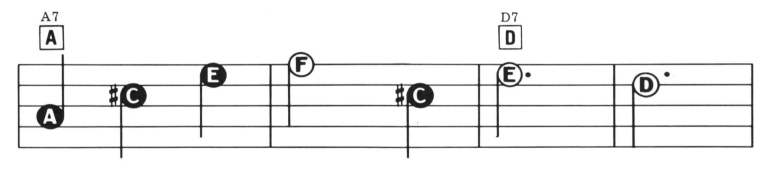

Meet me to - night in dream - land

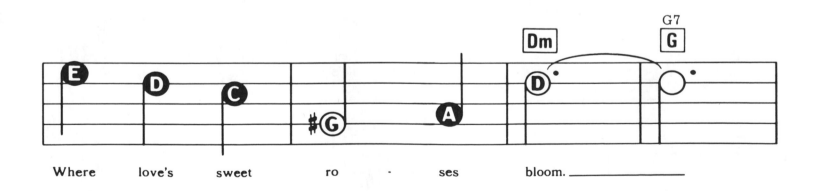

Where love's sweet ro - ses bloom.

Copyright © 1996 by HAL LEONARD CORPORATION
International Copyright Secured   All Rights Reserved

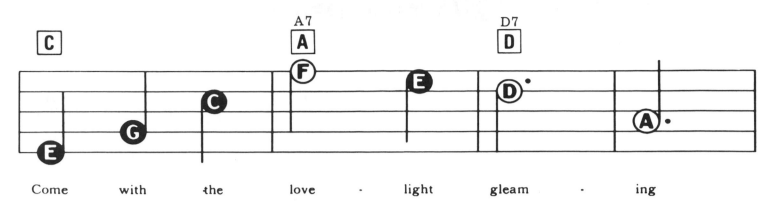

Come with the love - light gleam - ing

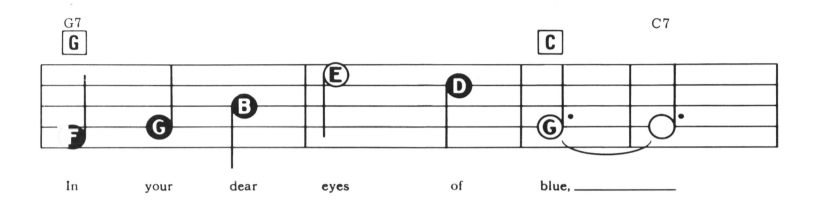

In your dear eyes of blue, _____

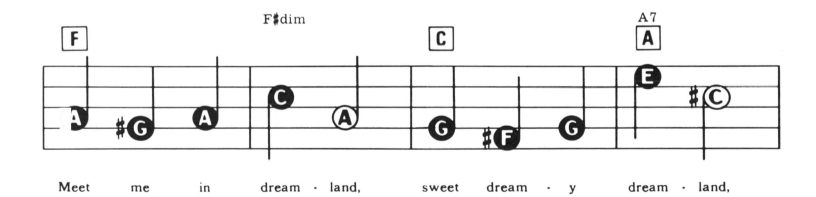

Meet me in dream - land, sweet dream - y dream - land,

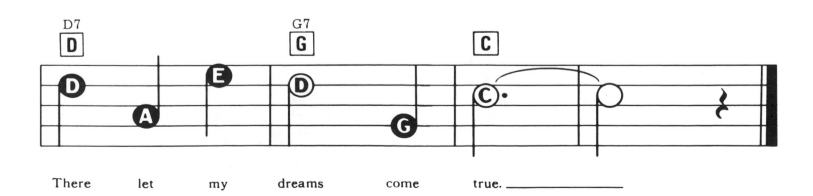

There let my dreams come true. _____

Memories

Registration 3
Rhythm: Waltz

Words by Gus Kahn
Music by Egbert Van Alstyne

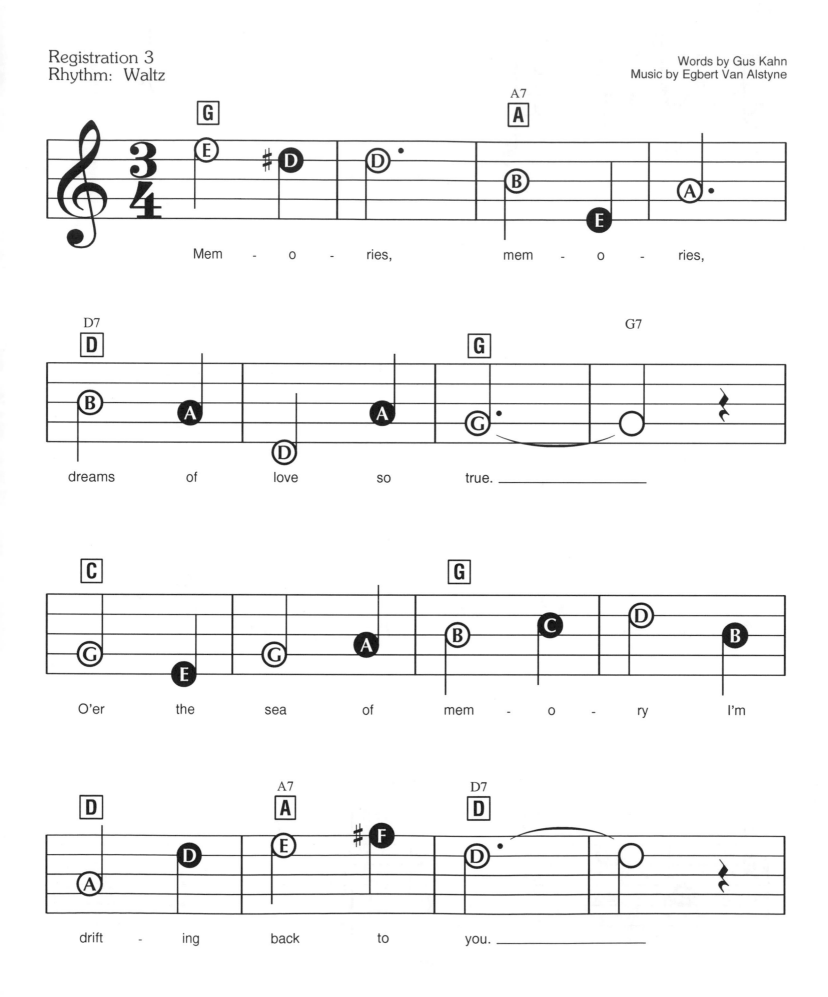

Copyright © 1996 by HAL LEONARD CORPORATION
International Copyright Secured   All Rights Reserved

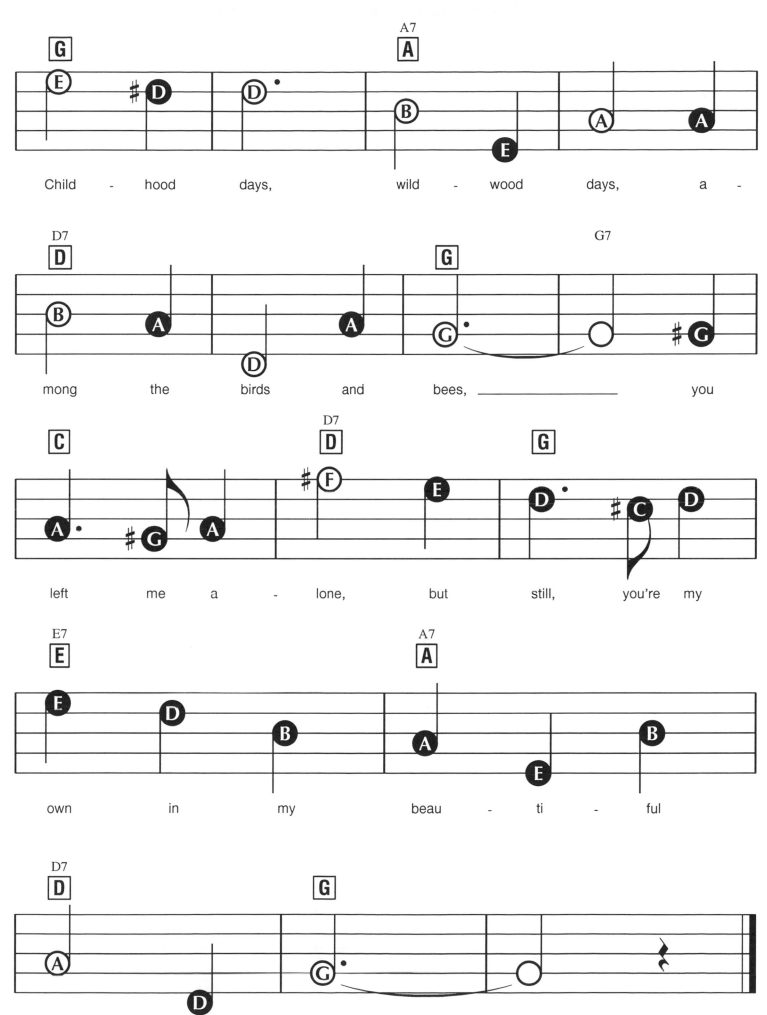

Child - hood days, wild - wood days, a -
mong the birds and bees, _____ you
left me a - lone, but still, you're my
own in my beau - ti - ful
mem - o - ries. _____

The Merry Widow Waltz

from THE MERRY WIDOW

Registration 10
Rhythm: Waltz

Words by Adrian Ross
Music by Franz Lehar

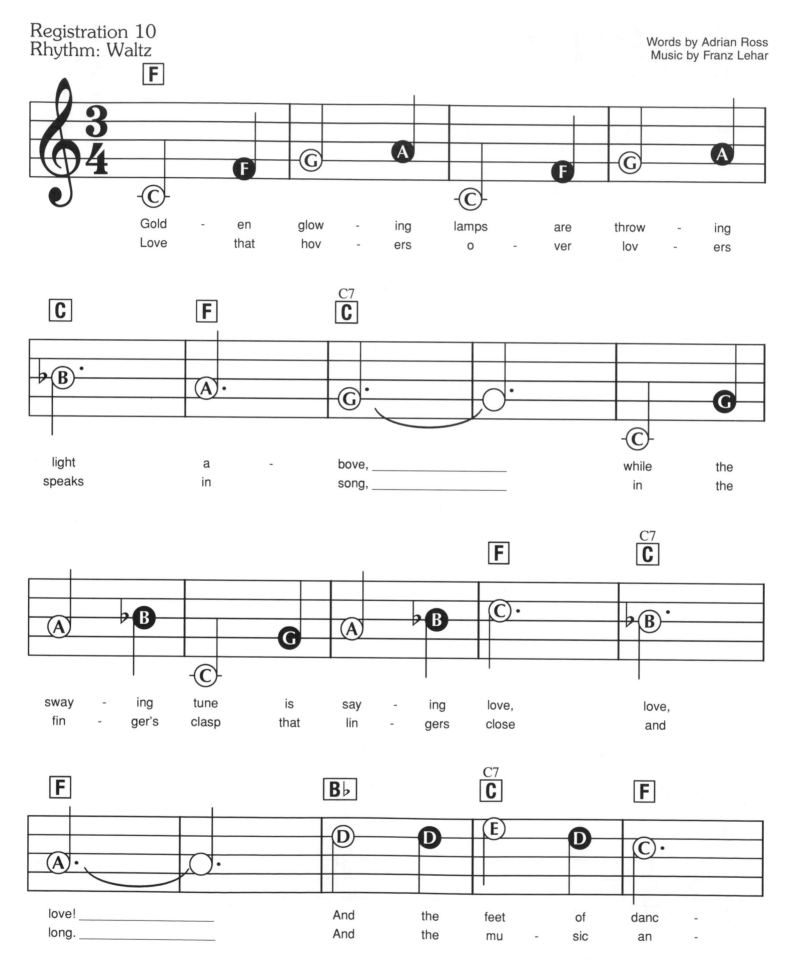

Copyright © 1994 by HAL LEONARD CORPORATION
International Copyright Secured All Rights Reserved

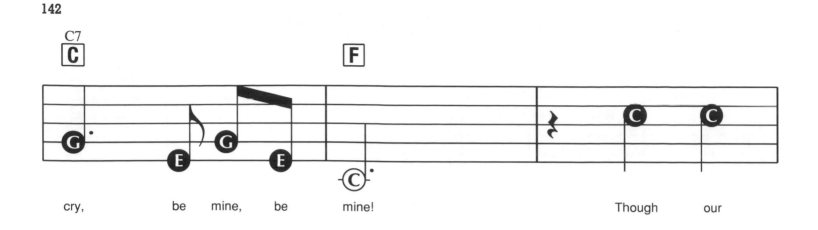

cry,   be mine,   be   mine!   Though   our

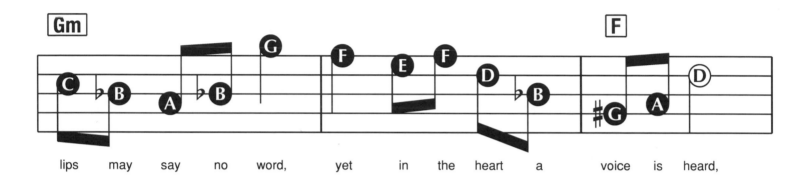

lips   may   say   no   word,   yet   in   the   heart   a   voice   is   heard,

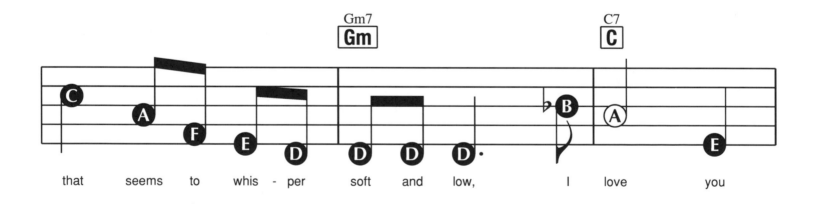

that   seems   to   whis - per   soft   and   low,   I   love   you

D.C. al Coda
(Return to beginning
Play to ⊕ and
Skip to Coda)

CODA
⊕

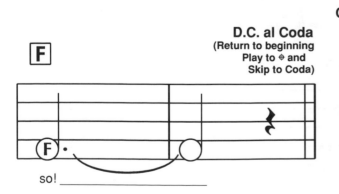

so! _____

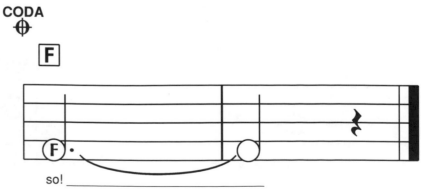

so! _____

My Little Girl

Registration 1
Rhythm: Fox Trot or Swing

Words by Sam M. Lewis and William Dillon
Music by Albert von Tilzer

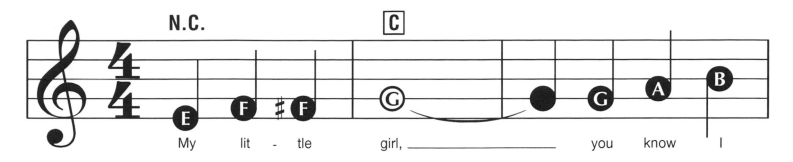

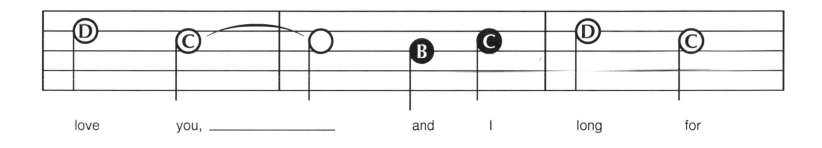

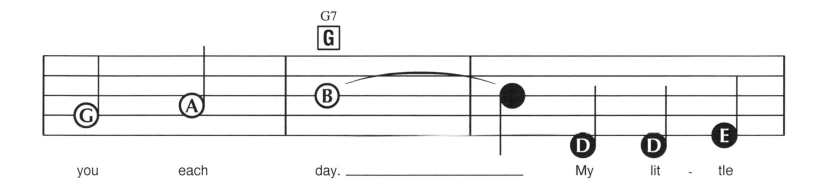

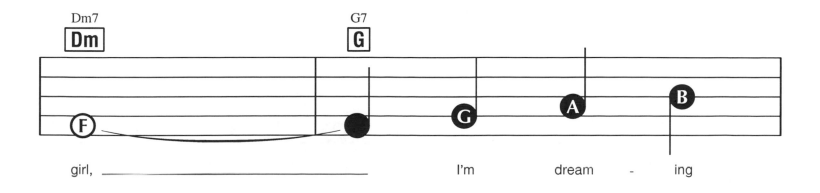

Copyright © 1996 by HAL LEONARD CORPORATION
International Copyright Secured   All Rights Reserved

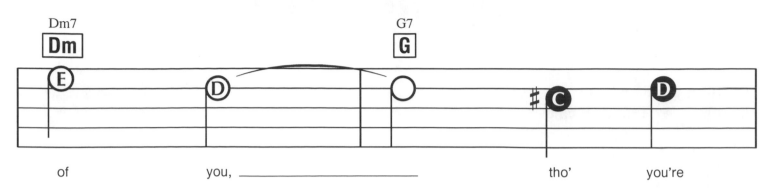

of you, _____ tho' you're

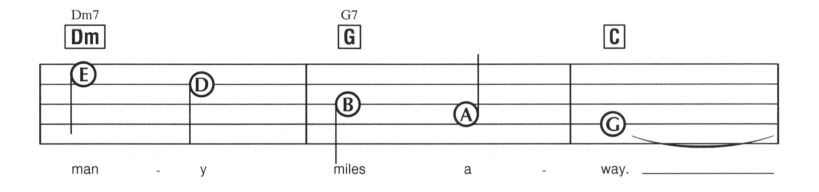

man - y miles a - way. _____

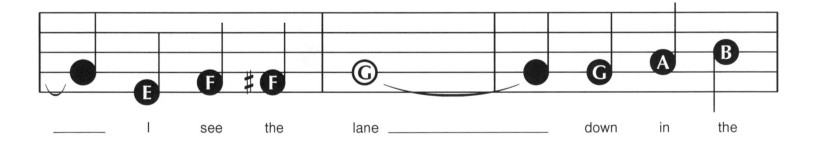

_____ I see the lane _____ down in the

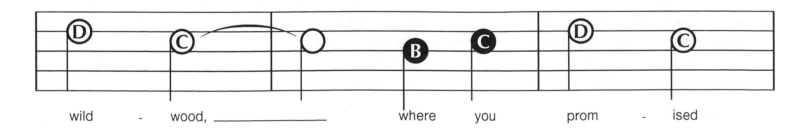

wild - wood, _____ where you prom - ised

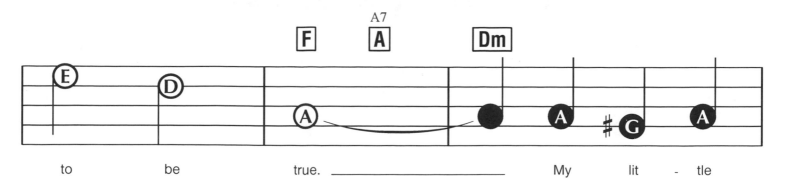

to   be   true. _____   My   lit - tle

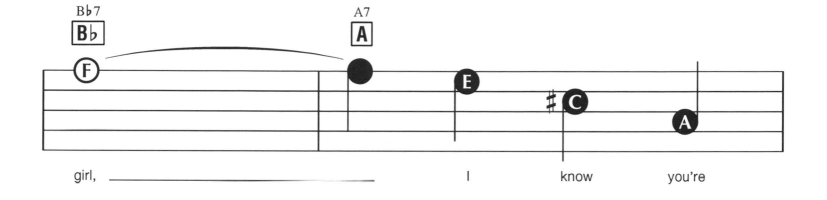

girl, _____   I   know   you're

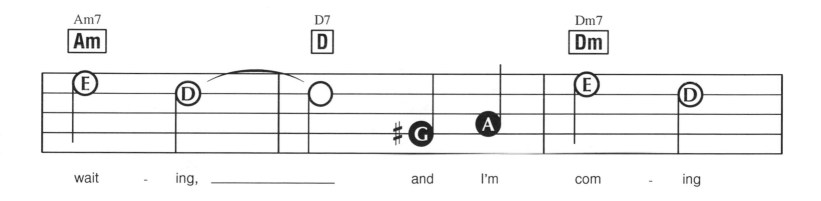

wait - ing, _____   and   I'm   com - ing

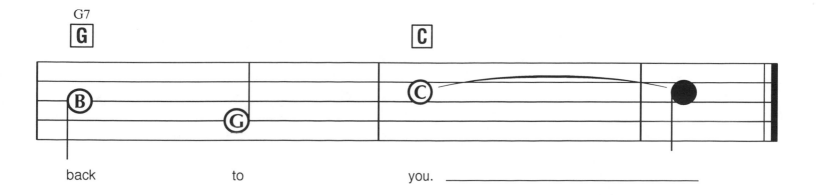

back   to   you. _____

Moonlight Bay

Registration 2
Rhythm: Swing

Words by Edward Madden
Music by Percy Wenrich

Copyright © 1994 by HAL LEONARD CORPORATION
International Copyright Secured   All Rights Reserved

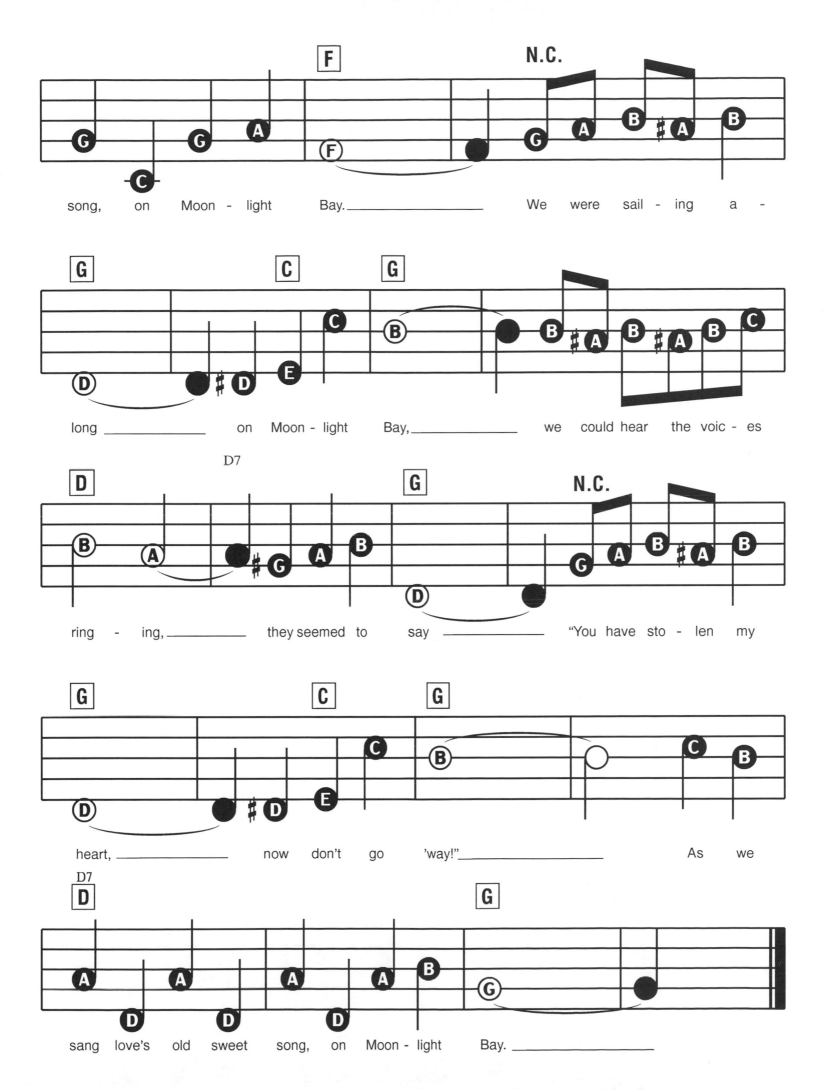

My Gal Sal

Registration 7
Rhythm: Swing

Words and Music by
Paul Dresser

C   F7 **F**   **C**

G   G.   G   A   C   D   E

They   called   her   friv - o - lous   Sal,_____

F7 **F**   **C**

G   G   G.   G   A   C   D   E

_____ a   pe - cu - liar   sort   of   a   gal._____

E7 **E**   **Am**

E   E   E   ♯D   E   B   C   D   D   C   B

_____ With   a   heart   that   was   mel - low,   an   all   'round good

D7 **D**   G7 **G**

C   D   E   D   A   D

fel - low   was   my   old   pal._____

Copyright © 1986 by HAL LEONARD CORPORATION
International Copyright Secured   All Rights Reserved

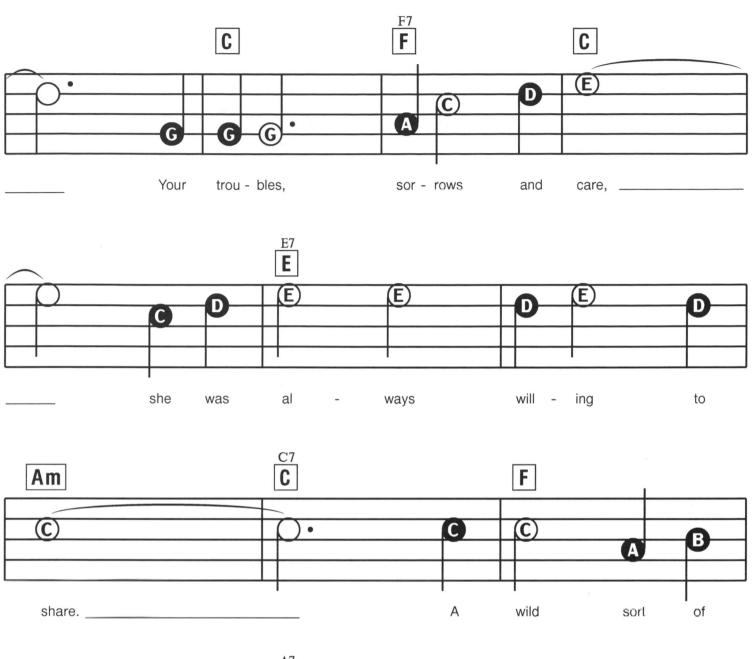

Your trou - bles, sor - rows and care, _____

_____ she was al - ways will - ing to

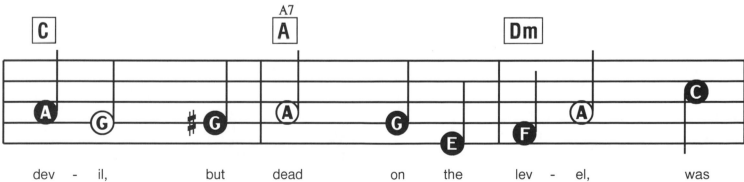

share. _____ A wild sort of

dev - il, but dead on the lev - el, was

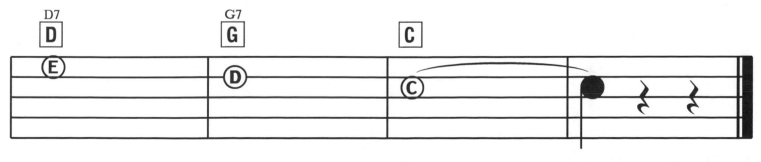

my gal Sal. _____

My Melancholy Baby

Words by George Norton
Music by Ernie Burnett

Copyright © 1994 by HAL LEONARD CORPORATION
International Copyright Secured   All Rights Reserved

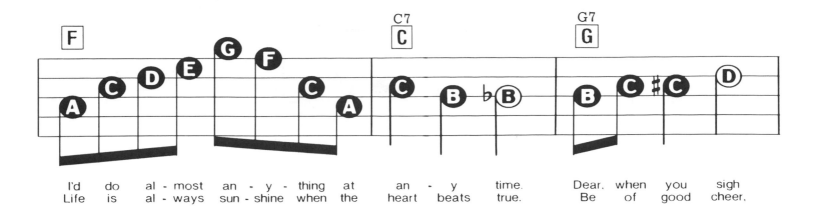

I'd do al - most an - y - thing at an - y time. Dear, when you sigh
Life is al - ways sun - shine when the heart beats true. Be of good cheer,

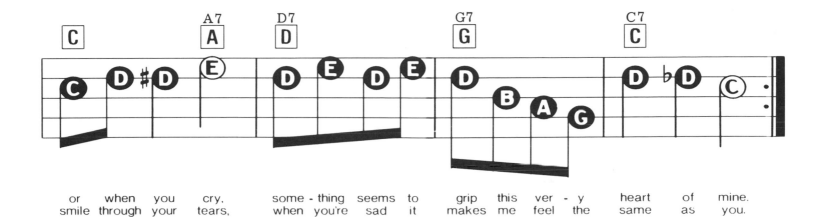

or when you cry, some - thing seems to grip this ver - y heart of mine.
smile through your tears, when you're sad it makes me feel the same as you.

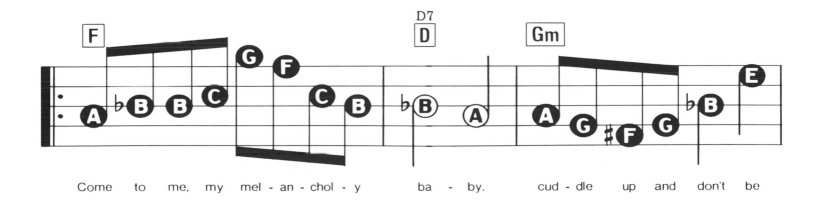

Come to me, my mel - an - chol - y ba - by. cud - dle up and don't be

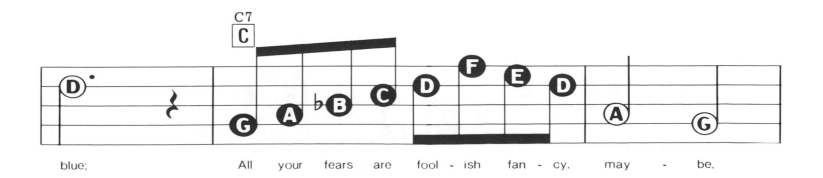

blue; All your fears are fool - ish fan - cy. may - be,

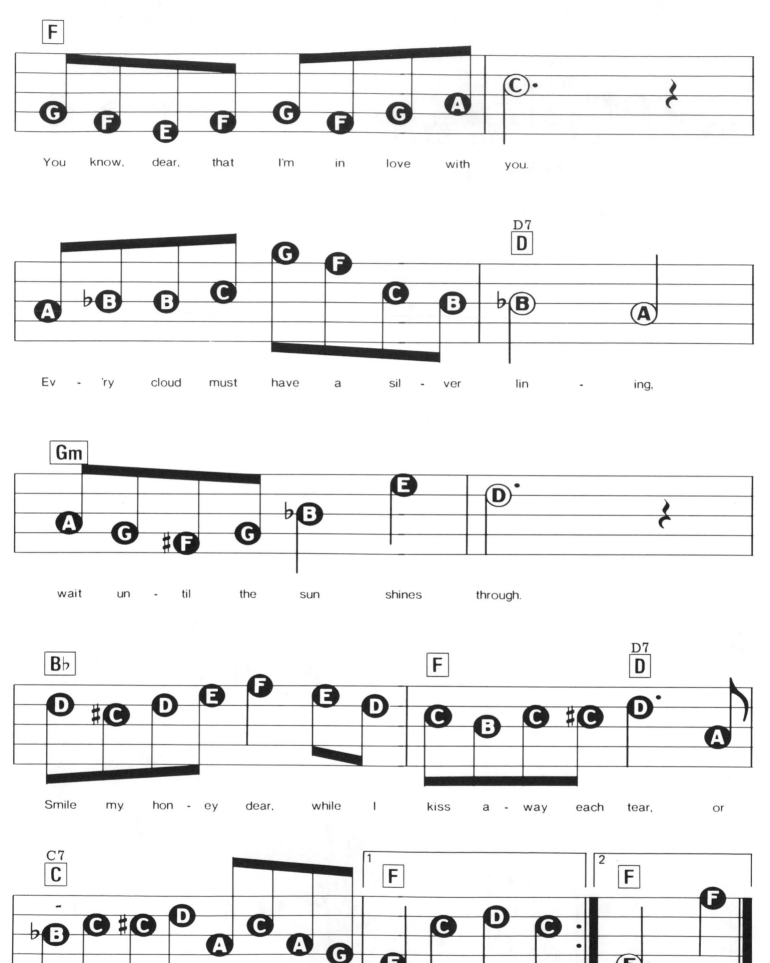

Oh Johnny, Oh Johnny, Oh!

Registration 7
Rhythm: Polka

Words by Ed Rose
Music by Abe Olman

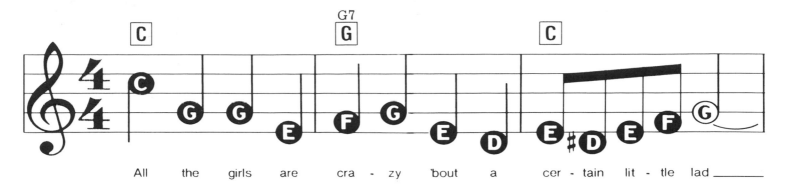

All the girls are cra - zy 'bout a cer - tain lit - tle lad ____

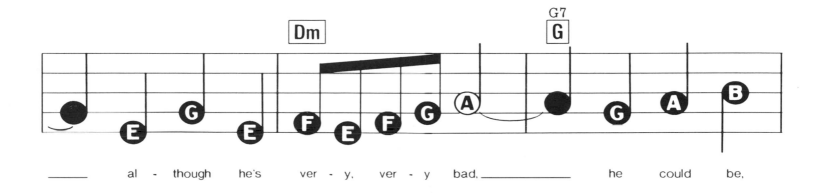

____ al - though he's ver - y, ver - y bad, ____ he could be,

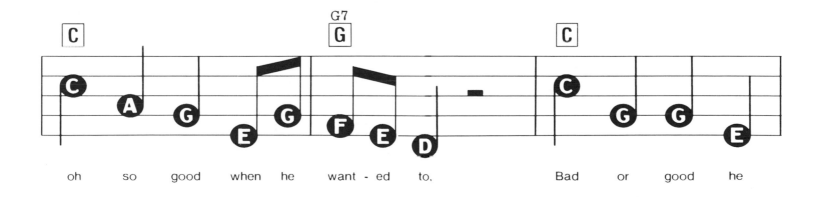

oh so good when he want - ed to, Bad or good he

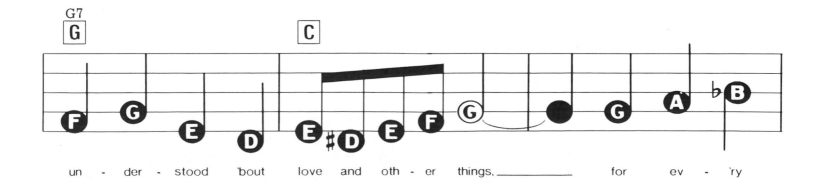

un - der - stood 'bout love and oth - er things, ____ for ev - 'ry

Copyright © 1996 by HAL LEONARD CORPORATION
International Copyright Secured   All Rights Reserved

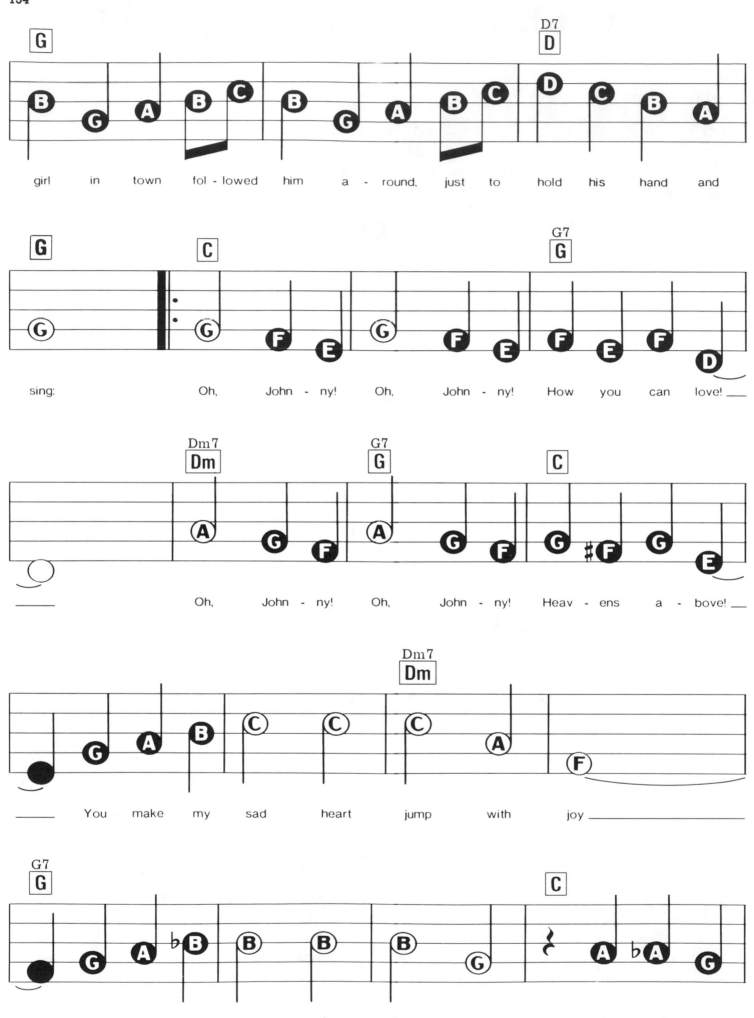

min - ute, I'm so, Oh, John - ny! Oh, John - ny! Please tell me, dear, ____

____ what makes me love you so? _____

____ You're not hand - some, it's true, _____ but when I look at you, ___

____ I just Oh, John - ny! Oh, John - ny!

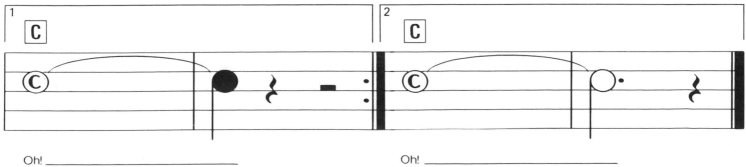

Oh! _____ Oh! _____

Oh! How I Hate to Get Up in the Morning

from the Stage Production THIS IS THE ARMY

Registration 2
Rhythm: 6/8 March

Words and Music by
Irving Berlin

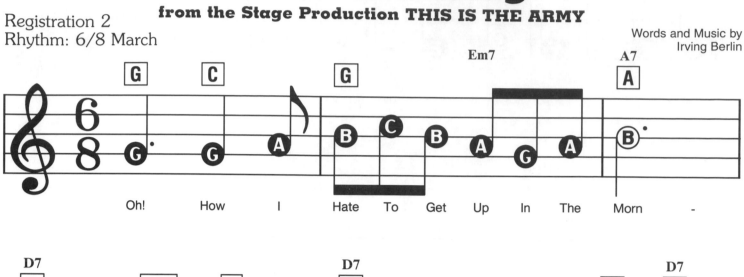

Oh! How I Hate To Get Up In The Morn -

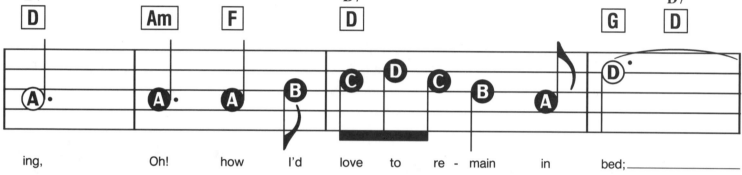

ing, Oh! how I'd love to re - main in bed;

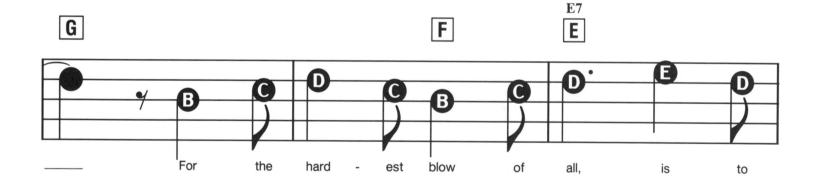

For the hard - est blow of all, is to

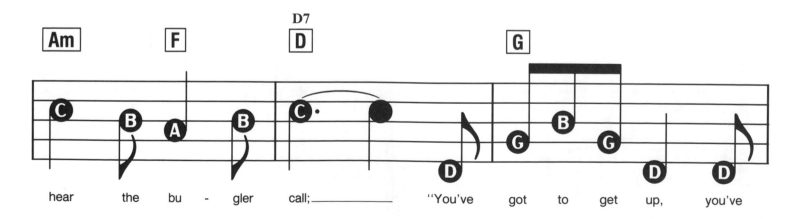

hear the bu - gler call;_____ "You've got to get up, you've

© Copyright 1918 by Irving Berlin
Copyright Renewed
Copyright Assigned to Winthrop Rutherfurd, Jr., Anne Phipps Sidamon-Eristoff and Theodore R. Jackson as Trustees of God Bless America Fund
International Copyright Secured   All Rights Reserved
Dedicated to my friend "Private Howard Friend" who occupies the cot next to mine and feels as I do about the "bugler"

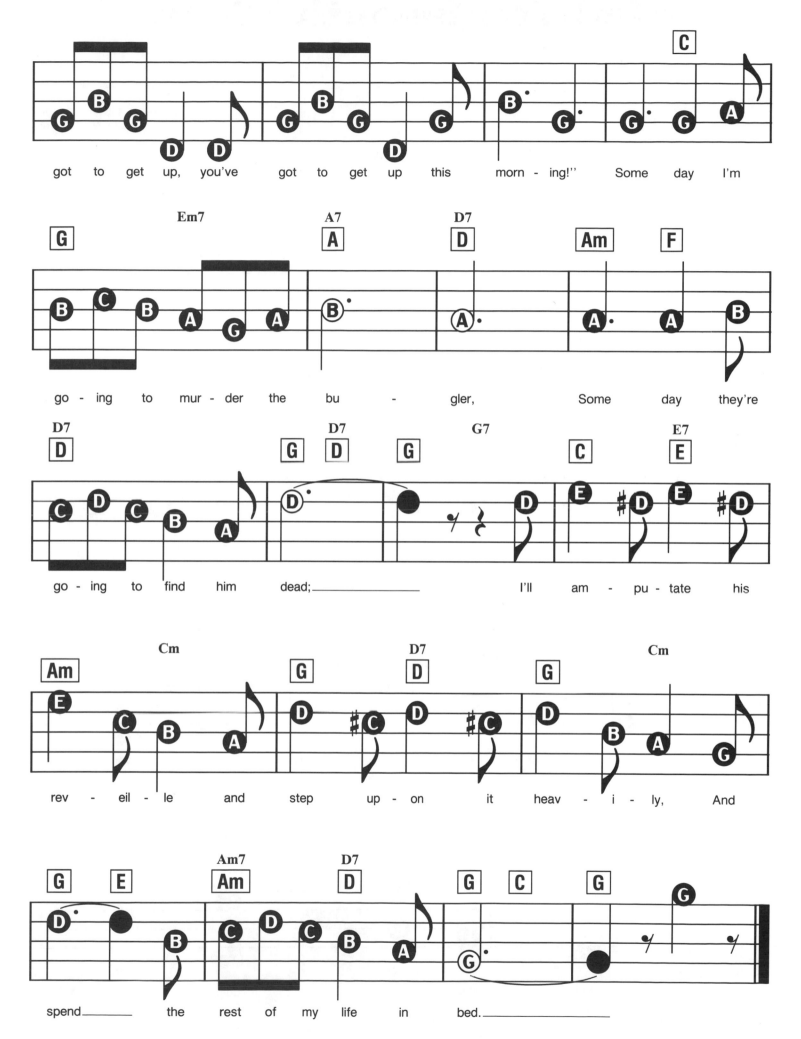

Oh! You Beautiful Doll

Registration 8
Rhythm: Fox Trot

Words by A. Seymour Brown
Music by Nat D. Ayer

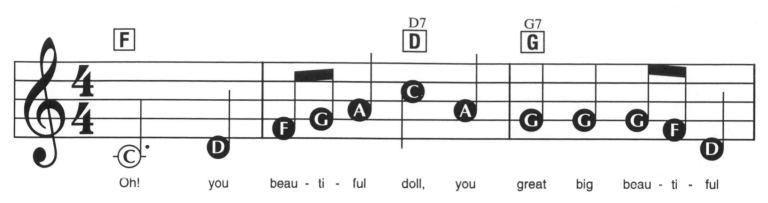

Oh! you beau - ti - ful doll, you great big beau - ti - ful

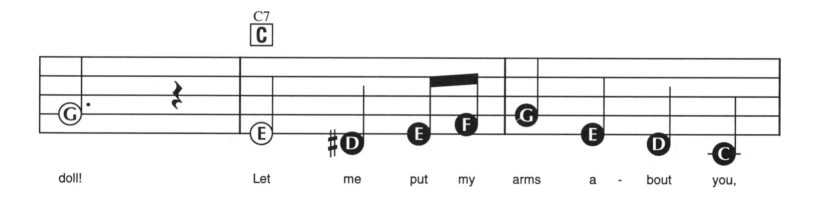

doll! Let me put my arms a - bout you,

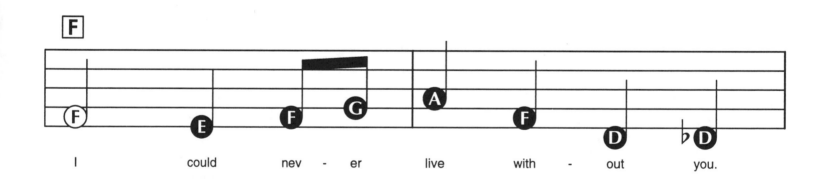

I could nev - er live with - out you.

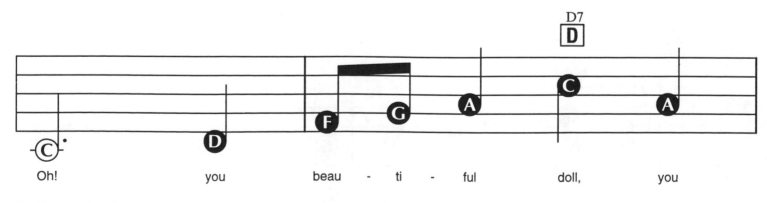

Oh! you beau - ti - ful doll, you

Copyright © 1911 Warner Bros.
Copyright renewed; extended term of Copyright deriving from Nat Ayer assigned and effective January 4, 1980 to Herald Square Music, Inc.
International Copyright Secured   All Rights Reserved
Used by Permission

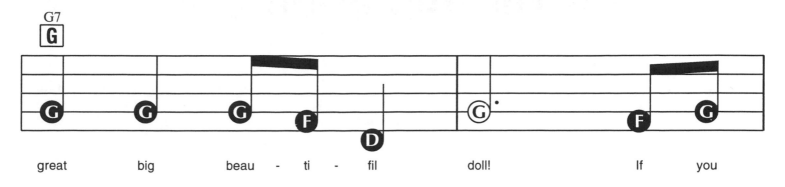

great big beau - ti - fil doll! If you

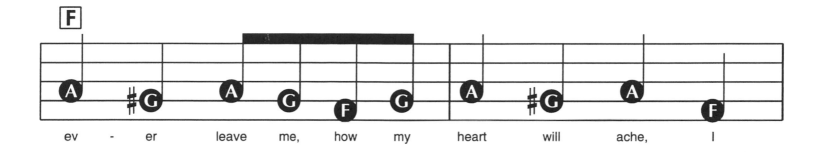

ev - er leave me, how my heart will ache, I

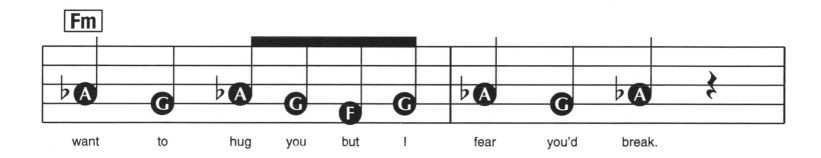

want to hug you but I fear you'd break.

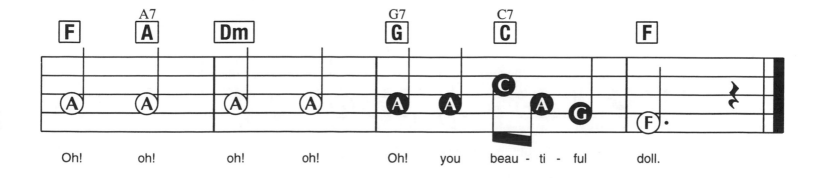

Oh! oh! oh! oh! Oh! you beau - ti - ful doll.

On Wisconsin!

Registration 5
Rhythm: March

Words by Carl Beck
Music by W.T. Purdy

Copyright © 1996 by HAL LEONARD CORPORATION
International Copyright Secured   All Rights Reserved

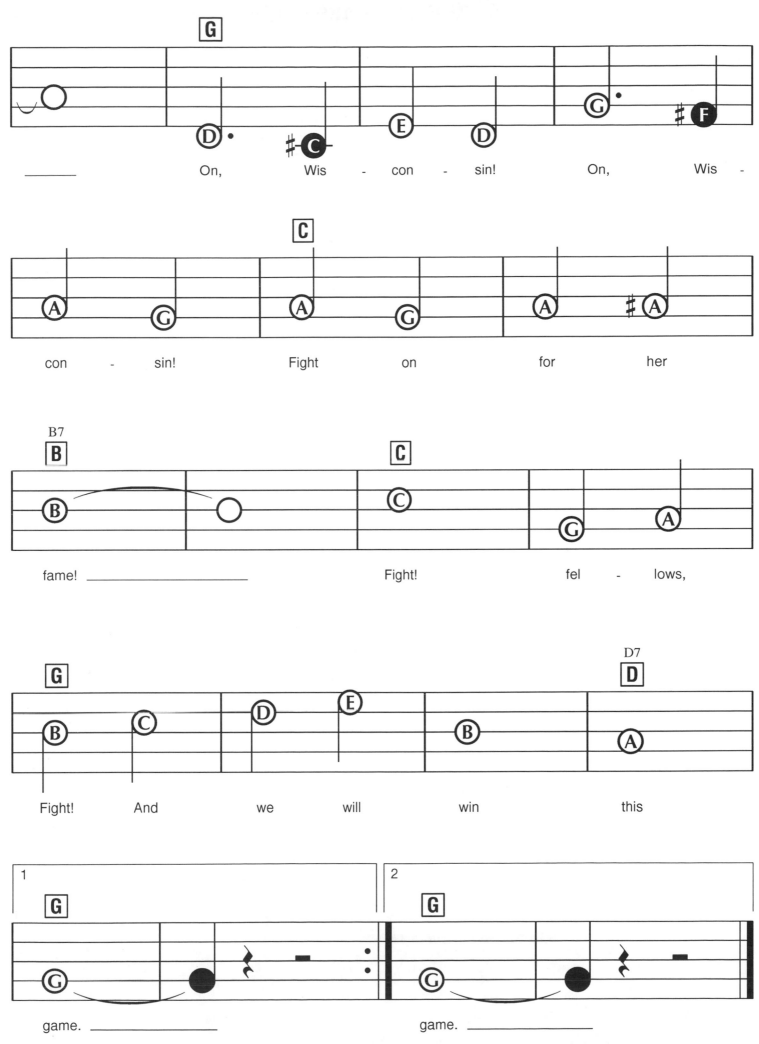

Over There

Registration 9
Rhythm: March

Words and Music by
George M. Cohan

Copyright © 1994 by HAL LEONARD CORPORATION
International Copyright Secured   All Rights Reserved

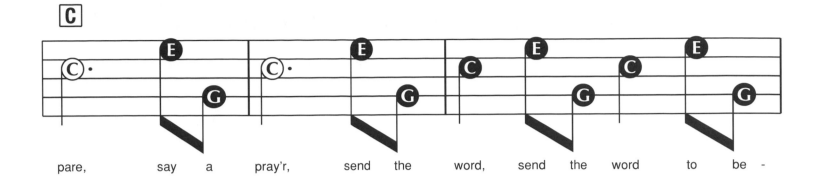

pare, say a pray'r, send the word, send the word to be -

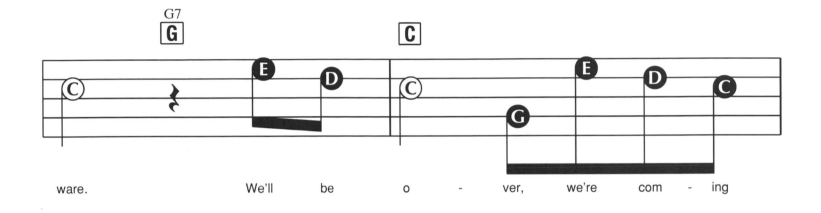

ware. We'll be o - ver, we're com - ing

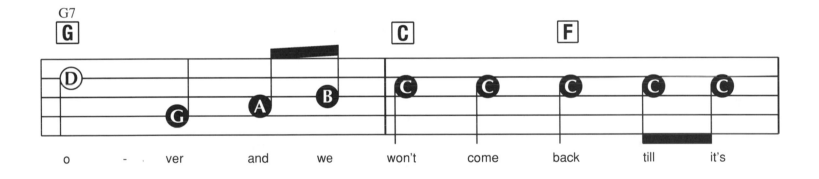

o - ver and we won't come back till it's

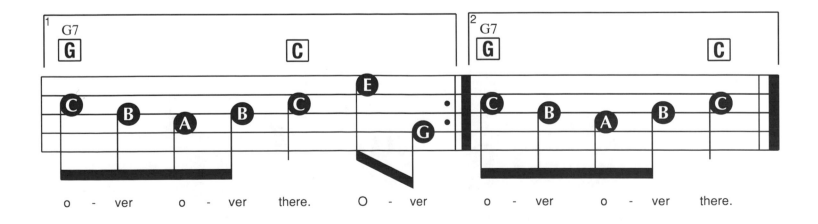

o - ver o - ver there. O - ver o - ver o - ver there.

Pack Up Your Troubles in Your Old Kit Bag and Smile, Smile, Smile

Registration 4
Rhythm: March

Words by George Asaf
Music by Felix Powell

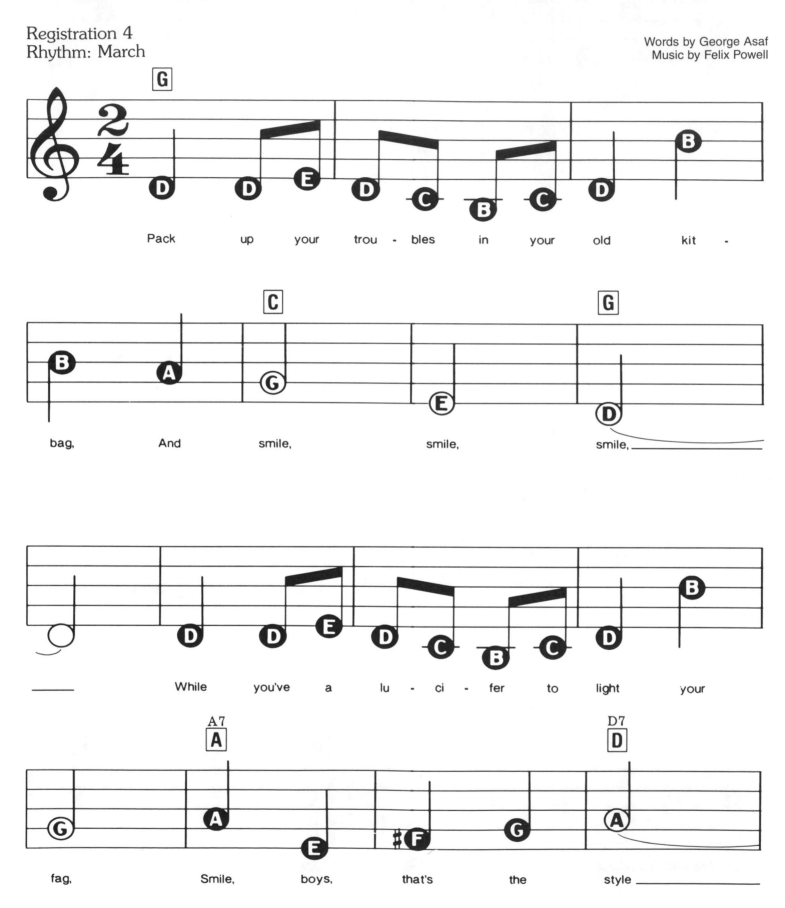

Copyright © 1994 by HAL LEONARD CORPORATION
International Copyright Secured   All Rights Reserved

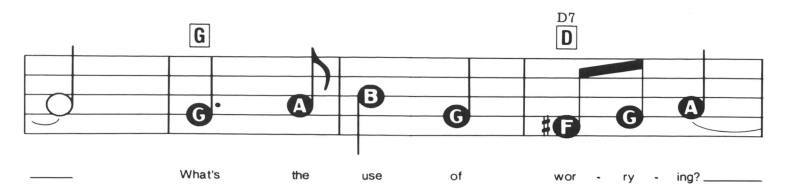

What's the use of wor - ry - ing? _____

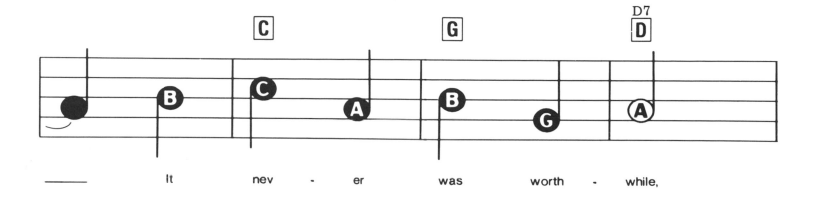

_____ It nev - er was worth - while,

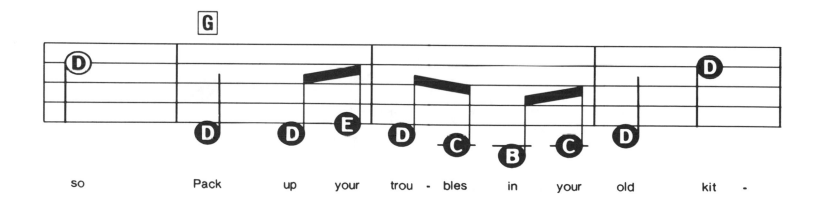

so Pack up your trou - bles in your old kit -

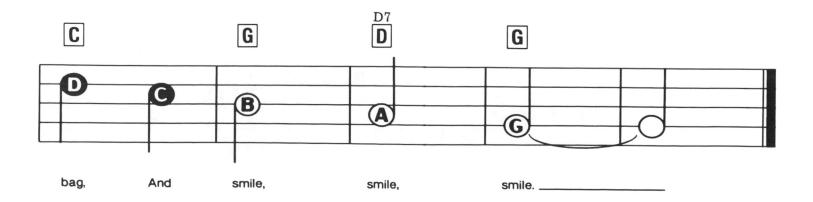

bag, And smile, smile, smile. _____

Paper Doll

Registration 4
Rhythm: Fox Trot or Swing

Words and Music by
Johnny S. Black

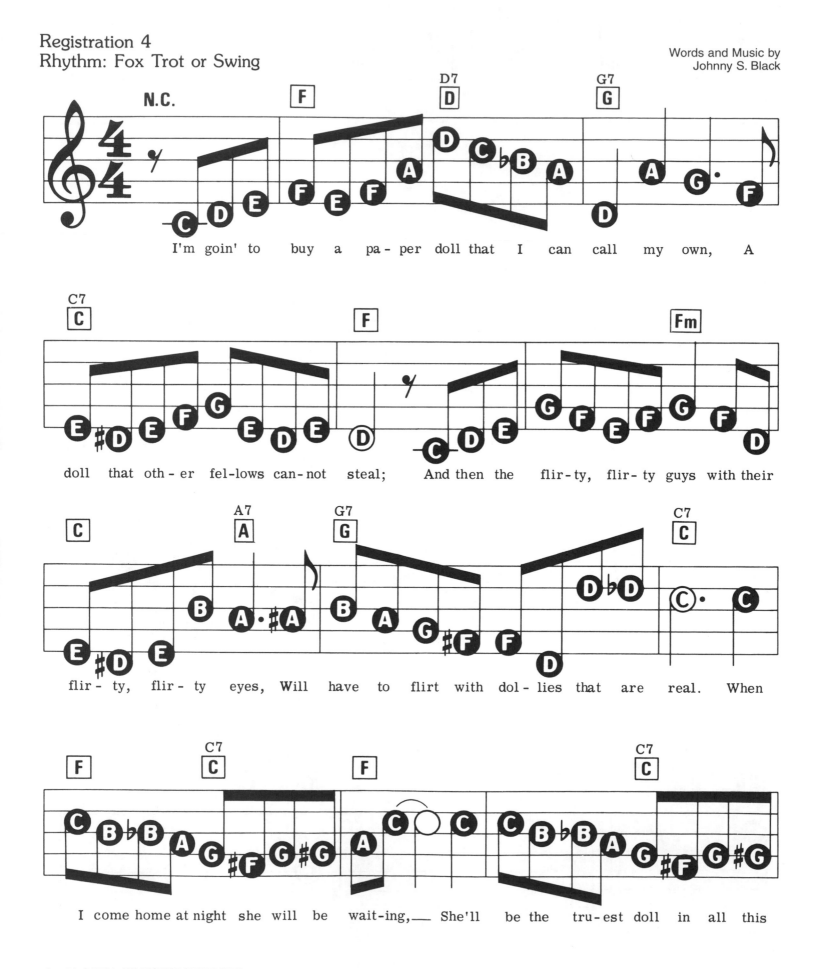

Copyright © 1996 by HAL LEONARD CORPORATION
International Copyright Secured   All Rights Reserved

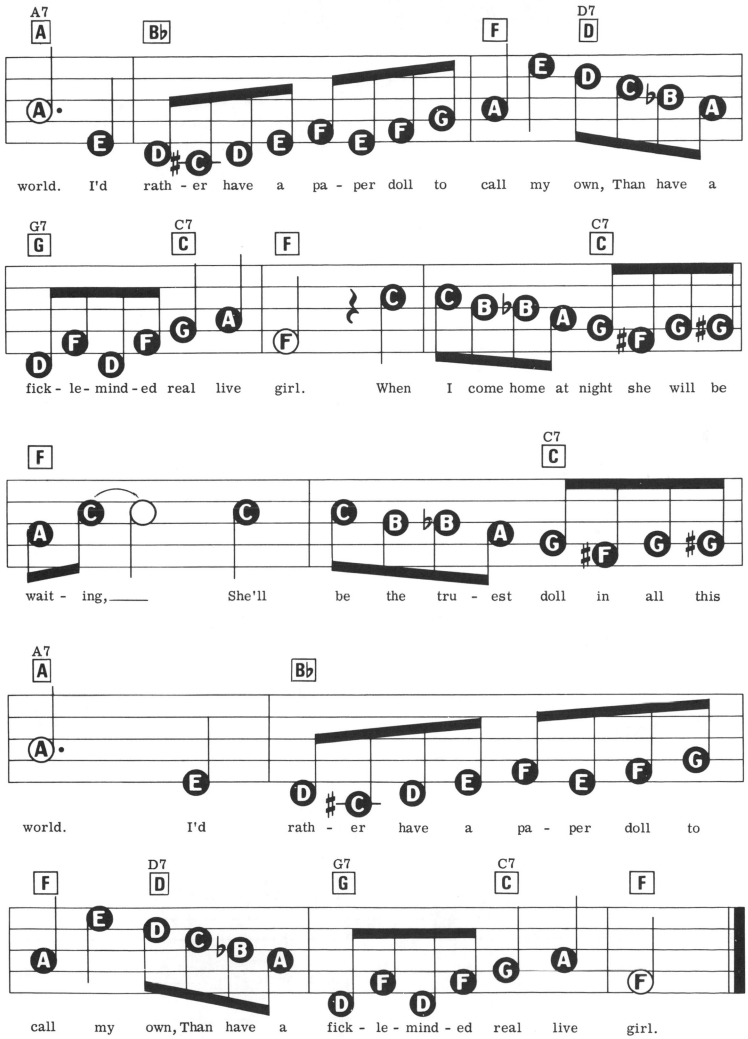

Peg o' My Heart

Registration 2
Rhythm: Fox Trot or Swing

Words by Alfred Bryan
Music by Fred Fisher

Copyright © 1994 by HAL LEONARD CORPORATION
International Copyright Secured All Rights Reserved

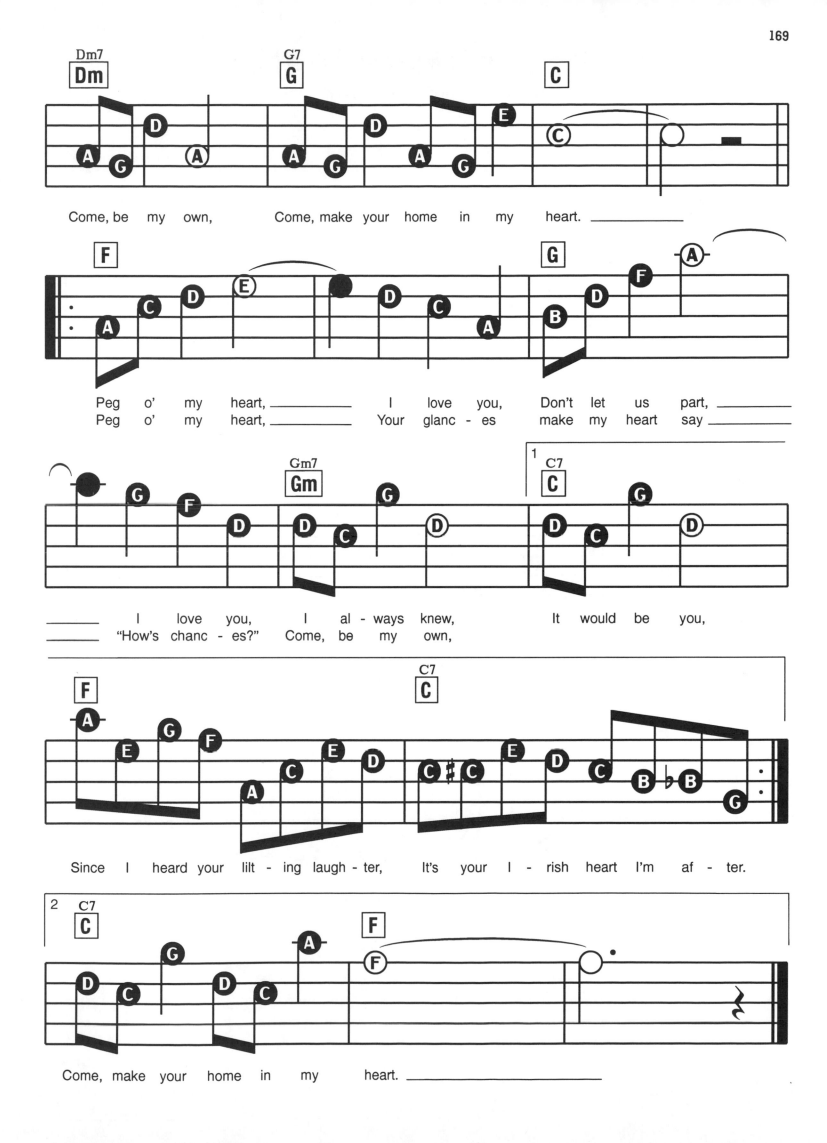

Come, be my own, Come, make your home in my heart. _____

Peg o' my heart, _____ I love you, Don't let us part, _____
Peg o' my heart, _____ Your glanc - es make my heart say _____

_____ I love you, I al - ways knew, It would be you,
_____ "How's chanc - es?" Come, be my own,

Since I heard your lilt - ing laugh - ter, It's your I - rish heart I'm af - ter.

Come, make your home in my heart. _____

Play a Simple Melody
from the Stage Production WATCH YOUR STEP

Registration 1
Rhythm: Swing

Words and Music by
Irving Berlin

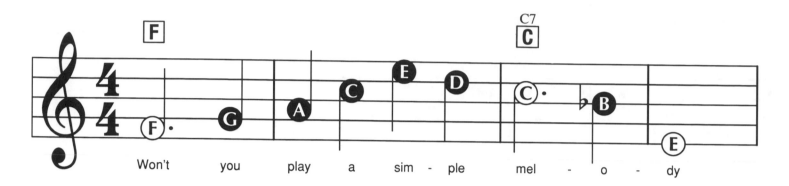

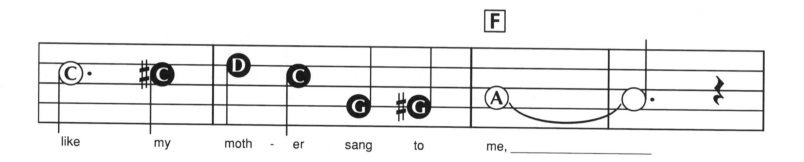

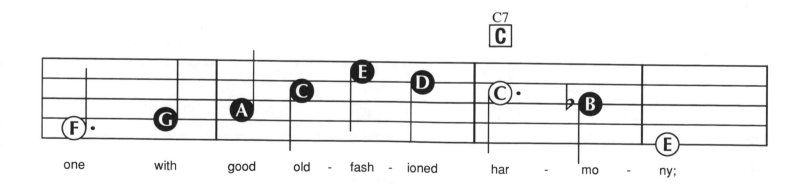

© Copyright 1914 by Irving Berlin
Copyright Renewed
International Copyright Secured All Rights Reserved

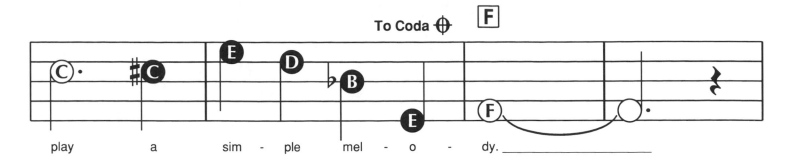

play a sim - ple mel - o - dy. _____

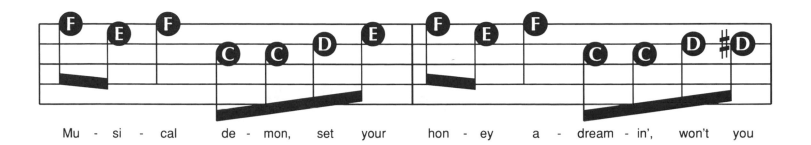

Mu - si - cal de - mon, set your hon - ey a - dream - in', won't you

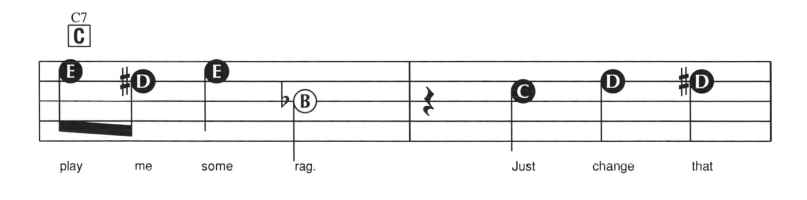

play me some rag. Just change that

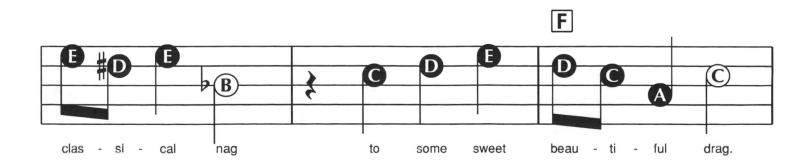

clas - si - cal nag to some sweet beau - ti - ful drag.

172

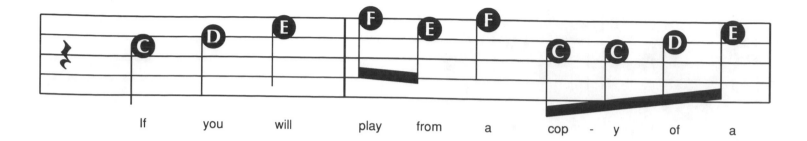

If you will play from a copy of a

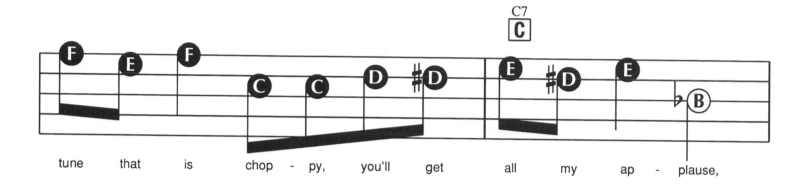

C7

tune that is chop - py, you'll get all my ap - plause,

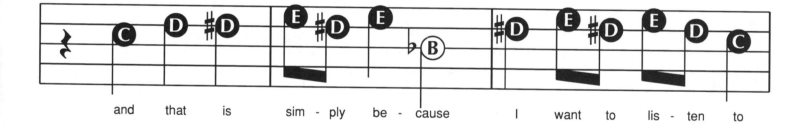

and that is sim - ply be - cause I want to lis - ten to

D.C. al Coda
(Return to beginning
Play to ⊕
Skip to Coda)

CODA
⊕

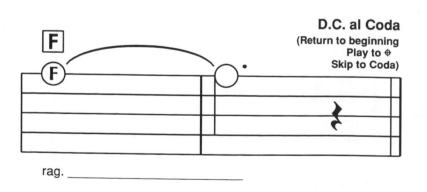

rag. _____

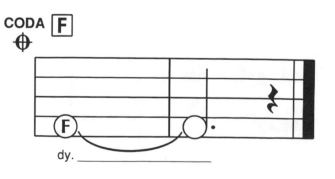

dy. _____

Rock-A-Bye Your Baby
with a Dixie Melody

from SINBAD

Registration 9
Rhythm: Fox Trot or Swing

Words by Sam M. Lewis and Joe Young
Music by Jean Schwartz

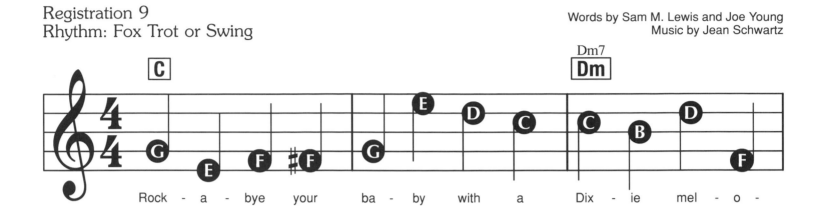

Rock - a - bye your ba - by with a Dix - ie mel - o -

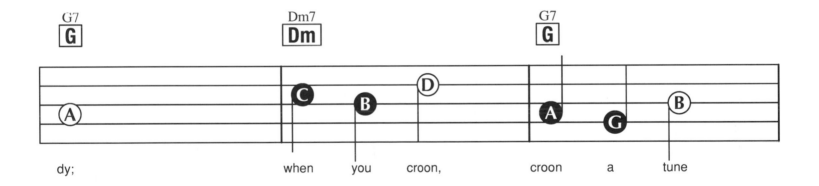

dy; when you croon, croon a tune

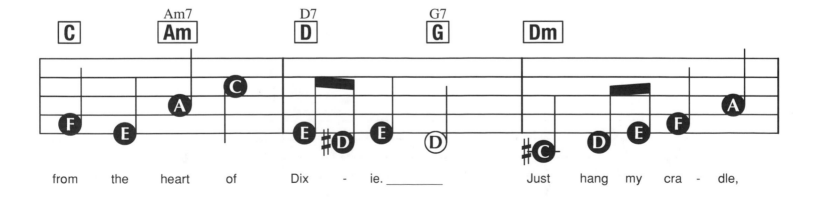

from the heart of Dix - ie._____ Just hang my cra - dle,

Copyright © 1994 by HAL LEONARD CORPORATION
International Copyright Secured   All Rights Reserved

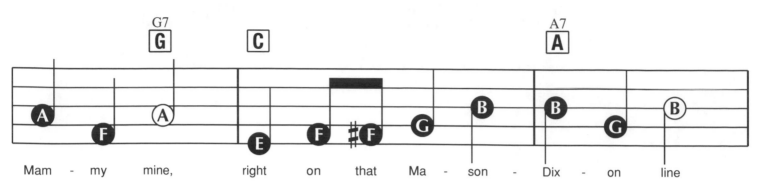

Mam - my mine, right on that Ma - son - Dix - on line

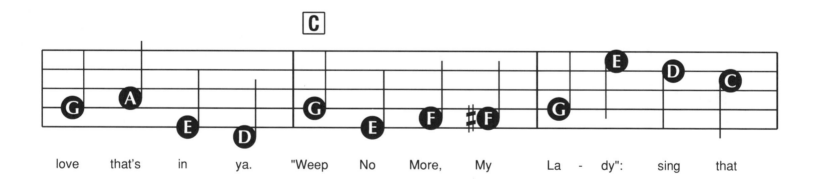

and swing it from Vir - gin - ia to Ten - nes - see with all the

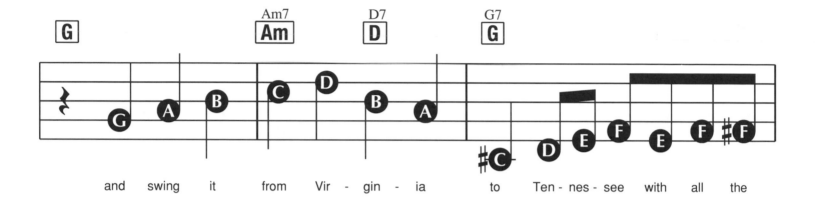

love that's in ya. "Weep No More, My La - dy": sing that

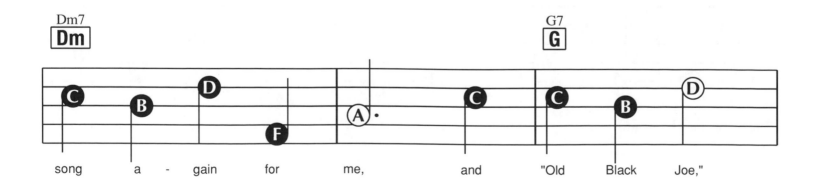

song a - gain for me, and "Old Black Joe,"

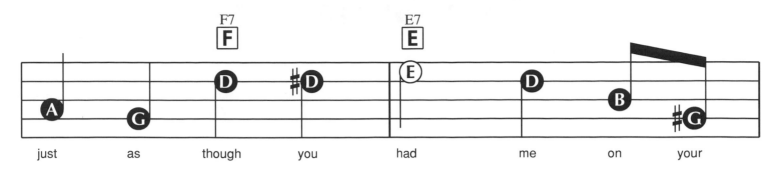

just as though you had me on your

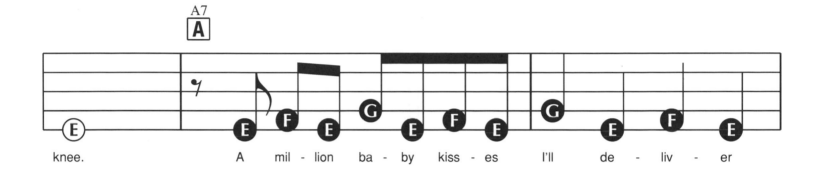

knee. A mil - lion ba - by kiss - es I'll de - liv - er

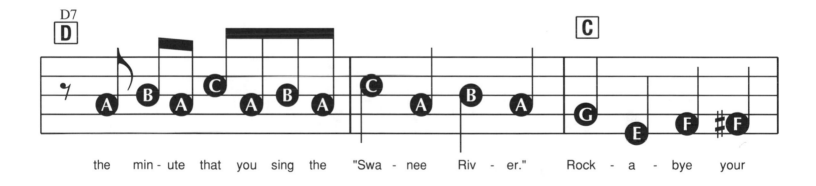

the min - ute that you sing the "Swa - nee Riv - er." Rock - a - bye your

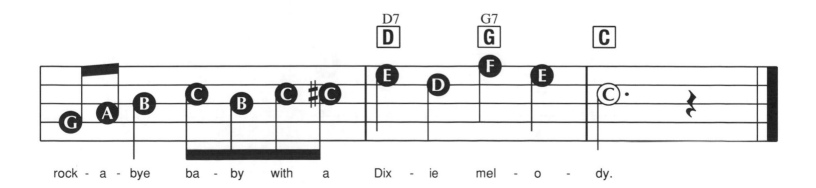

rock - a - bye ba - by with a Dix - ie mel - o - dy.

Poor Butterfly

Registration 1
Rhythm: Fox Trot or Swing

Words by John L. Golden
Music by Raymond Hubbell

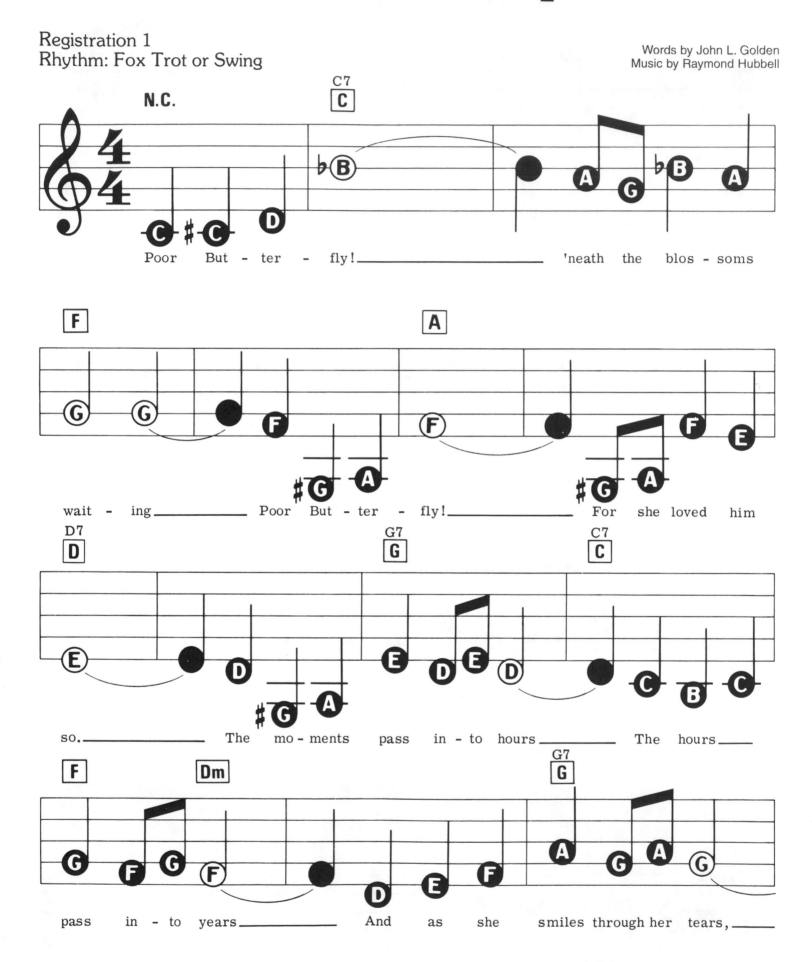

Copyright © 1996 by HAL LEONARD CORPORATION
International Copyright Secured   All Rights Reserved

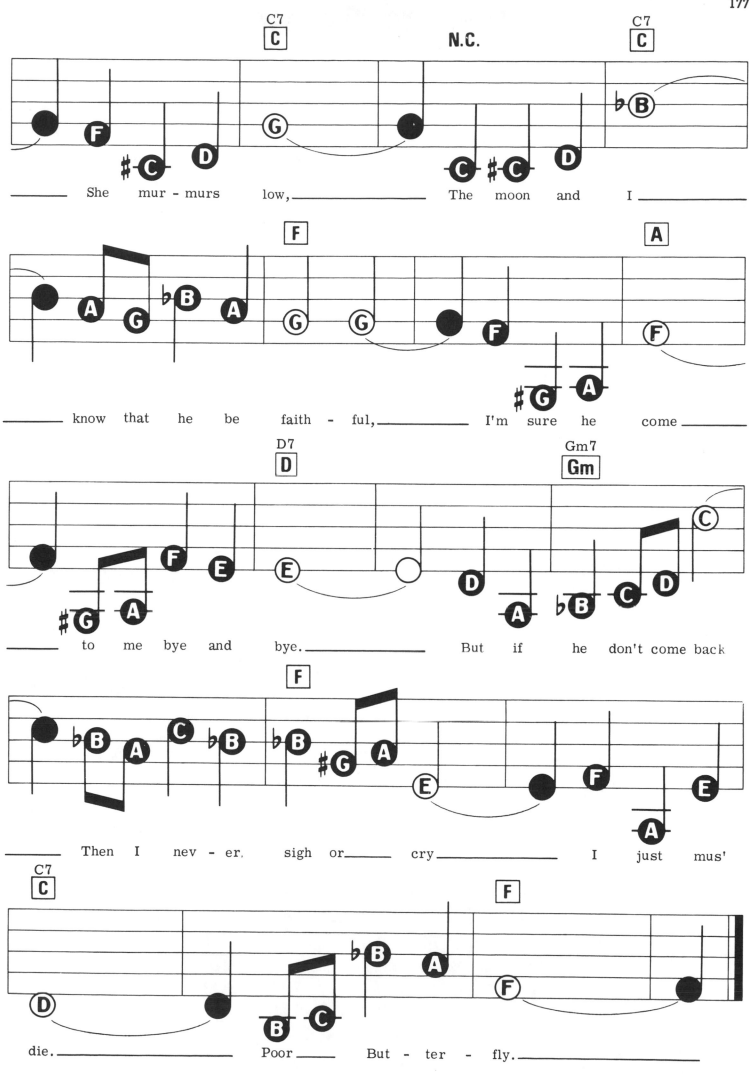

Pretty Baby

Words by Gus Kahn
Music by Egbert Van Alstyne
and Tony Jackson

Registration 2
Rhythm: Swing

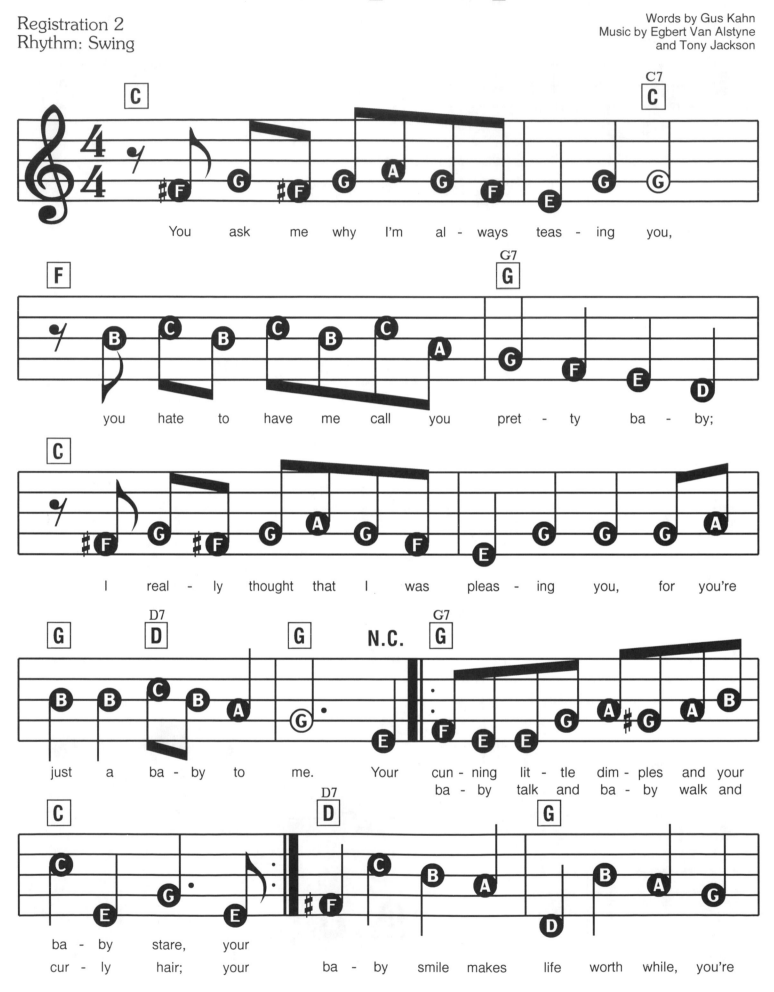

Copyright © 1996 by HAL LEONARD CORPORATION
International Copyright Secured   All Rights Reserved

A Pretty Girl Is Like a Melody
from the 1919 Stage Production ZIEGFELD FOLLIES

Registration 8
Rhythm: Fox Trot or Ballad

Words and Music by
Irving Berlin

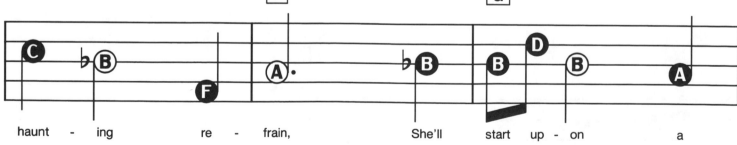

© Copyright 1919 by Irving Berlin
© Copyright Renewed
International Copyright Secured   All Rights Reserved

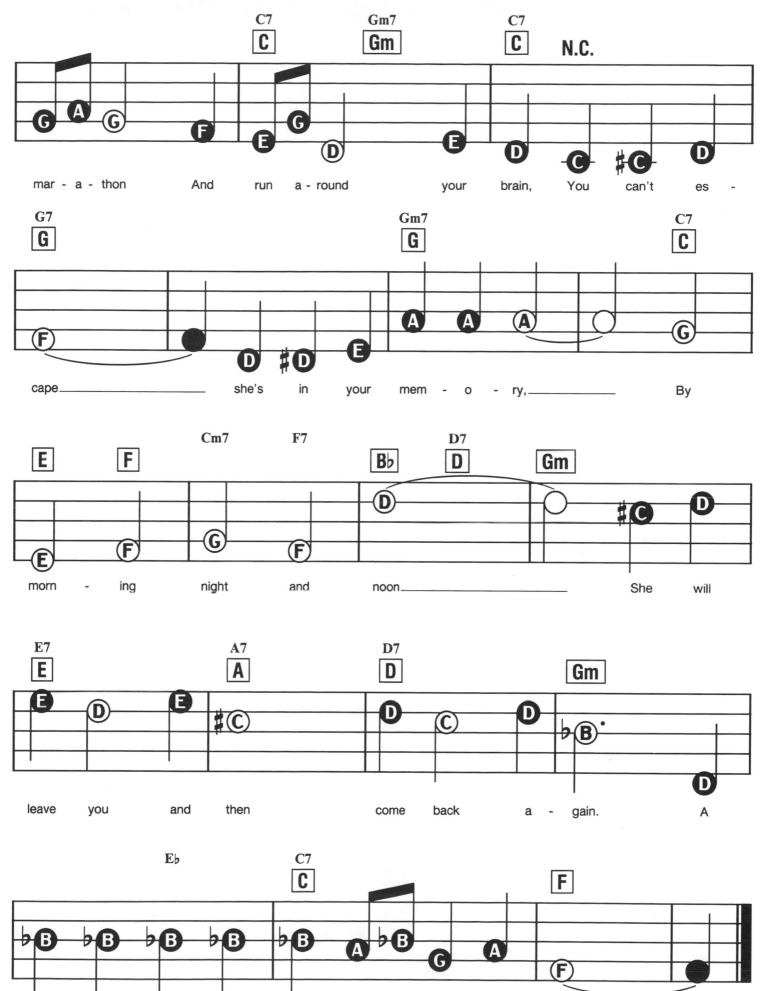

Put on Your Old Grey Bonnet

Registration 3
Rhythm: Polka or March

Words by Stanley Murphy
Music by Percy Wenrich

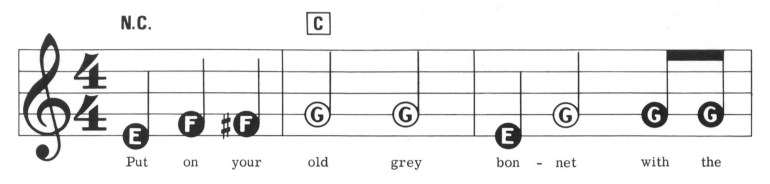

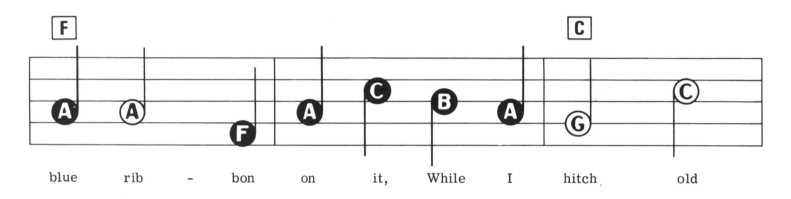

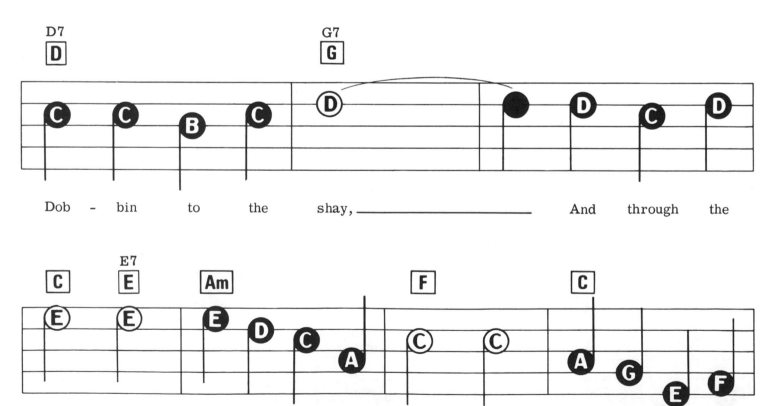

Copyright © 1994 by HAL LEONARD CORPORATION
International Copyright Secured   All Rights Reserved

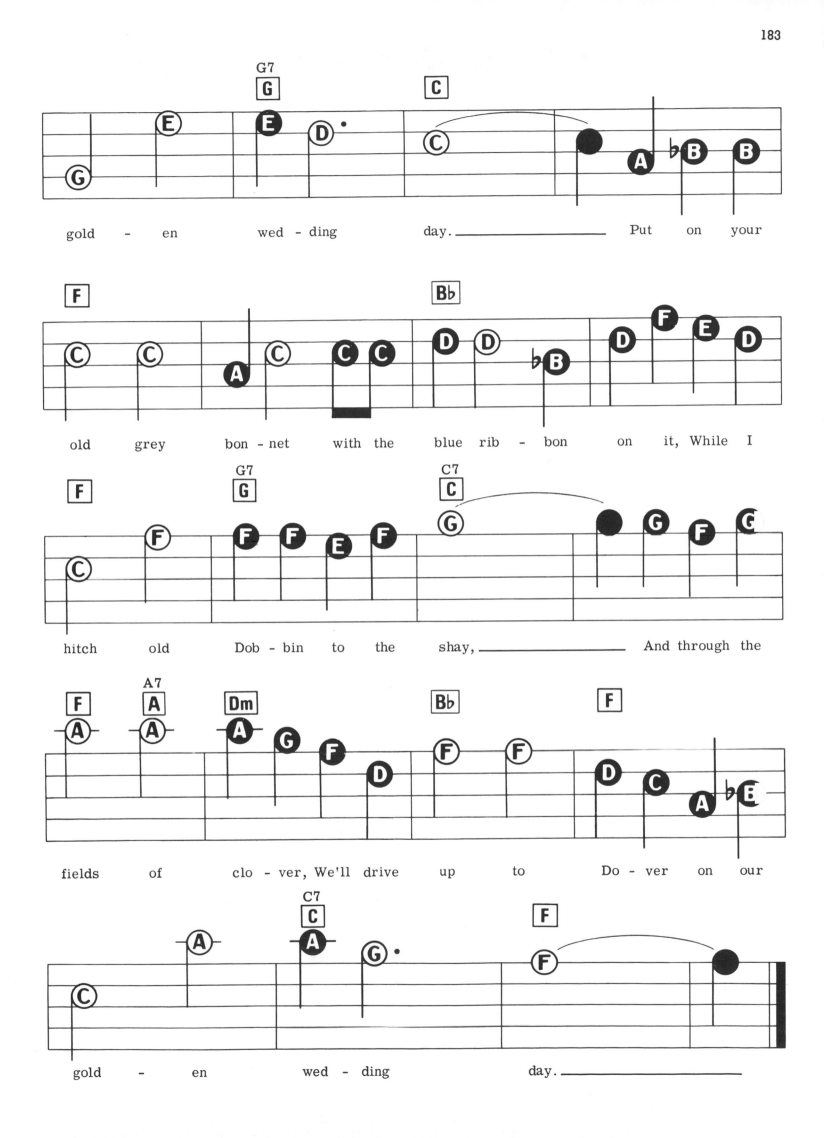

Put Your Arms Around Me, Honey

Registration 9
Rhythm: Fox Trot

Words by Junie McCree
Music by Albert von Tilzer

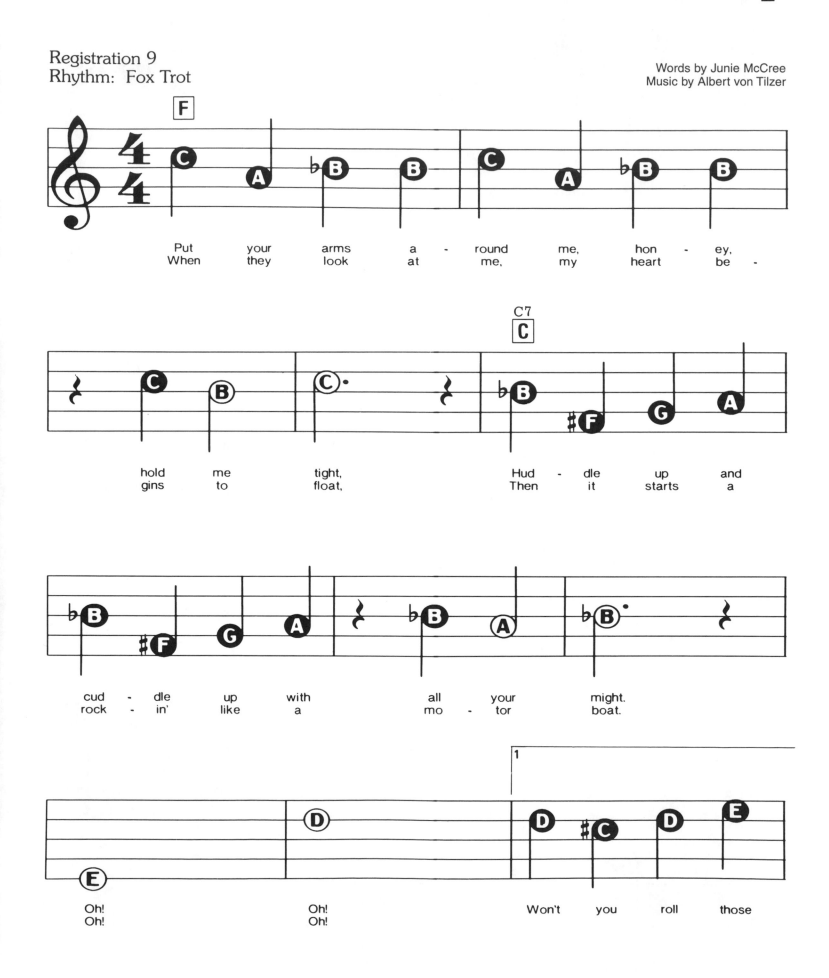

Copyright © 1996 by HAL LEONARD CORPORATION
International Copyright Secured   All Rights Reserved

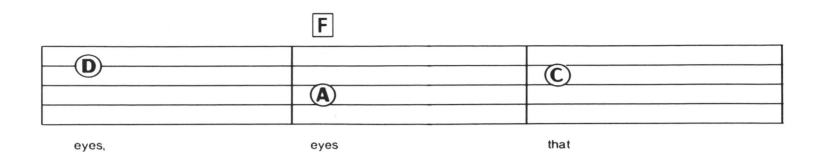

eyes,   eyes   that

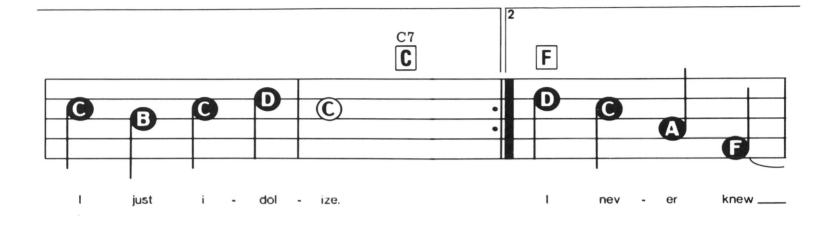

I   just   i - dol - ize.   I   nev - er knew ____

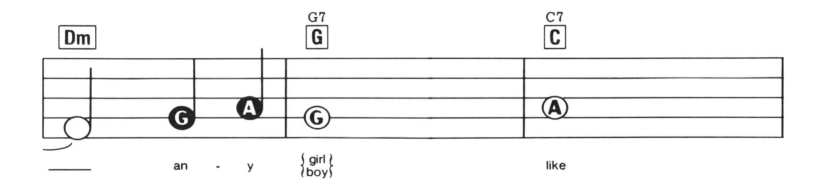

____ an - y { girl boy }   like

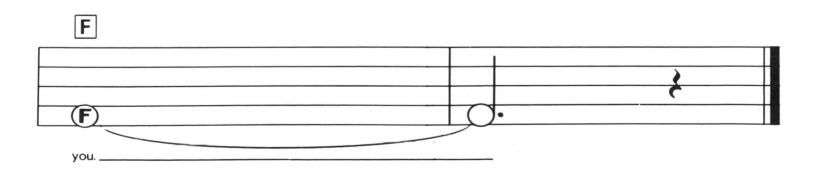

you. _____

Ragtime Cowboy Joe

Registration 5
Rhythm: Swing or Shuffle

Words and Music by Lewis F. Muir,
Grant Clarke and Maurice Abrahams

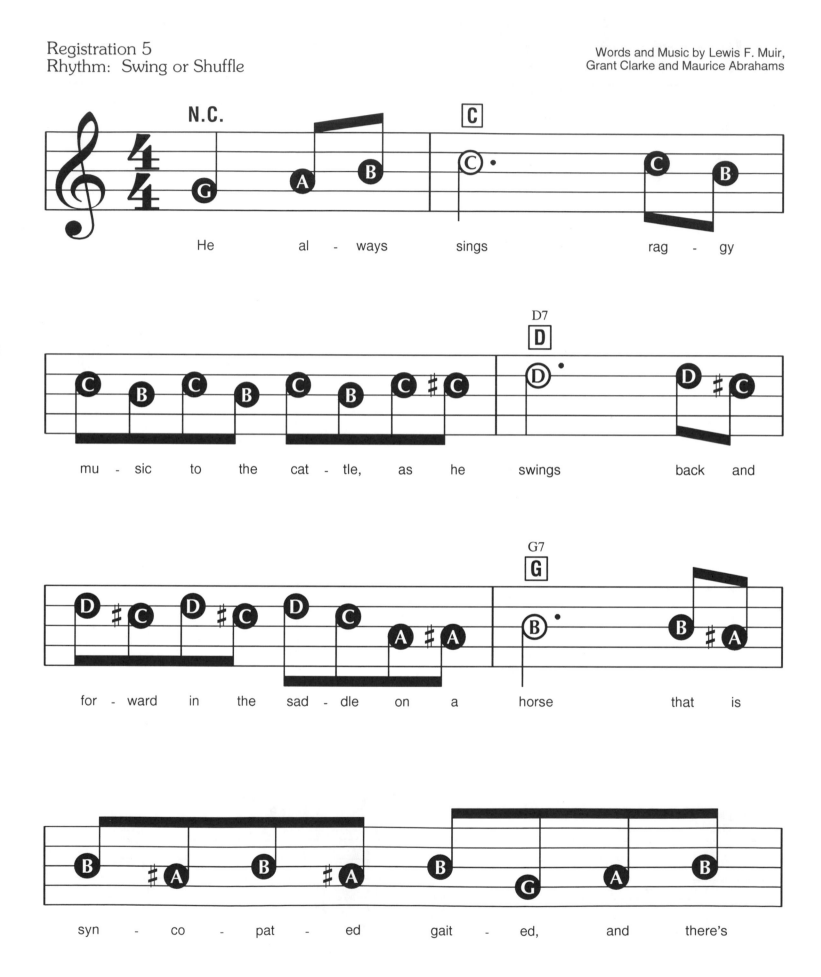

Copyright © 1996 by HAL LEONARD CORPORATION
International Copyright Secured   All Rights Reserved

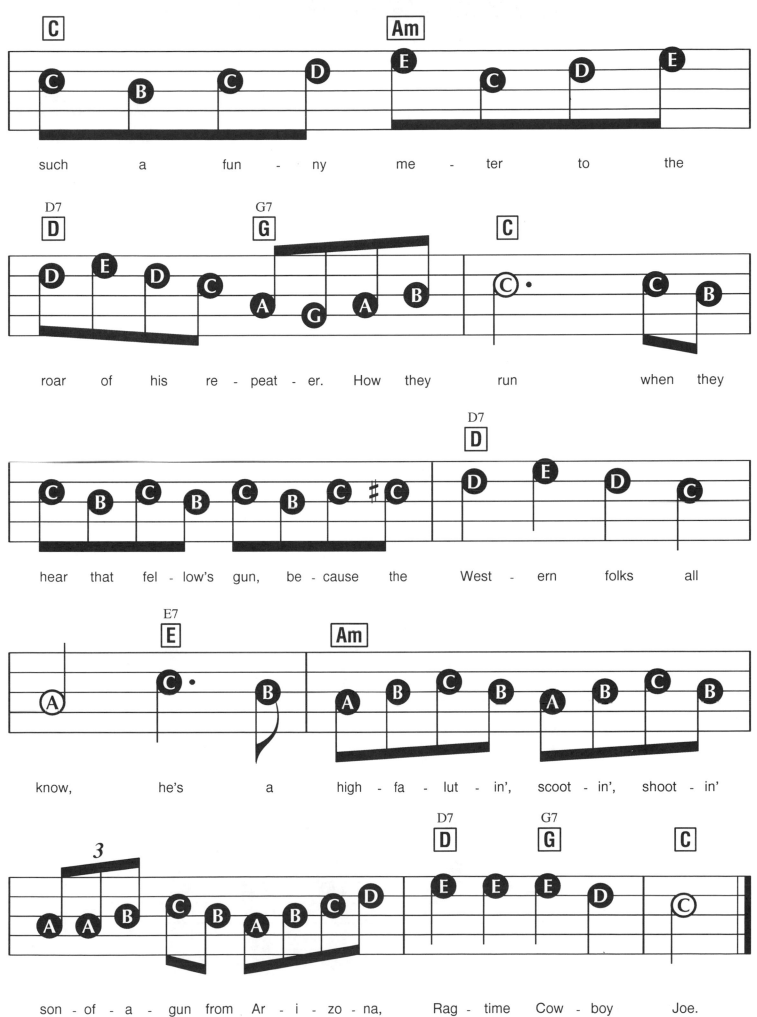

Rose of Washington Square

Registration 4
Rhythm: Swing

Lyric by Ballard MacDonald
Music by James F. Hanley

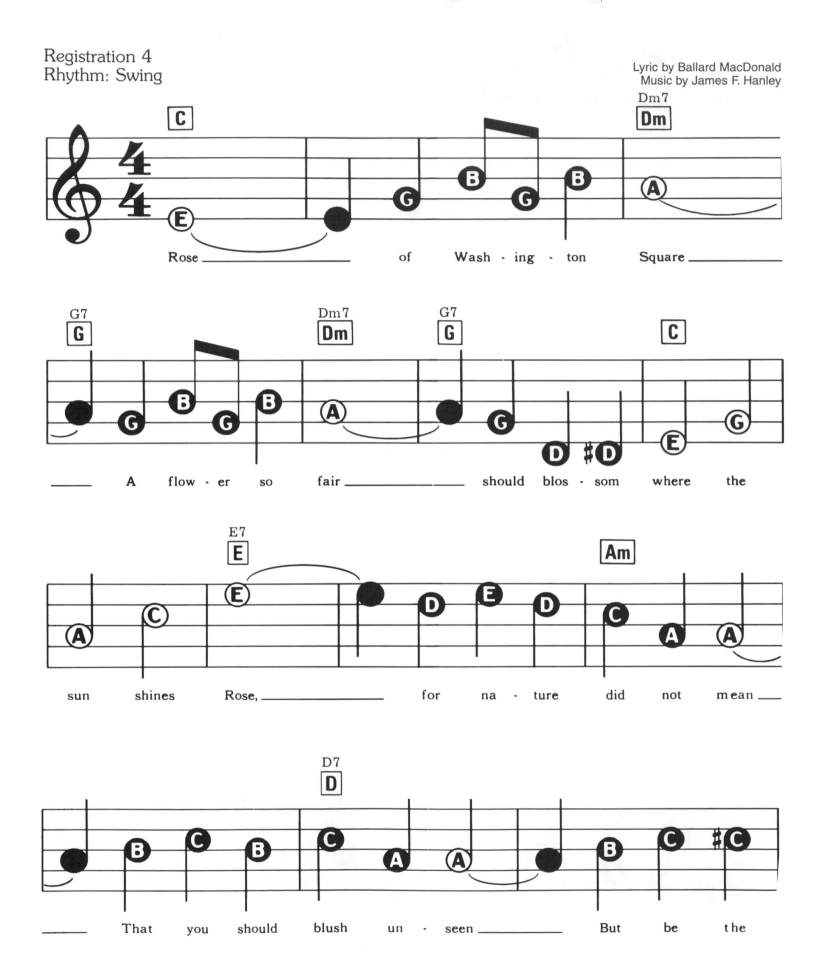

Copyright © 1996 by HAL LEONARD CORPORATION
International Copyright Secured   All Rights Reserved

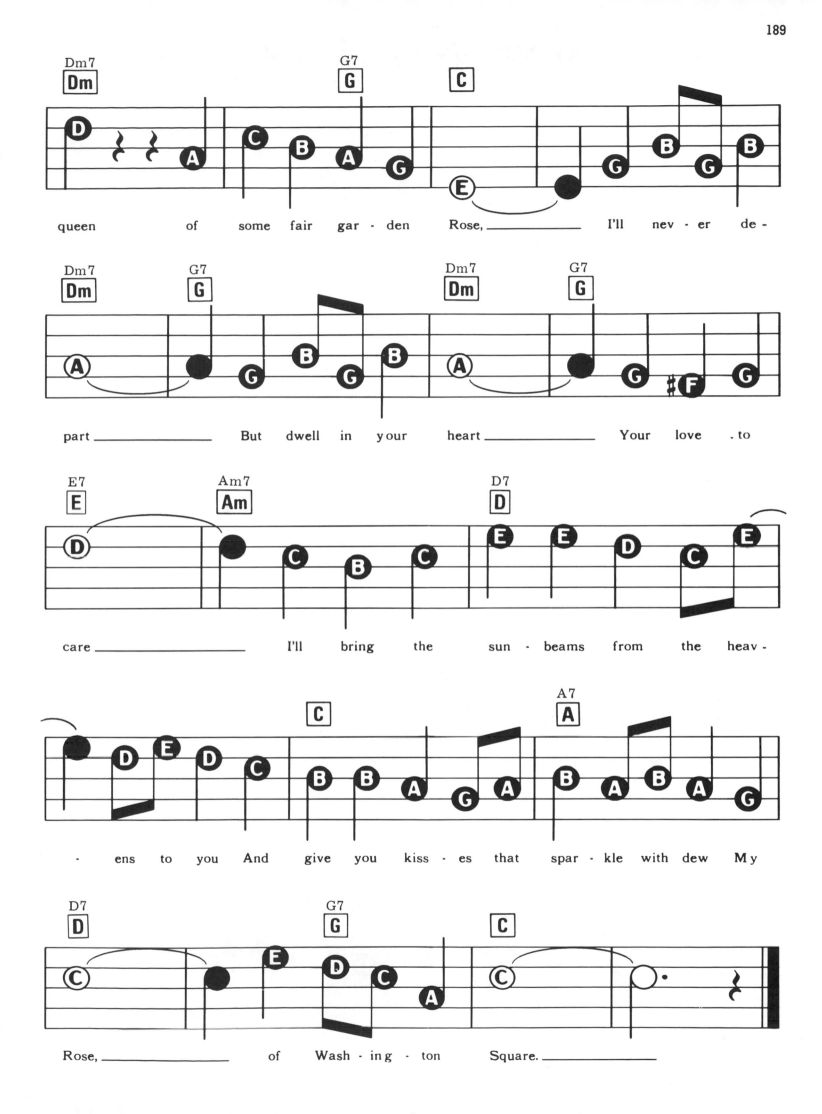

Row, Row, Row

Registration 5
Rhythm: Fox Trot or Swing

Words by William Jerome
Music by Jimmie V. Monaco

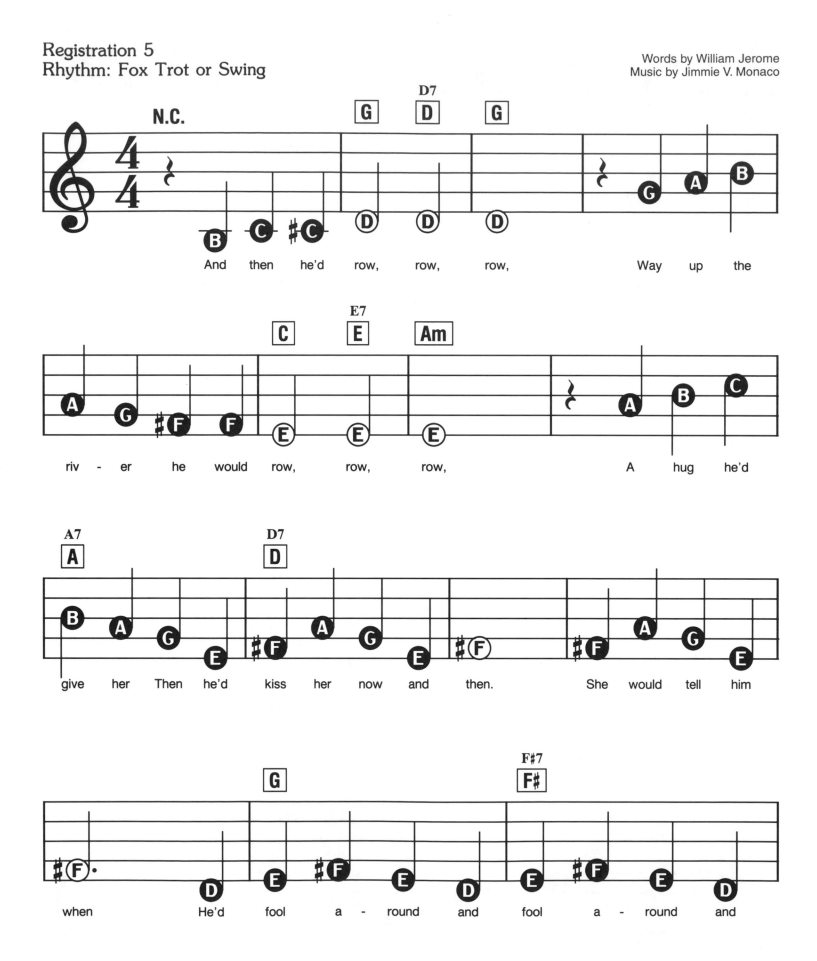

Copyright © 1996 by HAL LEONARD CORPORATION
International Copyright Secured   All Rights Reserved

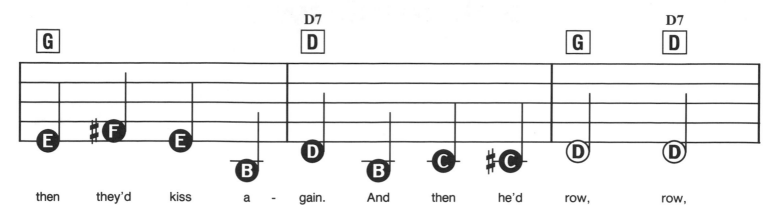

then   they'd   kiss   a - gain.   And   then   he'd   row,   row,

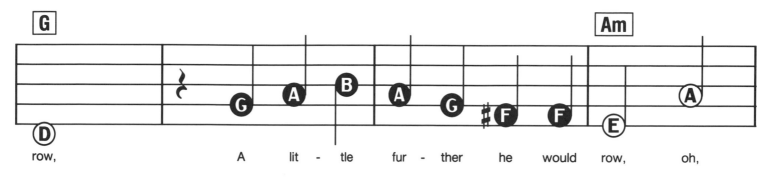

row,   A   lit - tle   fur - ther   he   would   row,   oh,

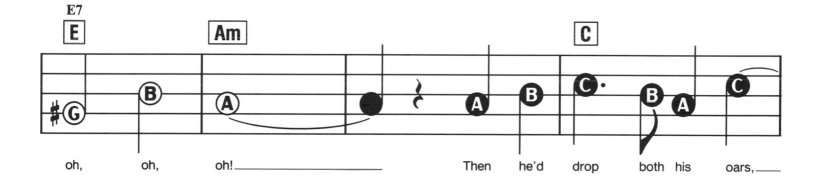

oh,   oh,   oh!_____   Then   he'd   drop   both   his   oars,____

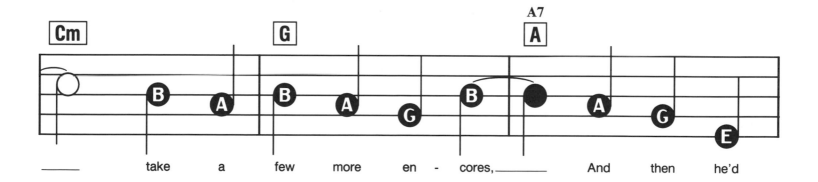

____   take   a   few   more   en - cores,_____   And   then   he'd

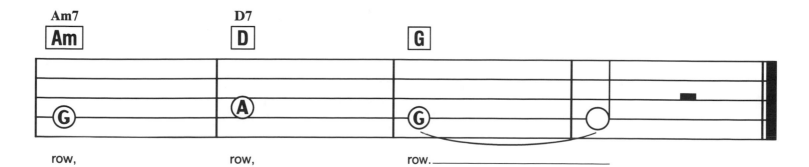

row,   row,   row._____

School Days
(When We Were a Couple of Kids)

Registration 2
Rhythm: Waltz

Words by Will D. Cobb
Music by Gus Edwards

School days, School days,

dear old gold - en rule days.

Read - in' and 'rit - in' and 'rith - me - tic,

Taught to the tune of a hick - 'ry stick.

Copyright © 1994 by HAL LEONARD CORPORATION
International Copyright Secured   All Rights Reserved

Shine on, Harvest Moon

Registration 9
Rhythm: Fox Trot or Swing

Words by Jack Norworth
Music by Nora Bayes and Jack Norworth

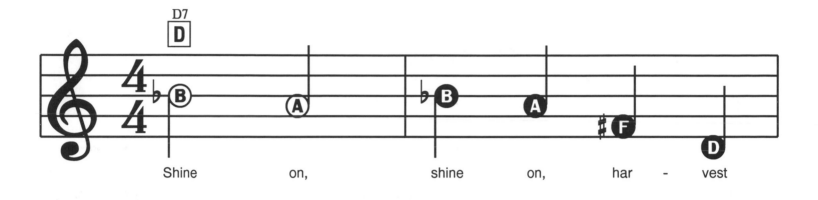

Shine on, shine on, har - vest

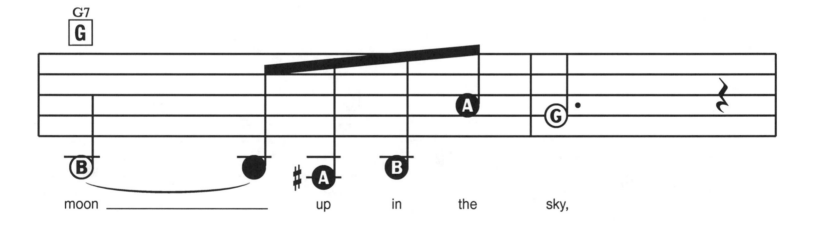

moon _____ up in the sky,

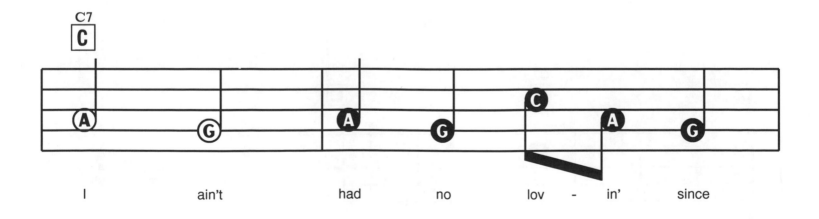

I ain't had no lov - in' since

Copyright © 1994 by HAL LEONARD CORPORATION
International Copyright Secured   All Rights Reserved

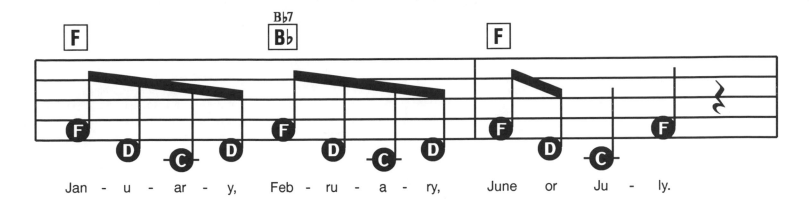

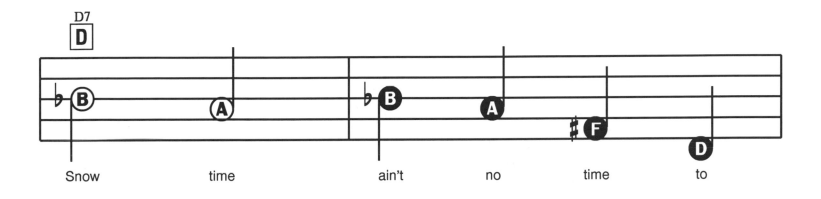

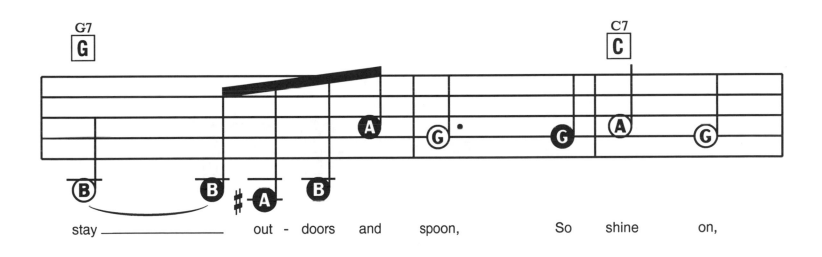

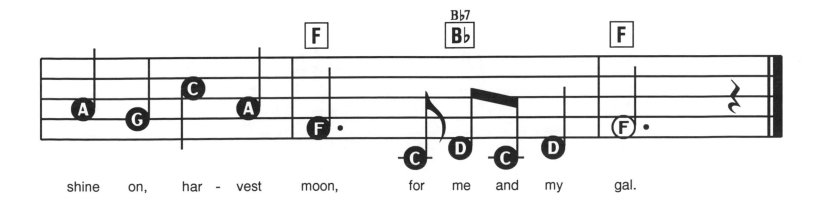

Smiles

Registration 5
Rhythm: Fox Trot or Swing

Words by J. Will Callahan
Music by Lee S. Roberts

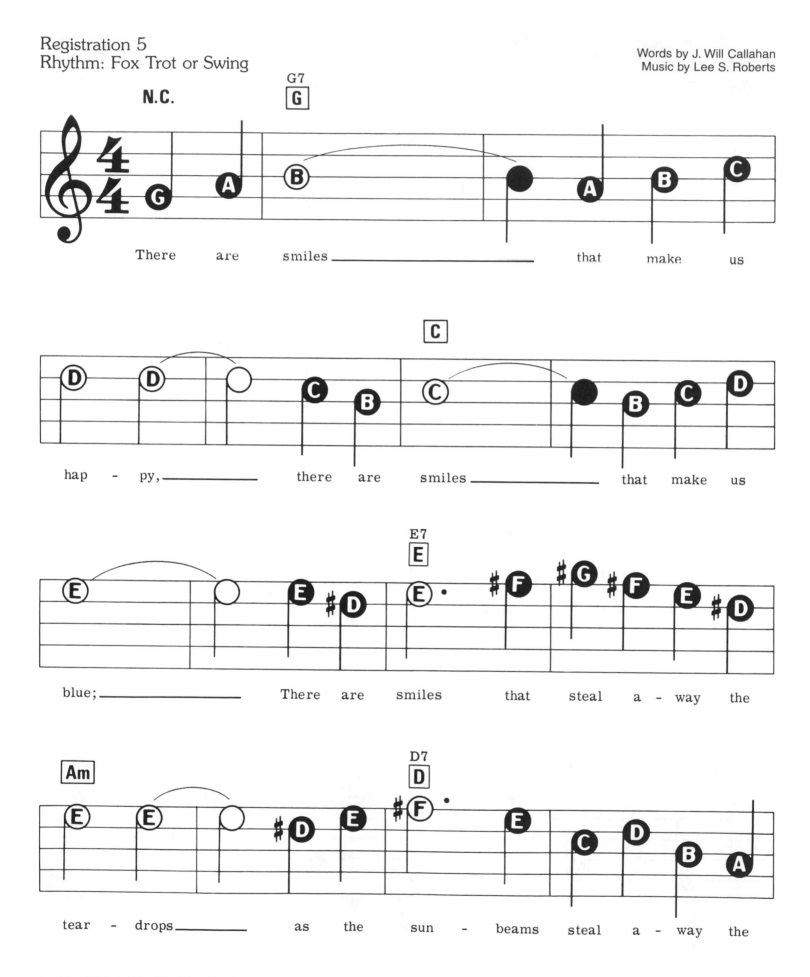

Copyright © 1996 by HAL LEONARD CORPORATION
International Copyright Secured   All Rights Reserved

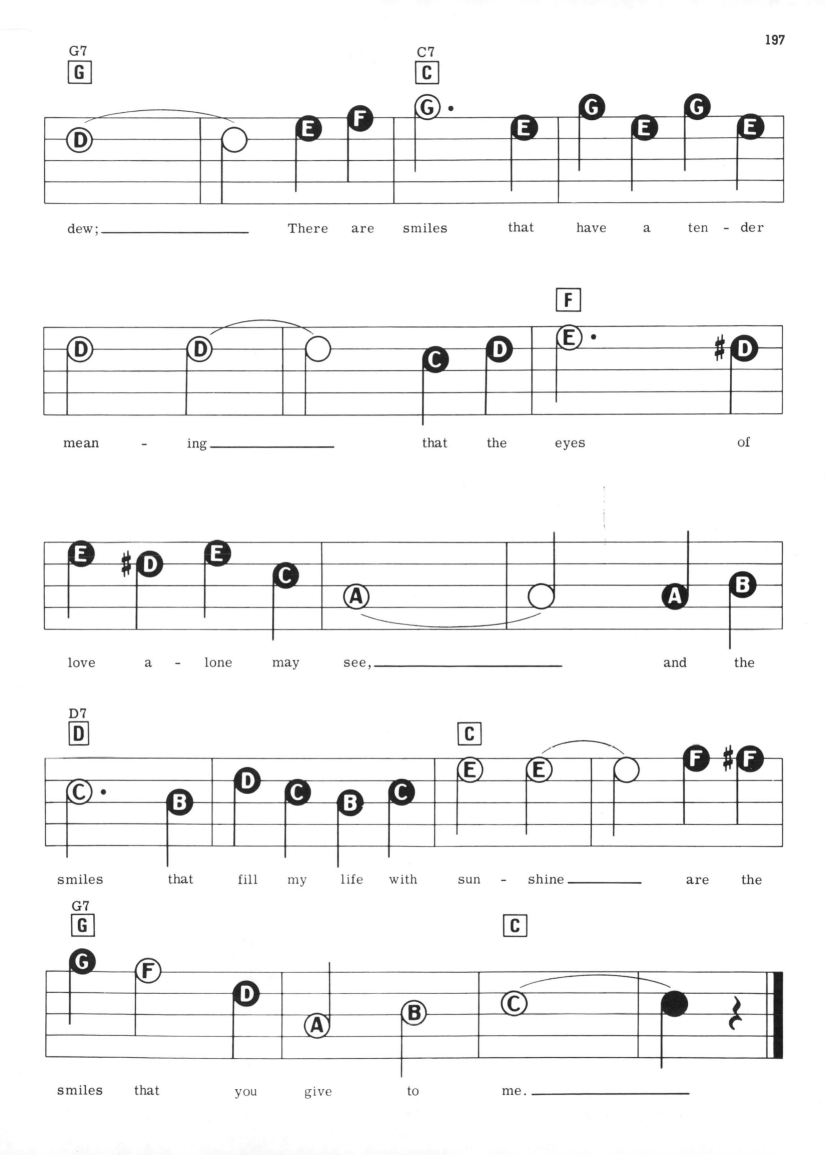

Snookey Ookums

Registration 8
Rhythm: Ragtime or Swing

Words and Music by
Irving Berlin

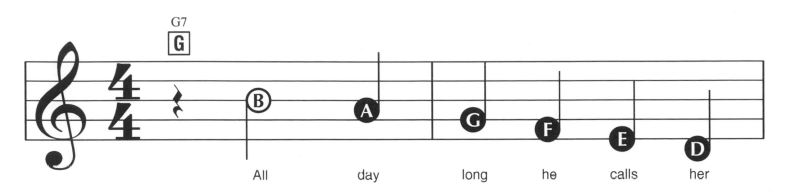

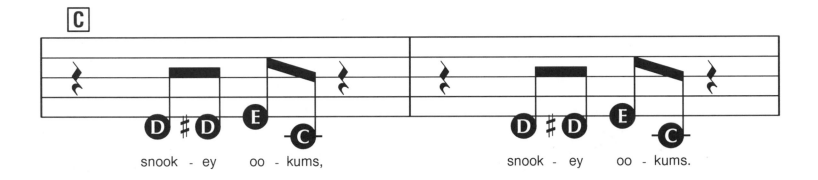

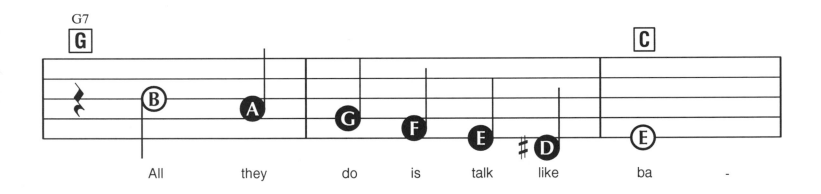

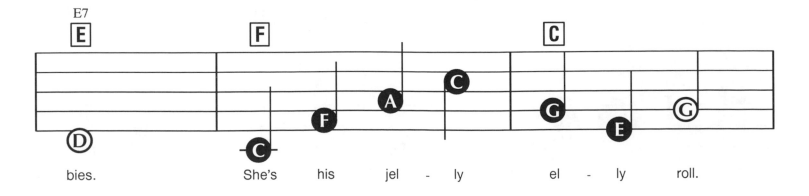

© Copyright 1913 by Irving Berlin
International Copyright Secured All Rights Reserved

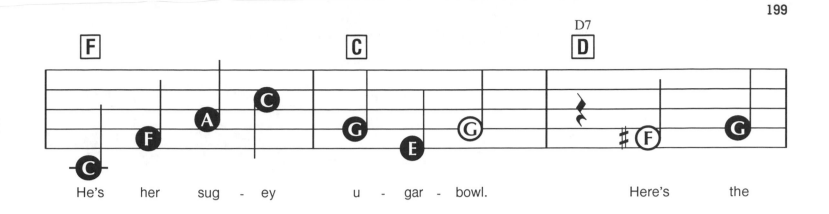

He's her sug - ey u - gar - bowl. Here's the

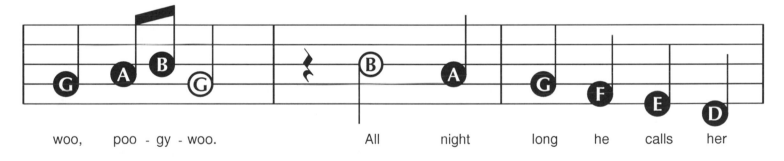

way they bill and coo, poo - gy - woo, poo - gy -

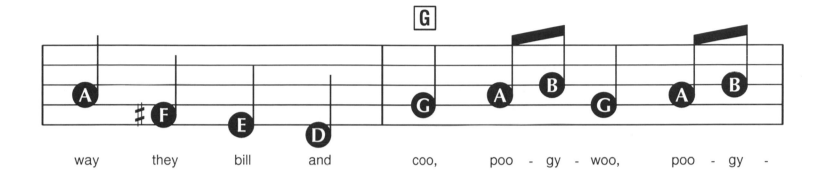

woo, poo - gy - woo. All night long he calls her

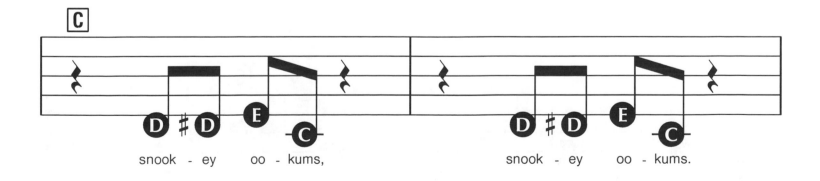

snook - ey oo - kums, snook - ey oo - kums.

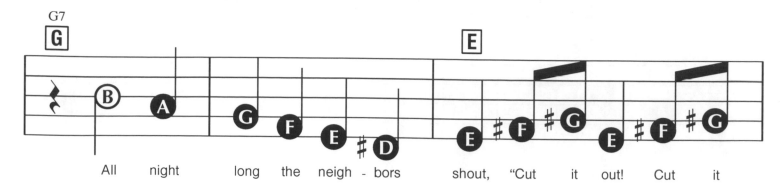

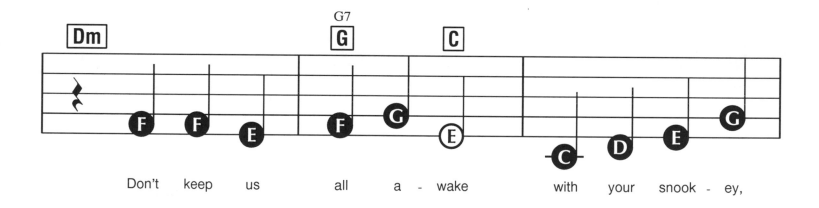

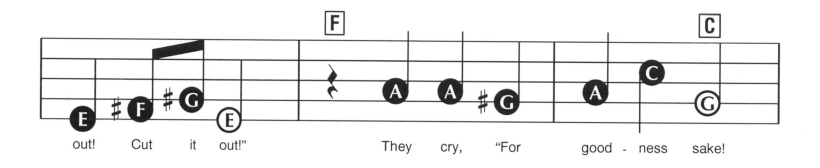

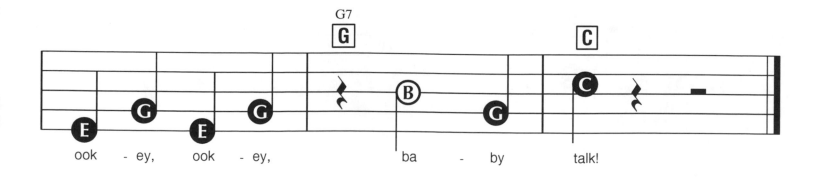

Some of These Days

Registration 1
Rhythm: Swing or Shuffle

Words and Music by
Shelton Brooks

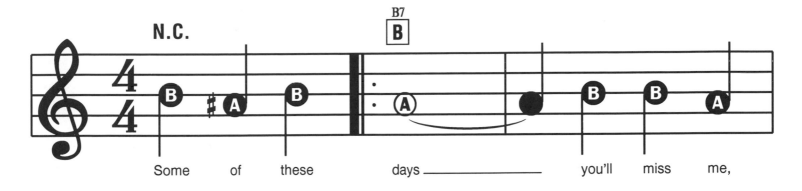

Some of these days _____ you'll miss me,

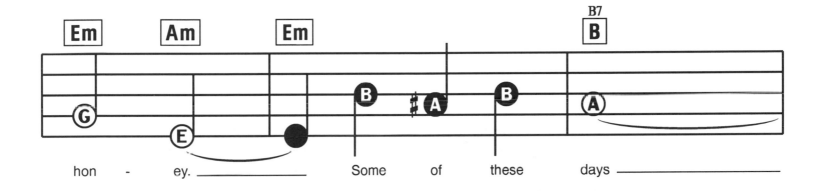

hon - ey. _____ Some of these days _____

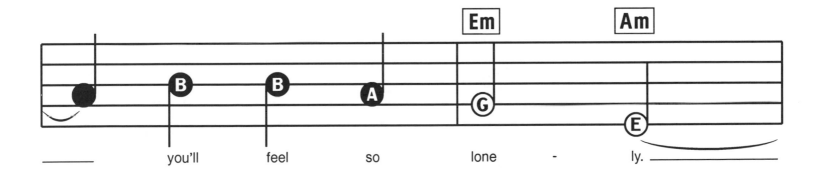

_____ you'll feel so lone - ly.

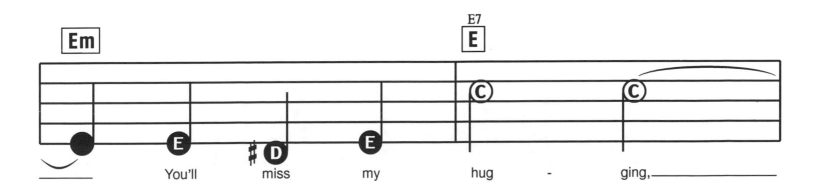

_____ You'll miss my hug - ging, _____

Copyright © 1991 by HAL LEONARD CORPORATION
International Copyright Secured   All Rights Reserved

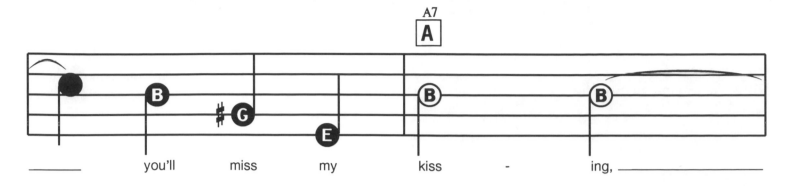

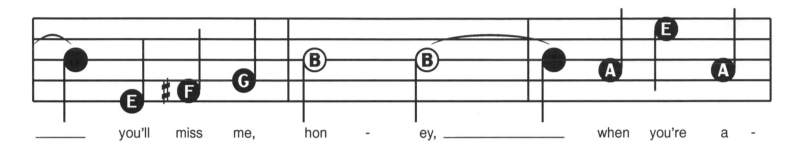

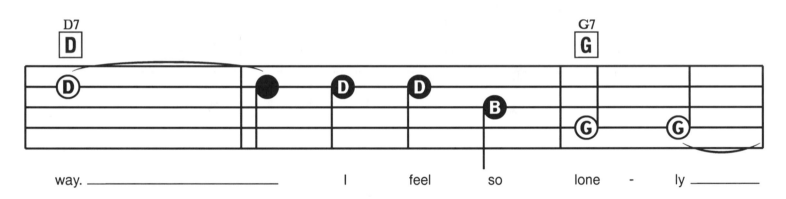

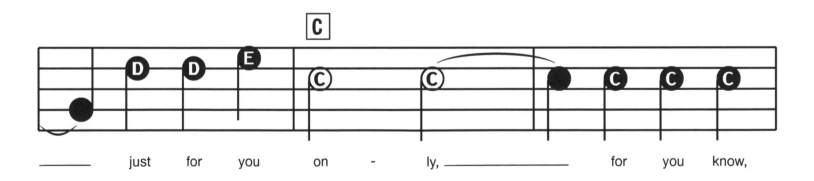

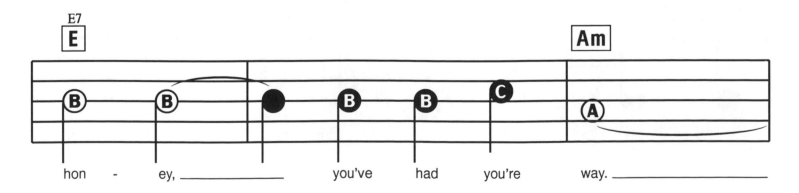

203

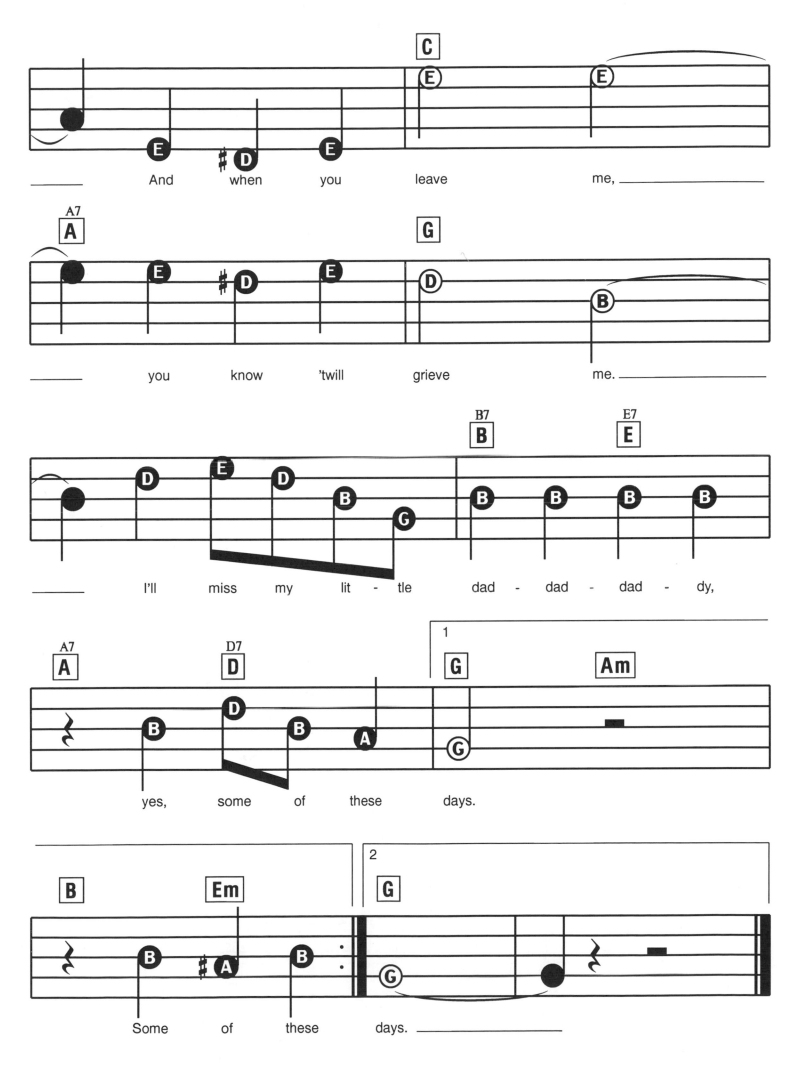

St. Louis Blues
from BIRTH OF THE BLUES

Registration 7
Rhythm: Swing

Words and Music by
W.C. Handy

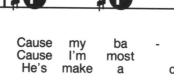

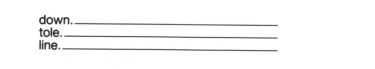

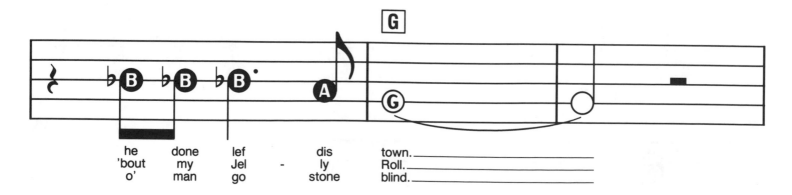

Copyright © 1990 by HAL LEONARD CORPORATION
International Copyright Secured   All Rights Reserved

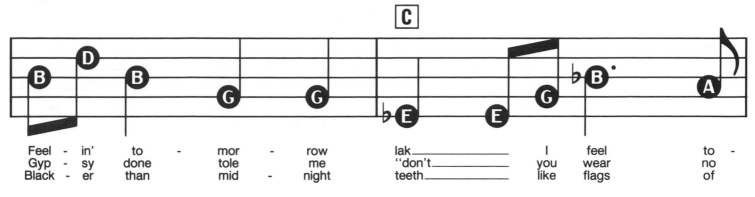

G7

C

Feel - in' to - mor - row lak_____ I feel to no -
Gyp - sy done tole me "don't_____ you feel wear no
Black - er than mid - night teeth_____ like flags of

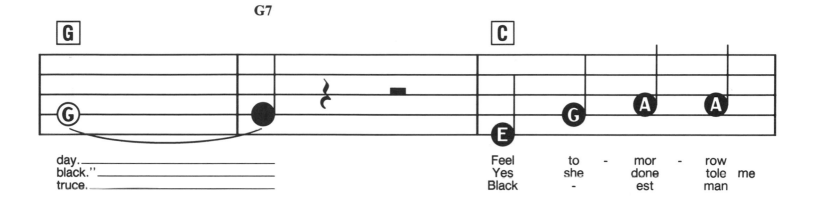

G   **G7**   **C**

day._____
black."_____
truce._____

Feel to - mor - row
Yes she done tole me
Black - est man

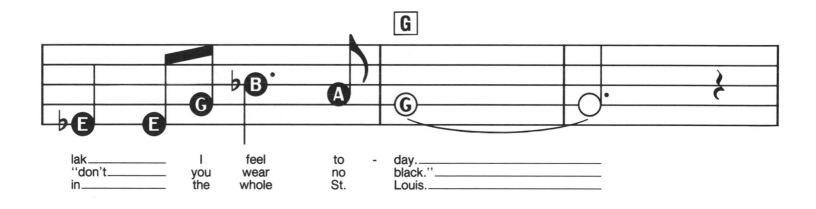

G

lak_____ I feel to - day._____
"don't_____ you wear no black."_____
in_____ the whole St. Louis._____

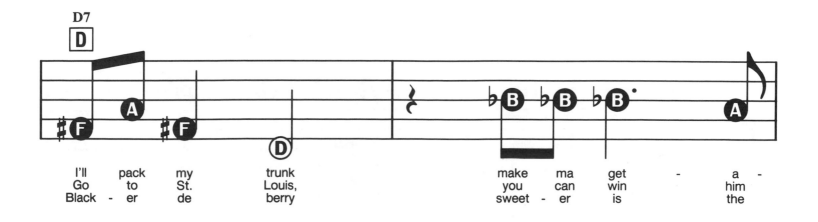

D7

D

I'll pack my trunk Louis, make ma get - a -
Go to St. Louis, you can win him
Black - er de berry sweet - er is the

G — **Gm**

way. _____
back. _____
juice. _____

St. Lou - is wom - an
Help me to Cai - ro,
A - bout a crap game

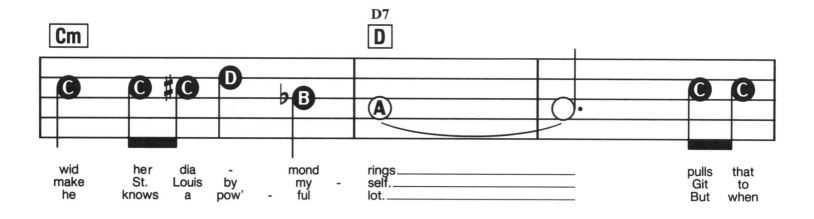

Cm — **D7** / **D**

wid her dia - mond rings _____ pulls that
make her St. Louis by my - self. _____ Git to
he knows a pow' - ful lot. _____ But when

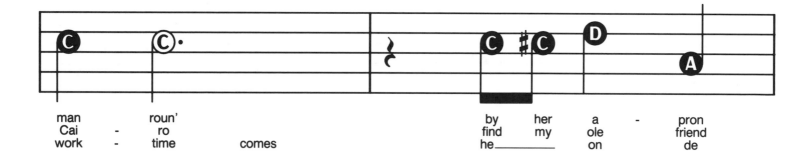

man roun'
Cai - ro
work - time comes

by her a - pron
find my ole friend
he _____ on de

Gm

strings. _____
Jeff. _____
dot. _____

'Twant for pow - der
Gwine to pin me
Gwine to ask him

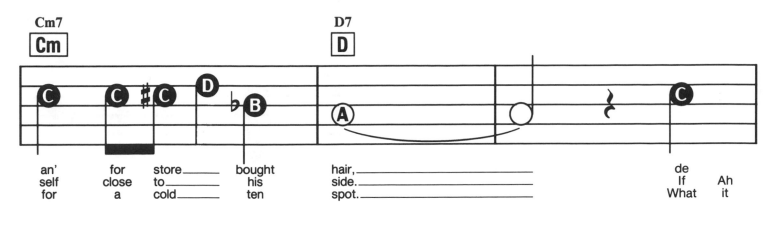

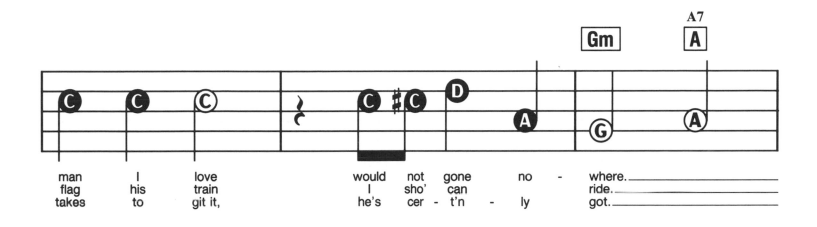

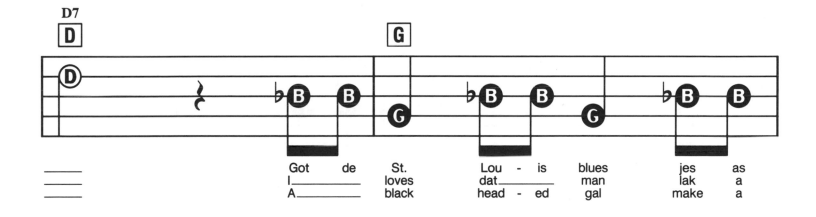

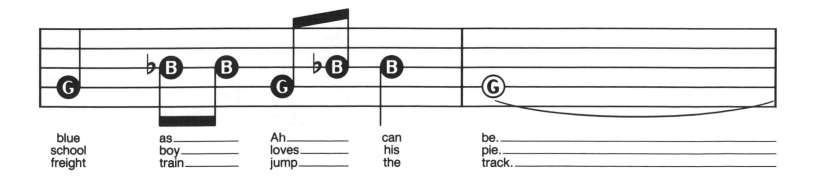

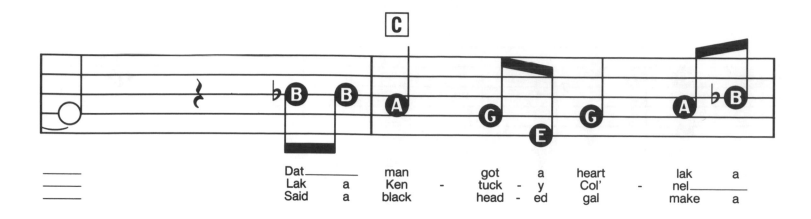

Dat_____ man got a heart_____ lak a
Lak a Ken - tuck - y Col' - nel_____
Said a black head - ed gal make a

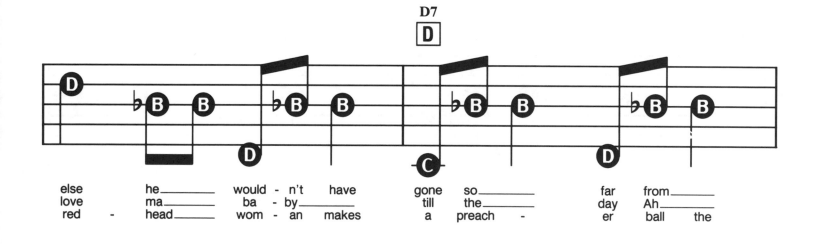

rock cast_____ in the_____ sea._____ or_____
loves his_____ mint an'_____ rye._____ I'll_____
freight train_____ jump_____ the track._____ But a

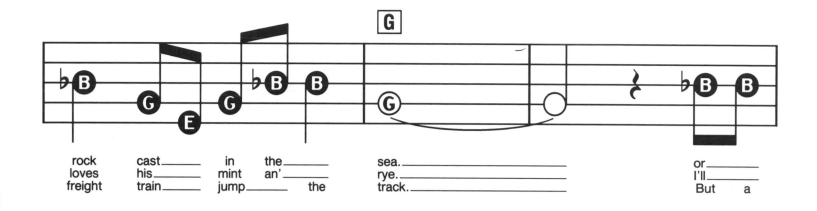

else he_____ would - n't have gone so_____ far from_____
love ma_____ ba - by_____ till the_____ day Ah_____
red - head_____ wom - an makes a preach - er ball the

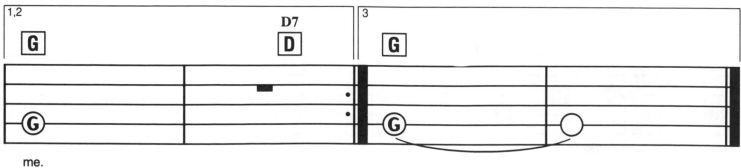

me.
die.   Jack._____

That's a Plenty

Registration 9
Rhythm: Swing

Words by Ray Gilbert
Music by Lew Pollack

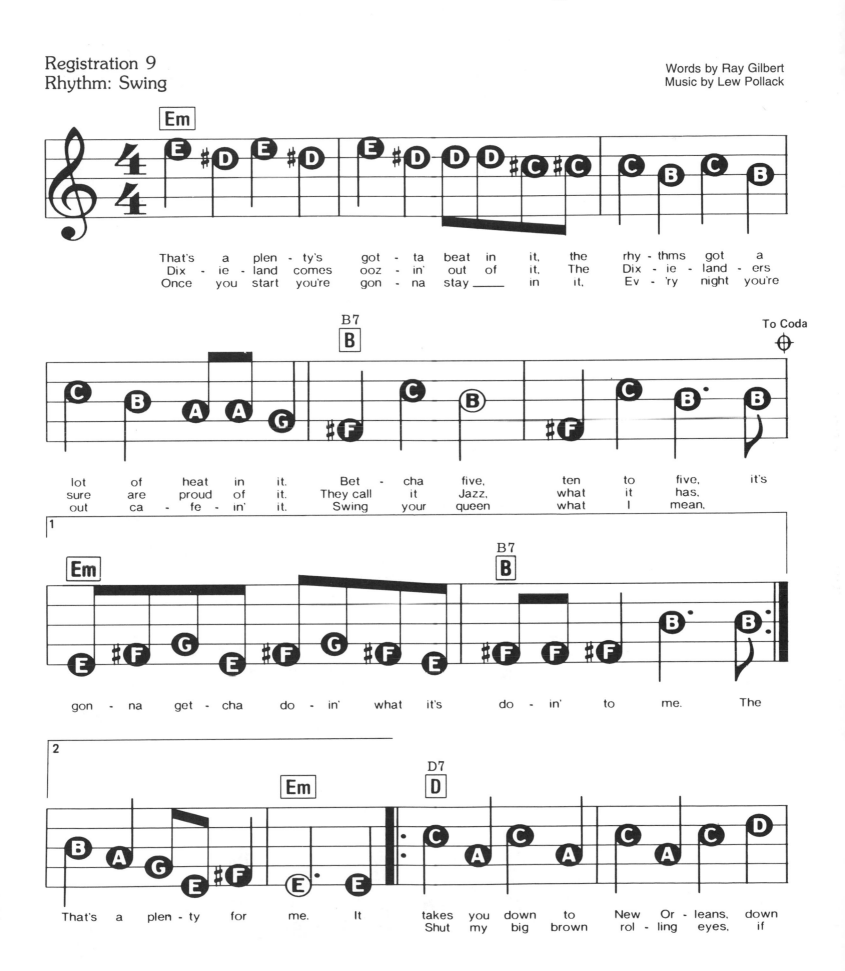

Copyright © 1996 by HAL LEONARD CORPORATION
International Copyright Secured   All Rights Reserved

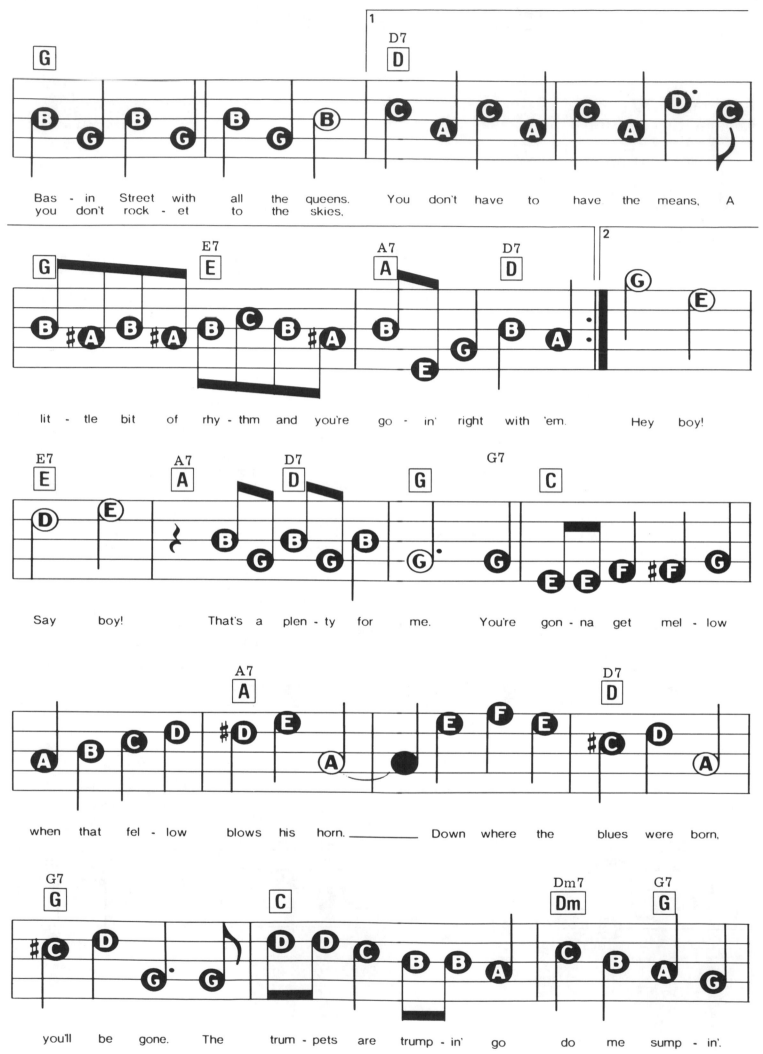

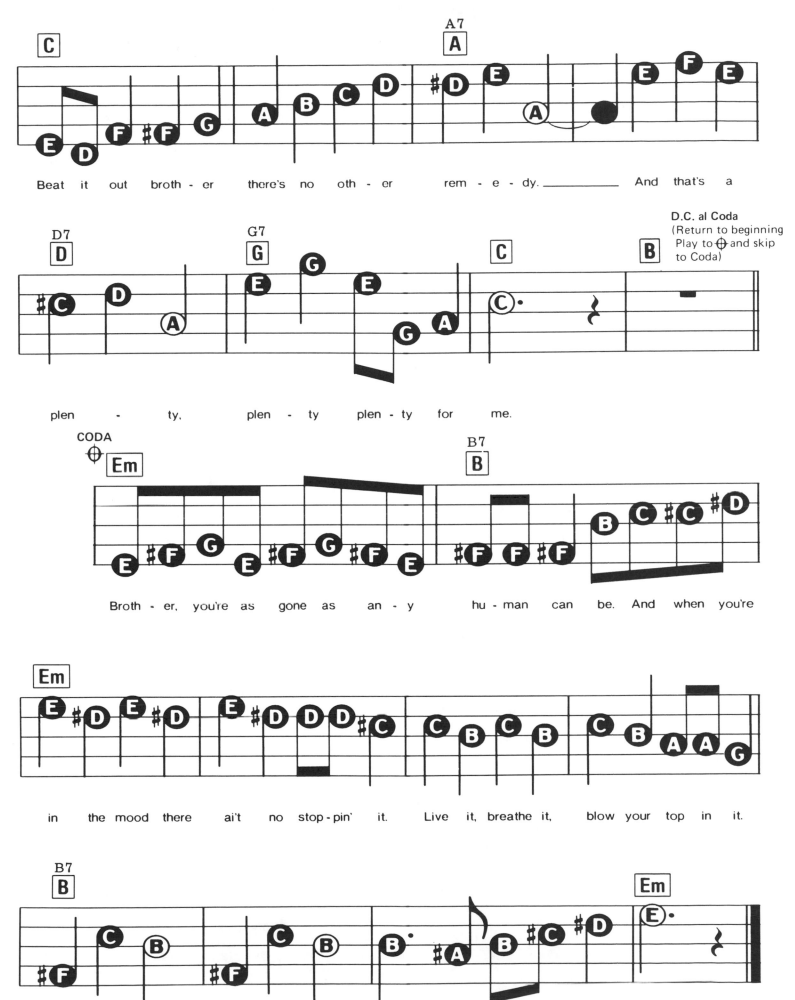

Sugar Blues

Registration 3
Rhythm: Swing or Fox Trot

Words by Lucy Fletcher
Music by Clarence Williams

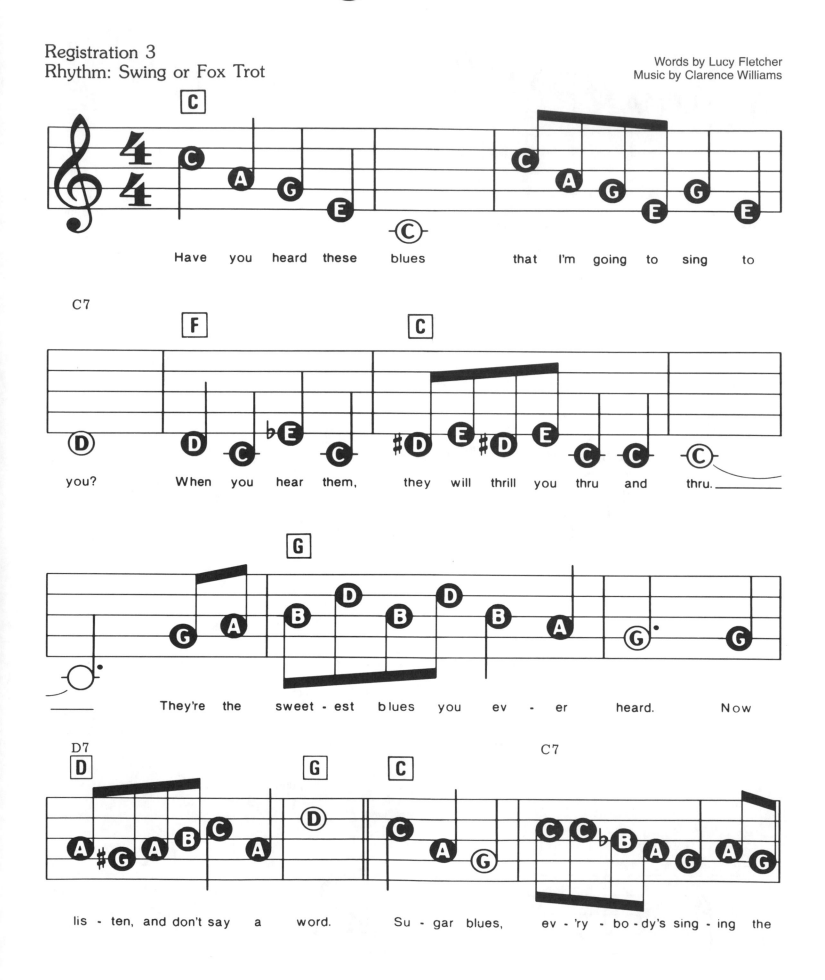

Copyright © 1996 by HAL LEONARD CORPORATION
International Copyright Secured   All Rights Reserved

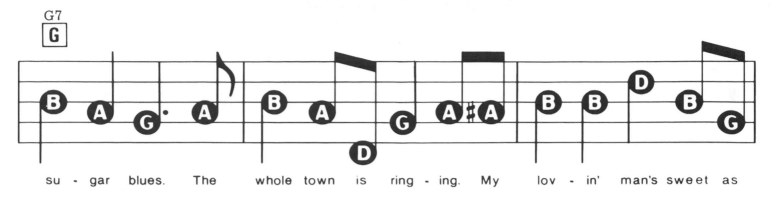

su - gar blues. The whole town is ring - ing. My lov - in' man's sweet as

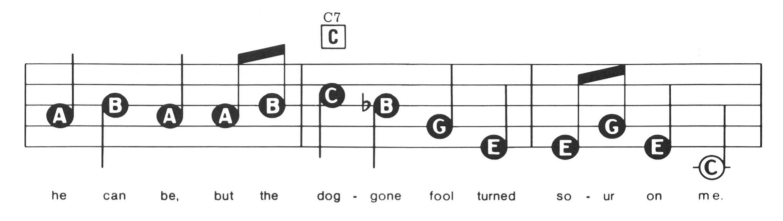

he can be, but the dog - gone fool turned so - ur on me.

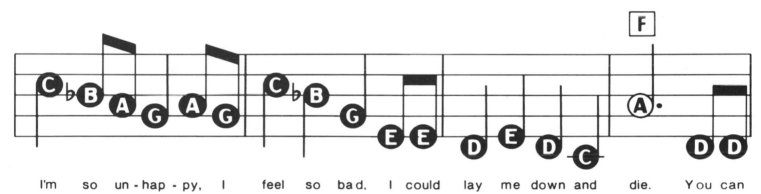

I'm so un - hap - py, I feel so bad, I could lay me down and die. You can

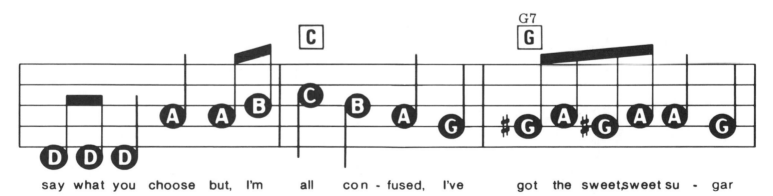

say what you choose but, I'm all con - fused, I've got the sweet, sweet su - gar

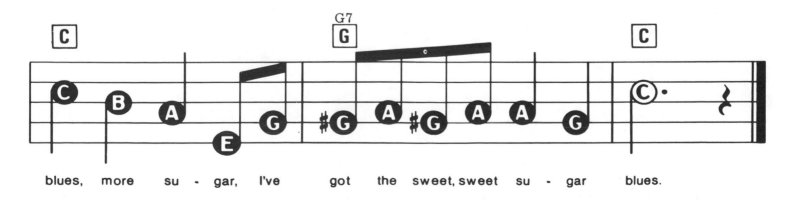

blues, more su - gar, I've got the sweet, sweet su - gar blues.

Swanee

Registration 9
Rhythm: Fox Trot or Swing

Words by Irving Caesar
Music by George Gershwin

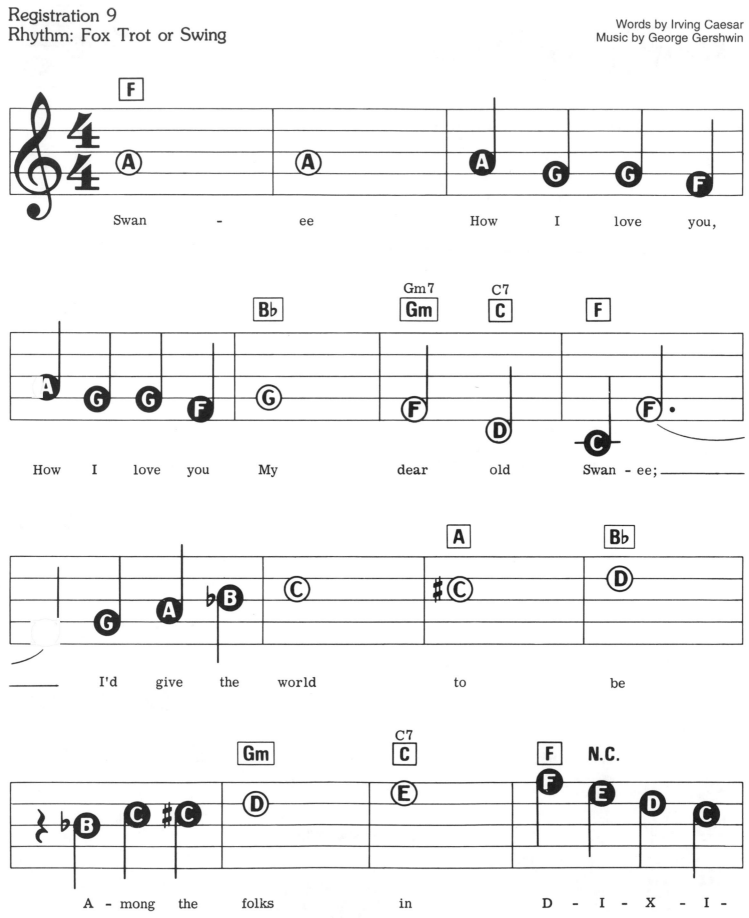

Copyright © 1996 by HAL LEONARD CORPORATION
International Copyright Secured   All Rights Reserved

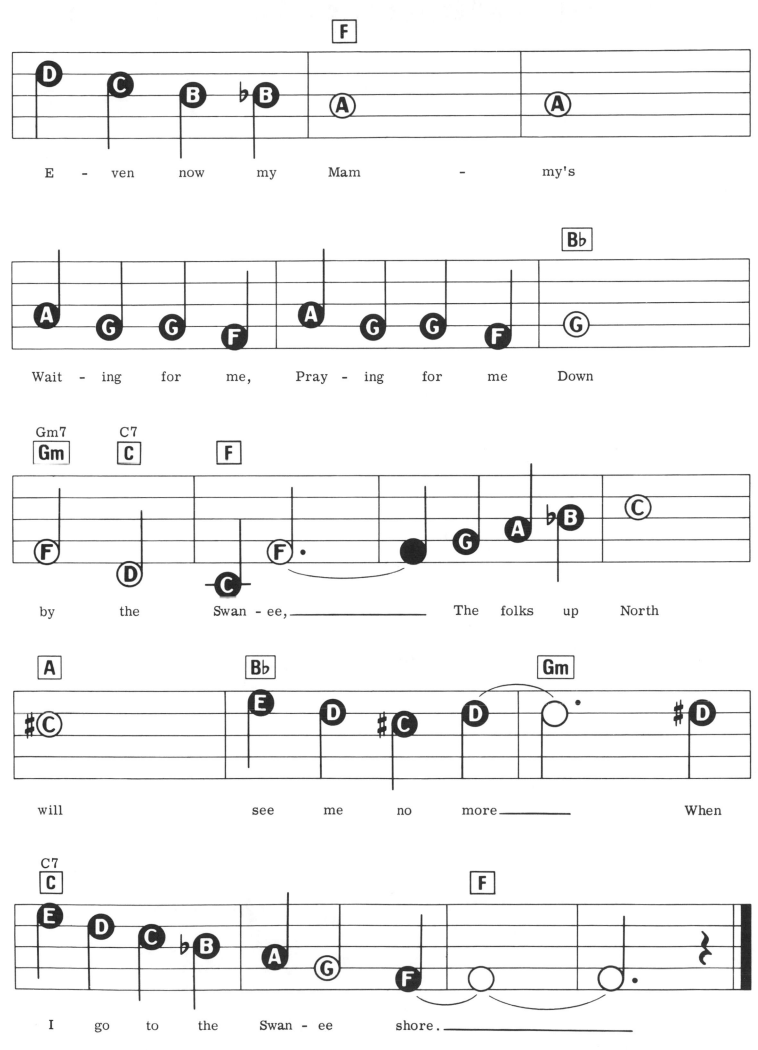

The Sweetheart of Sigma Chi

Registration 1
Rhythm: Waltz

Words by Byron D. Stokes
Music by F. Dudleigh Vernor

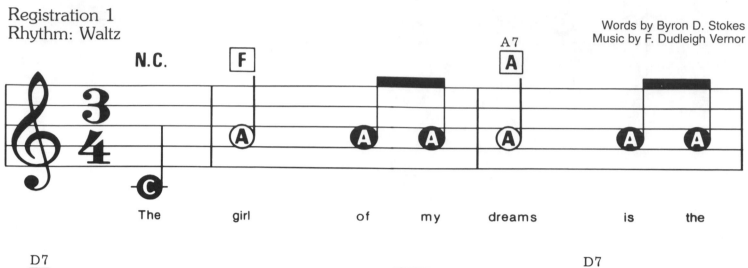

The girl of my dreams is the

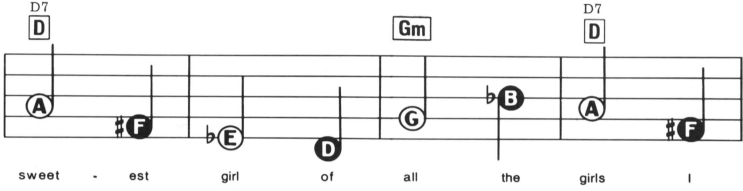

sweet - est girl of all the girls I

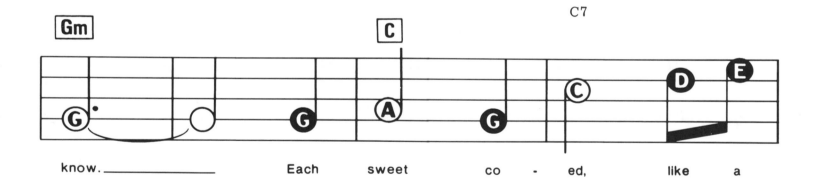

know. _____ Each sweet co - ed, like a

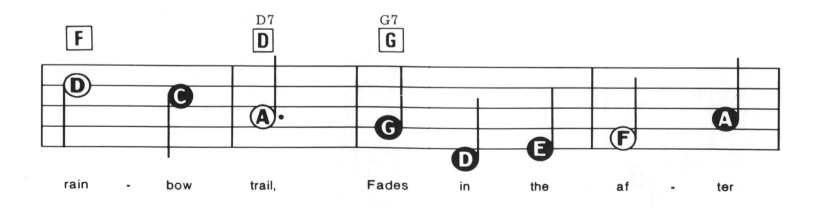

rain - bow trail, Fades in the af - ter

Copyright © 1994 by HAL LEONARD CORPORATION
International Copyright Secured   All Rights Reserved

217

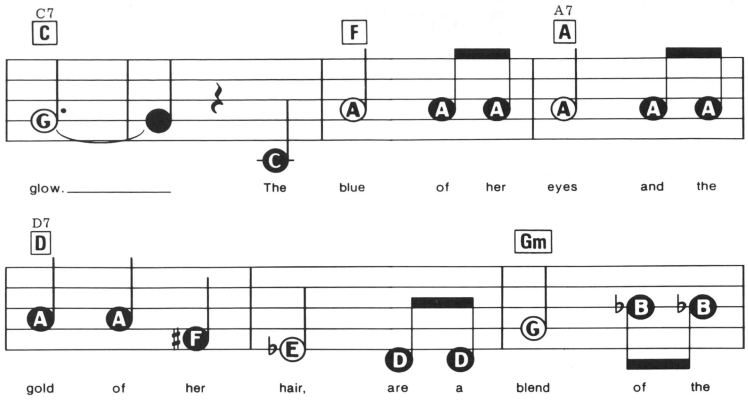

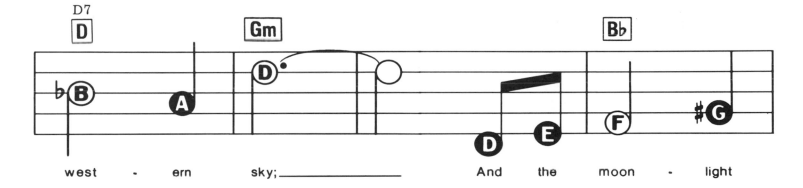

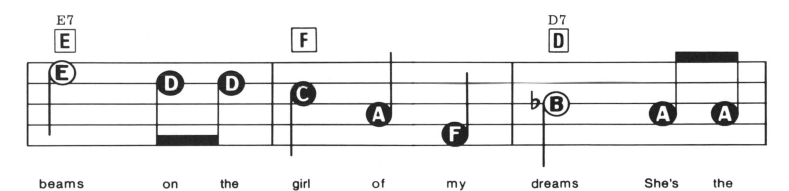

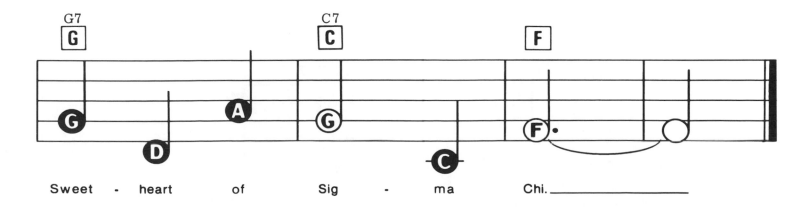

Sweethearts
from SWEETHEARTS

Registration 10
Rhythm: Waltz

Words by Robert B. Smith
Music by Victor Herbert

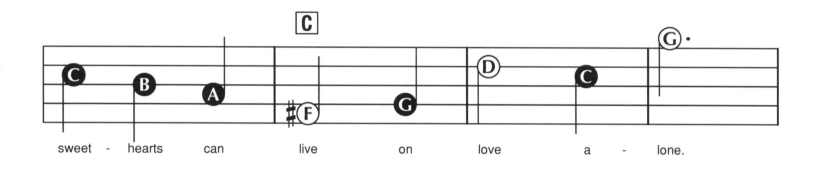

Sweet - hearts make love their ver - y own,

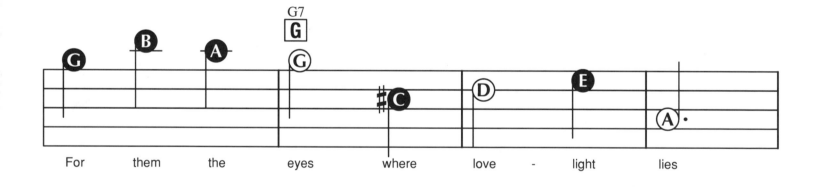

sweet - hearts can live on love a - lone.

For them the eyes where love - light lies

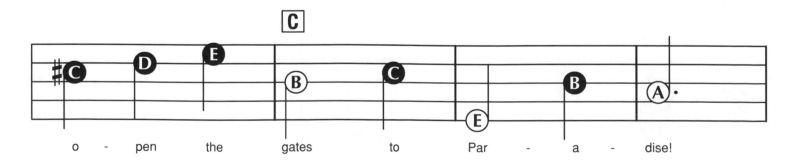

o - pen the gates to Par - a - dise!

Copyright © 1991 by HAL LEONARD CORPORATION
International Copyright Secured   All Rights Reserved

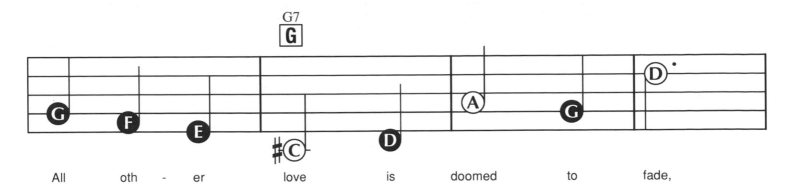

All oth - er love is doomed to fade,

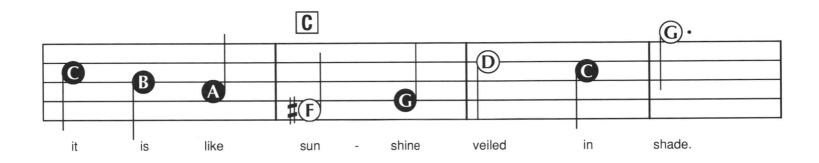

it is like sun - shine veiled in shade.

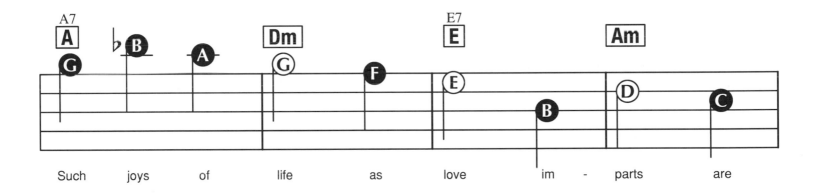

Such joys of life as love im - parts are

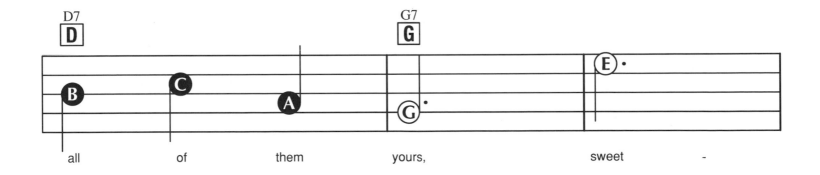

all of them yours, sweet -

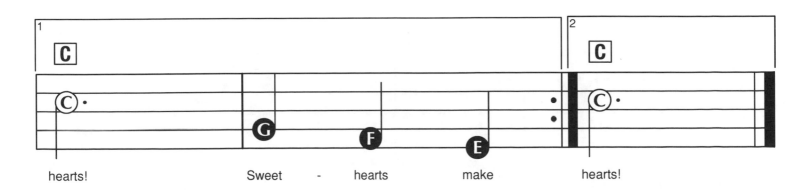

hearts! Sweet - hearts make hearts!

Take Me Out to the Ball Game

from TAKE ME OUT TO THE BALL GAME

Registration 4
Rhythm: Waltz

Words by Jack Norworth
Music by Albert von Tilzer

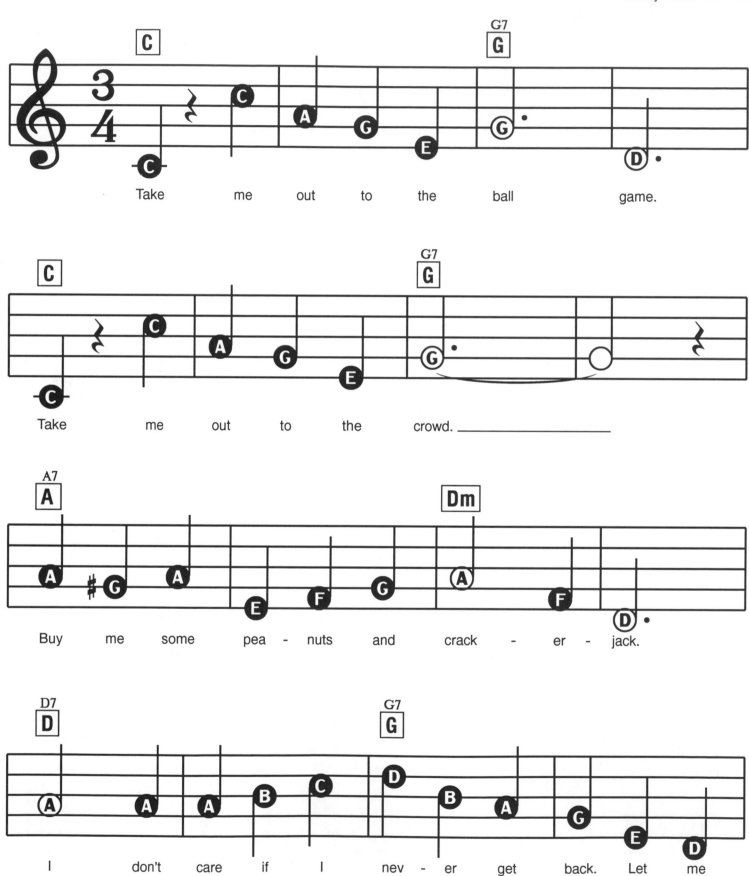

Copyright © 1994 by HAL LEONARD CORPORATION
International Copyright Secured   All Rights Reserved

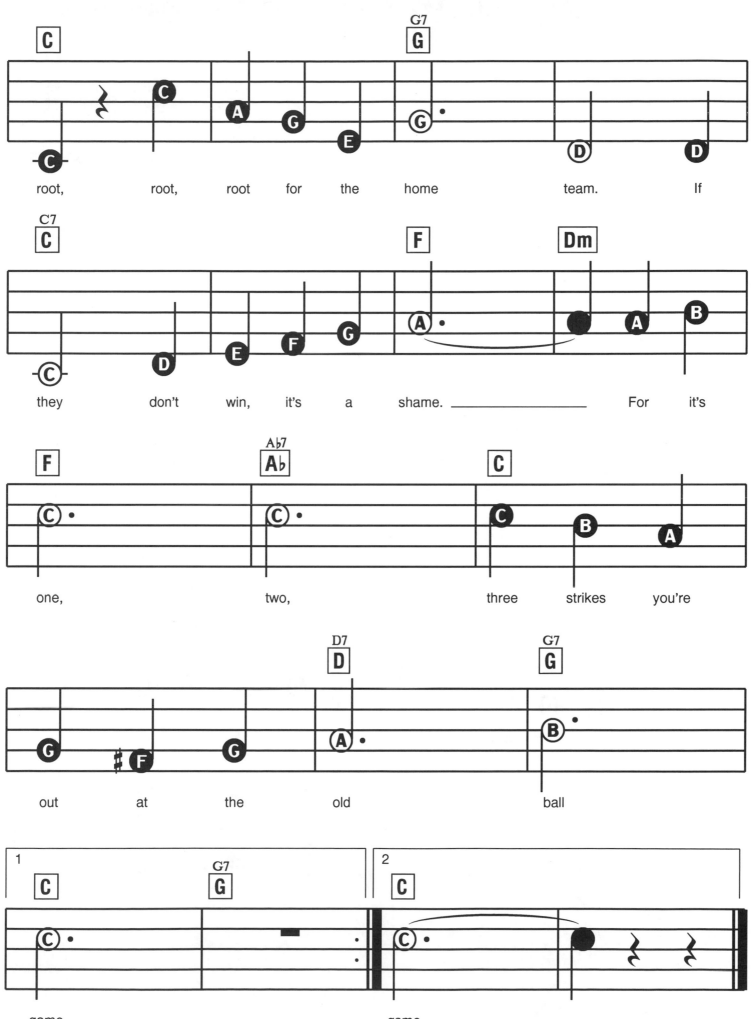

root, root, root for the home team. If

they don't win, it's a shame. _____ For it's

one, two, three strikes you're

out at the old ball

game.

game. _____

They Didn't Believe Me
from THE GIRL FROM UTAH

Registration 2
Rhythm: Ballad or Swing

Words by Herbert Reynolds
Music by Jerome Kern

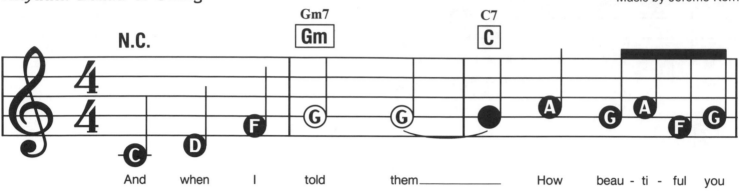

And when I told them___ How beau-ti-ful you

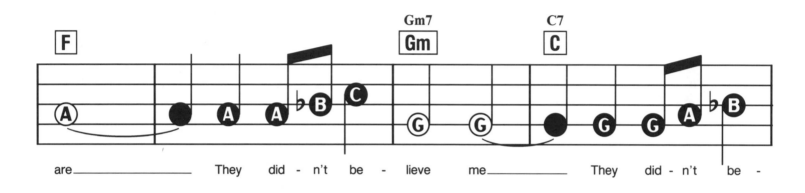

are___ They did-n't be-lieve me___ They did-n't be-

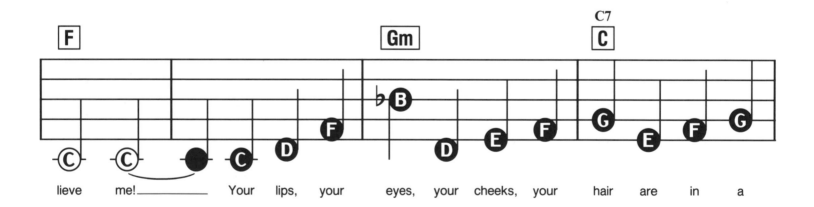

lieve me!___ Your lips, your eyes, your cheeks, your hair are in a

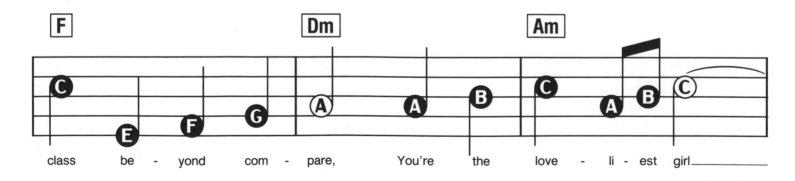

class be-yond com-pare, You're the love-li-est girl___

Copyright © 1994 by HAL LEONARD CORPORATION
International Copyright Secured   All Rights Reserved

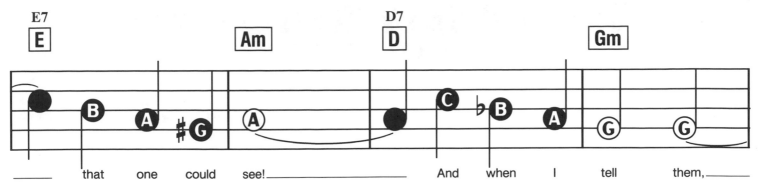

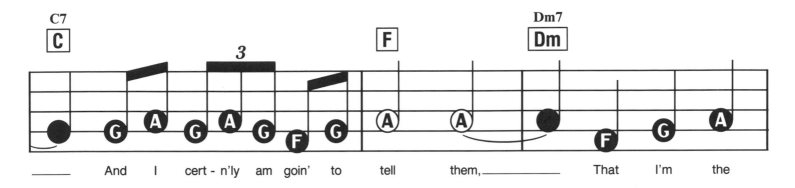

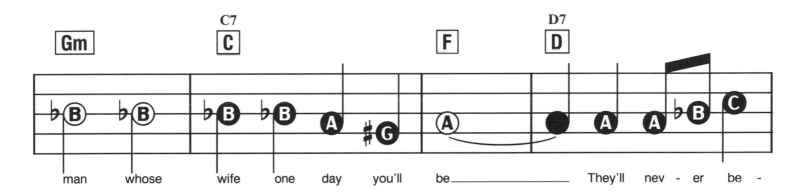

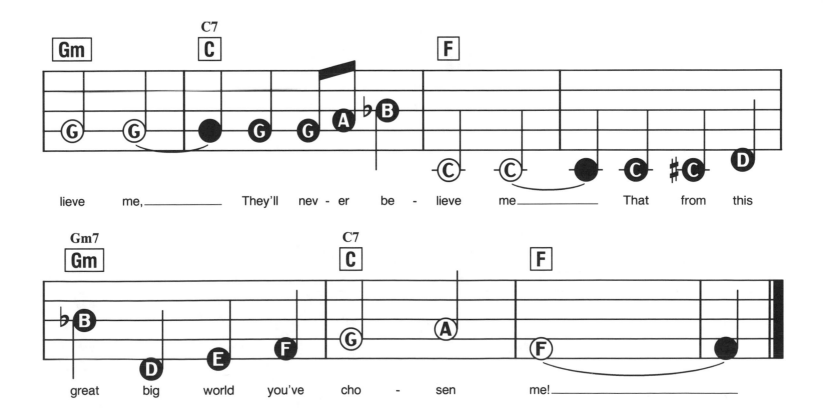

Tiger Rag
(Hold That Tiger)

Registration 4
Rhythm: Swing or Ragtime

Words by Harry DeCosta
Music by Original Dixieland Jazz Band

Where's that Ti - ger! Where's that
Ti - ger! Where's that Ti - ger! Where's that
Ti - ger! Hold that Ti - ger! Hold that
Ti - ger! Hold that Ti - ger! Choke him, poke him,

Copyright © 1996 by HAL LEONARD CORPORATION
International Copyright Secured All Rights Reserved

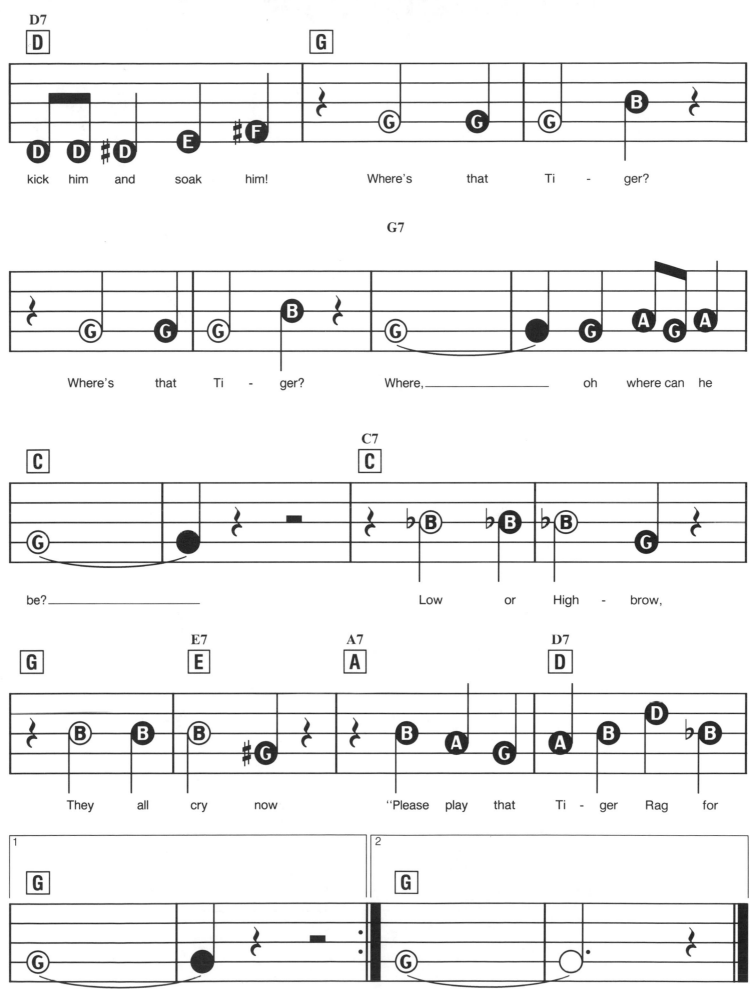

Till the Clouds Roll By
from OH BOY!

Registration 1
Rhythm: Fox Trot or Swing

Words by P.G. Wodehouse
Music by Jerome Kern

Oh, the rain comes a pit - ter, pat - ter, And I'd like to be safe in bed. Skies are weep - ing While the world is sleep - ing Trou - ble heap - ing on our

Copyright © 1996 by HAL LEONARD CORPORATION
International Copyright Secured All Rights Reserved

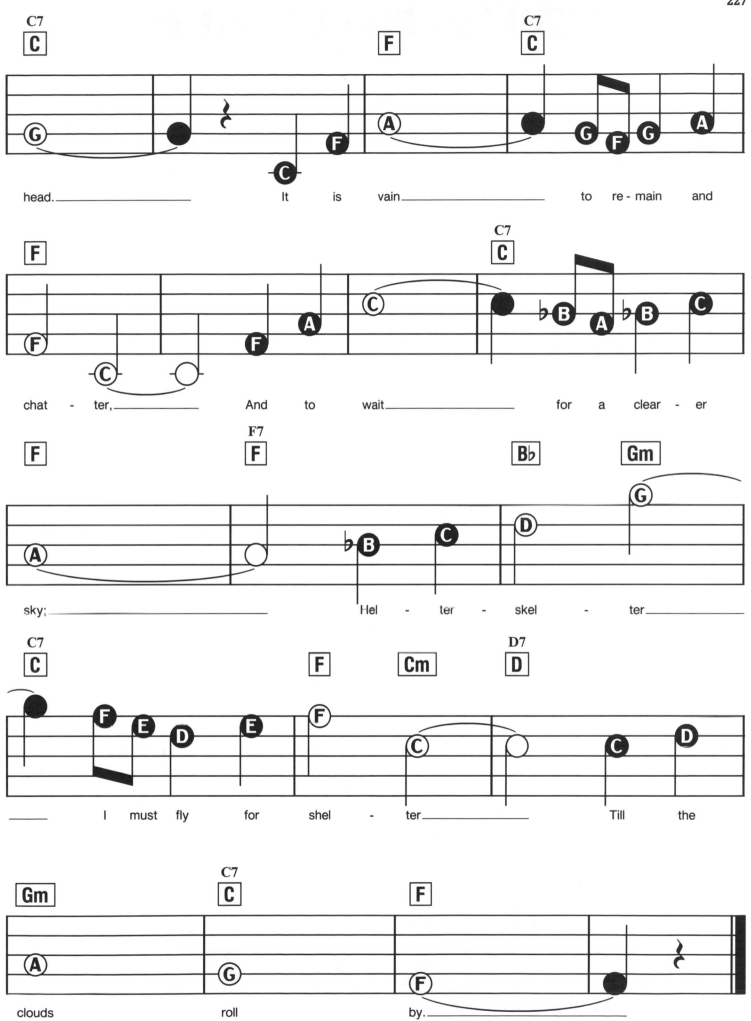

Till We Meet Again

Registration 4
Rhythm: Waltz

Words by Raymond B. Egan
Music by Richard A. Whiting

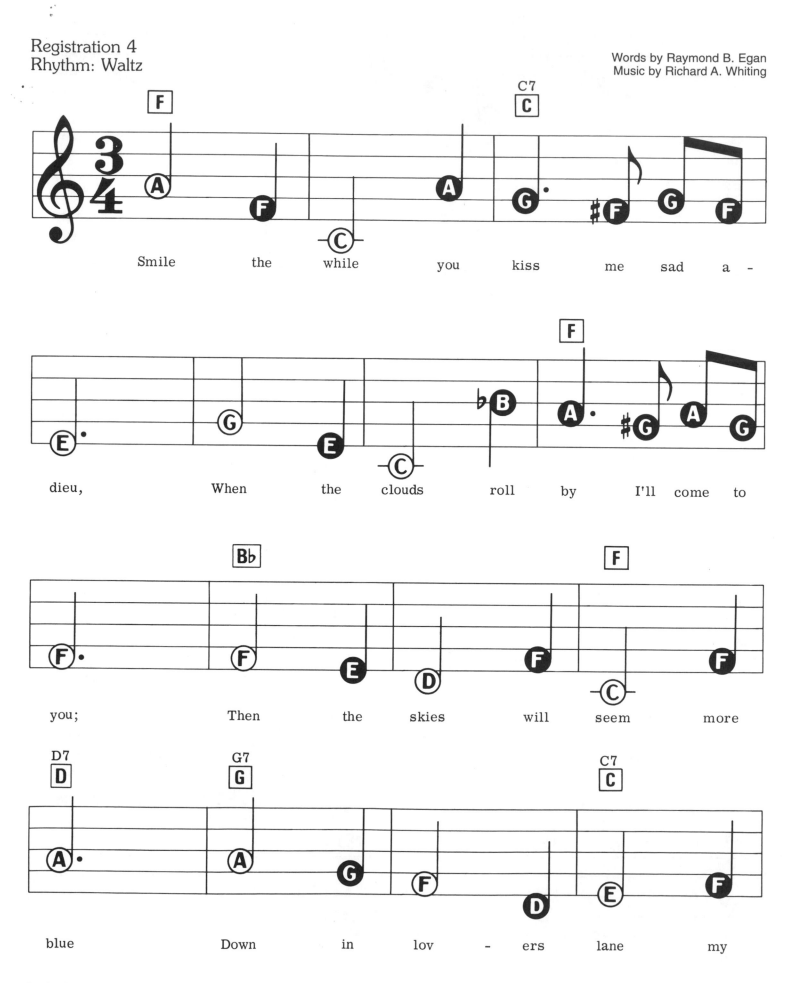

Copyright © 1996 by HAL LEONARD CORPORATION
International Copyright Secured   All Rights Reserved

229

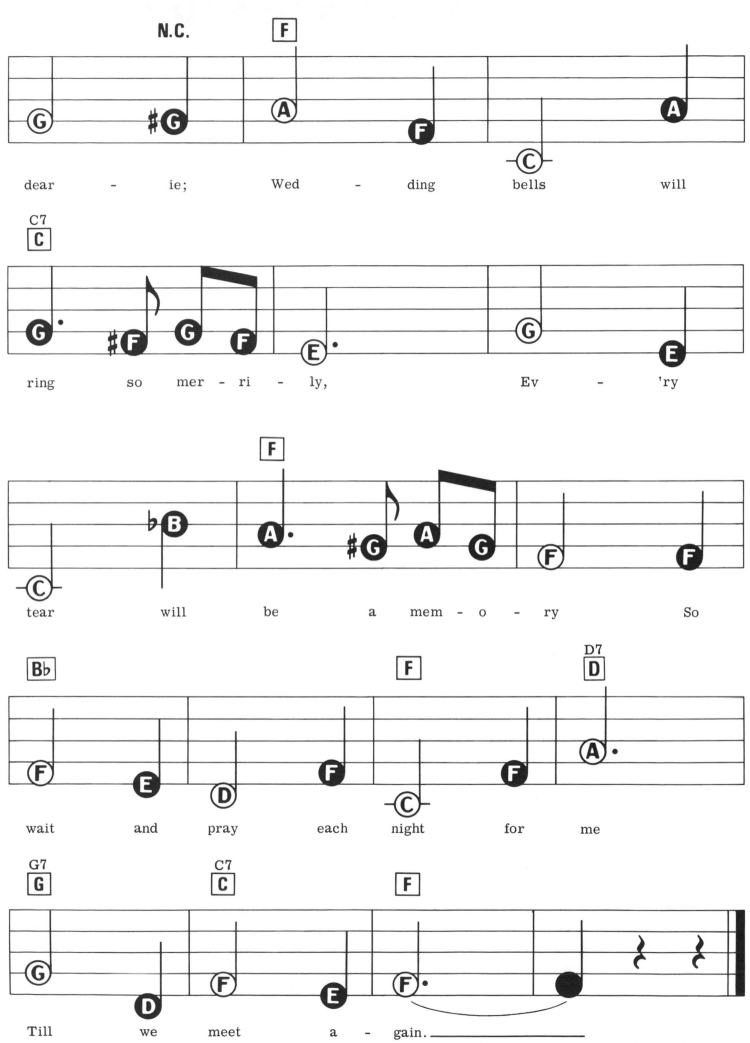

Too-Ra-Loo-Ra-Loo-Ral
(That's an Irish Lullaby)
from GOING MY WAY

Registration 1
Rhythm: Waltz

Words and Music by
James R. Shannon

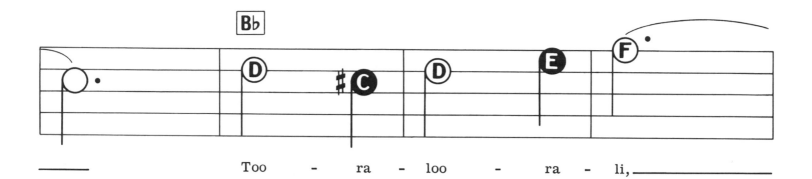

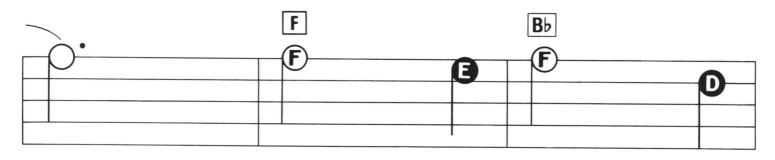

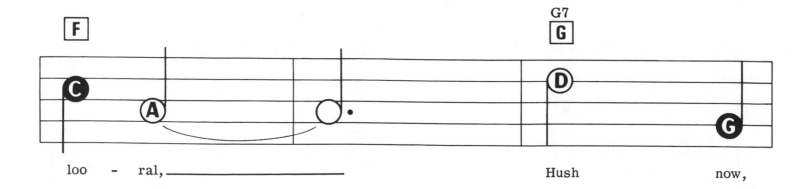

Copyright © 1993 by HAL LEONARD CORPORATION
International Copyright Secured   All Rights Reserved

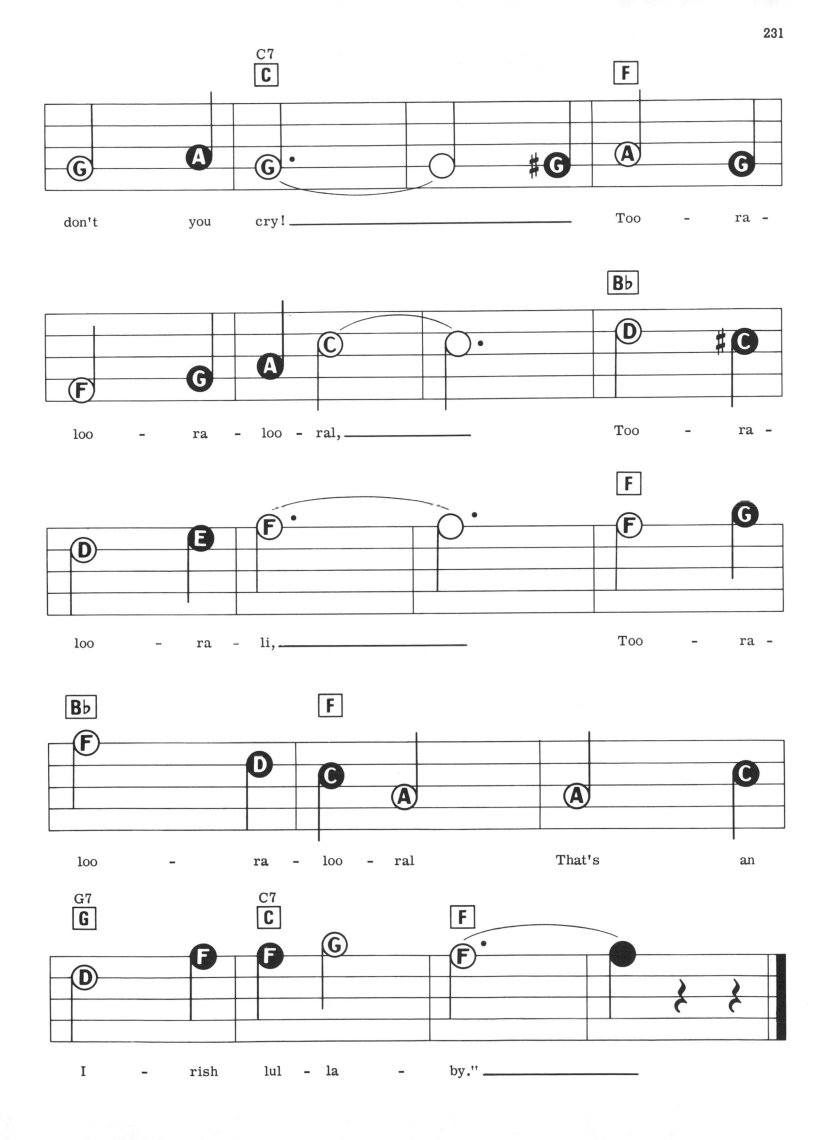

Twelfth Street Rag

Registration 5
Rhythm: Shuffle or Swing

By Euday L. Bowman

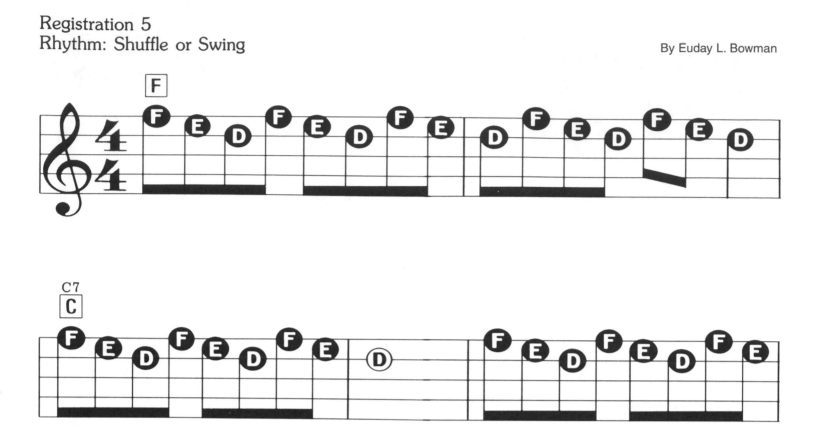

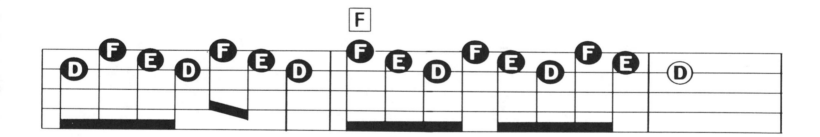

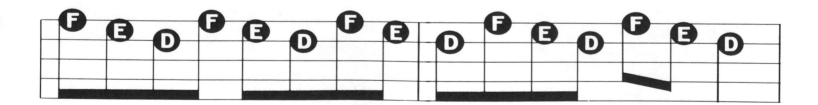

Copyright © 1994 by HAL LEONARD CORPORATION
International Copyright Secured   All Rights Reserved

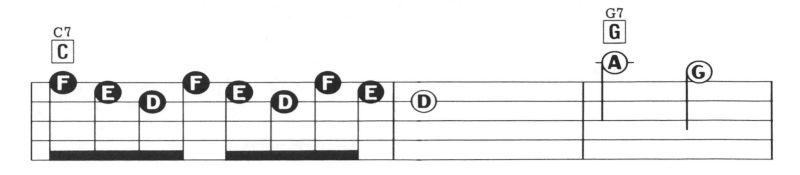

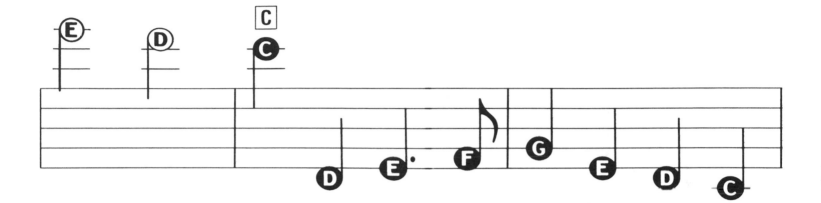

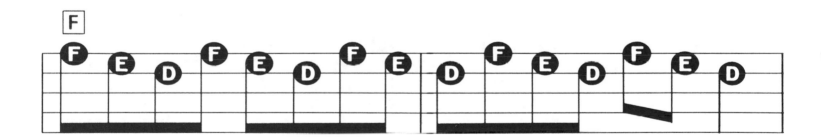

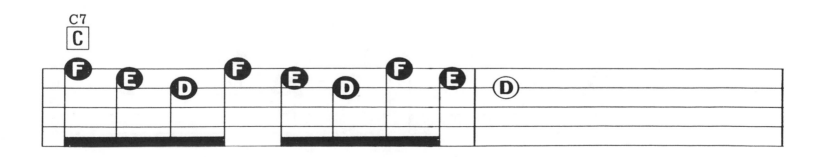

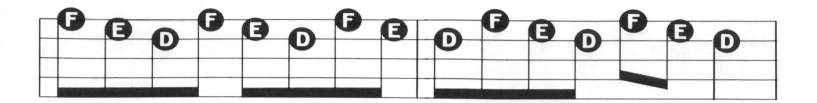

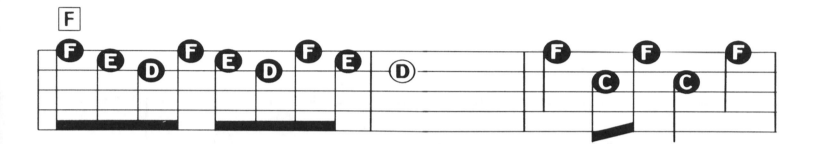

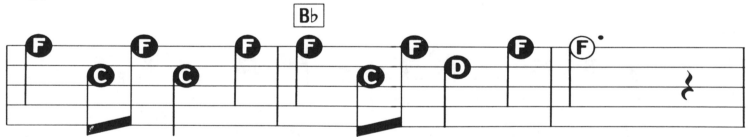

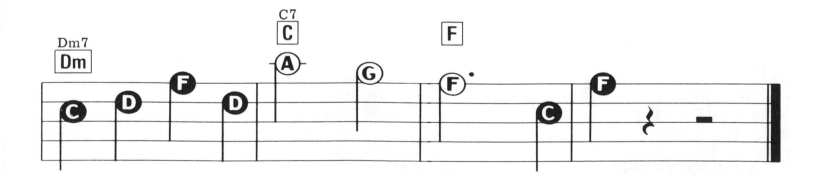

You Made Me Love You
(I Didn't Want to Do It)
from BROADWAY MELODY OF 1938

Registration 7
Rhythm: Fox Trot

Words by Joe McCarthy
Music by James V. Monaco

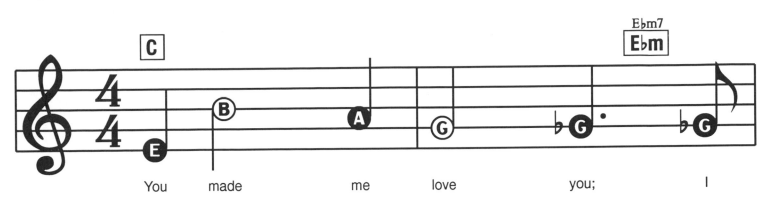

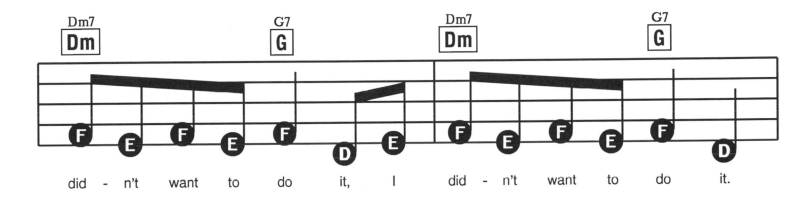

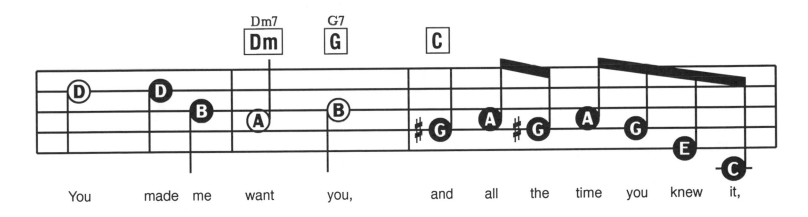

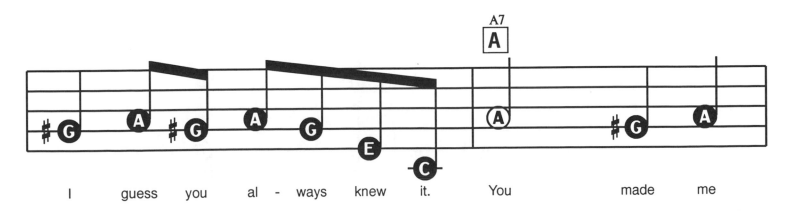

Copyright © 1994 by HAL LEONARD CORPORATION
International Copyright Secured   All Rights Reserved

236

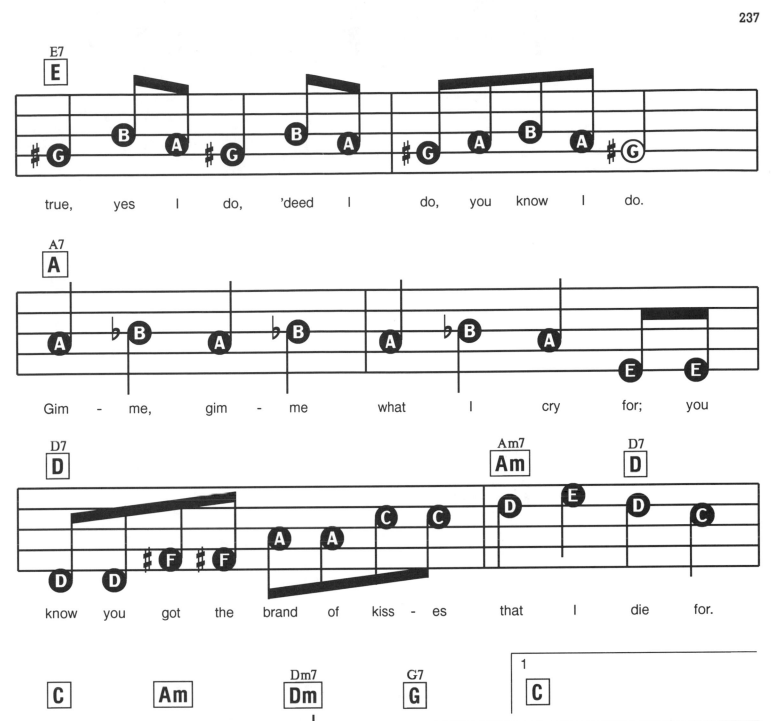

true, yes I do, 'deed I do, you know I do.

Gim - me, gim - me what I cry for; you

know you got the brand of kiss - es that I die for.

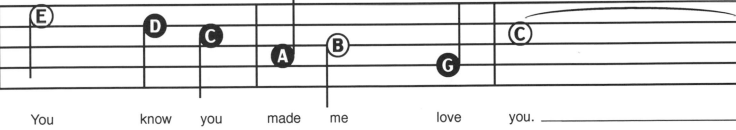

You know you made me love you. _____

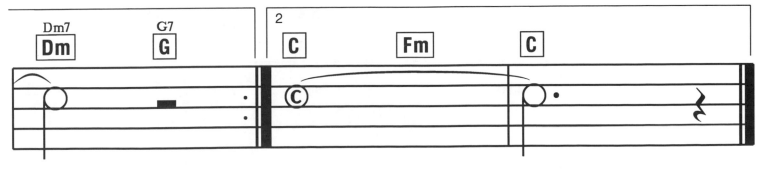

_____ you. _____

Waiting for the Robert E. Lee

Registration 3
Rhythm: Fox Trot or Jazz

Words by L. Wolfe Gilbert
Music by Lewis F. Muir

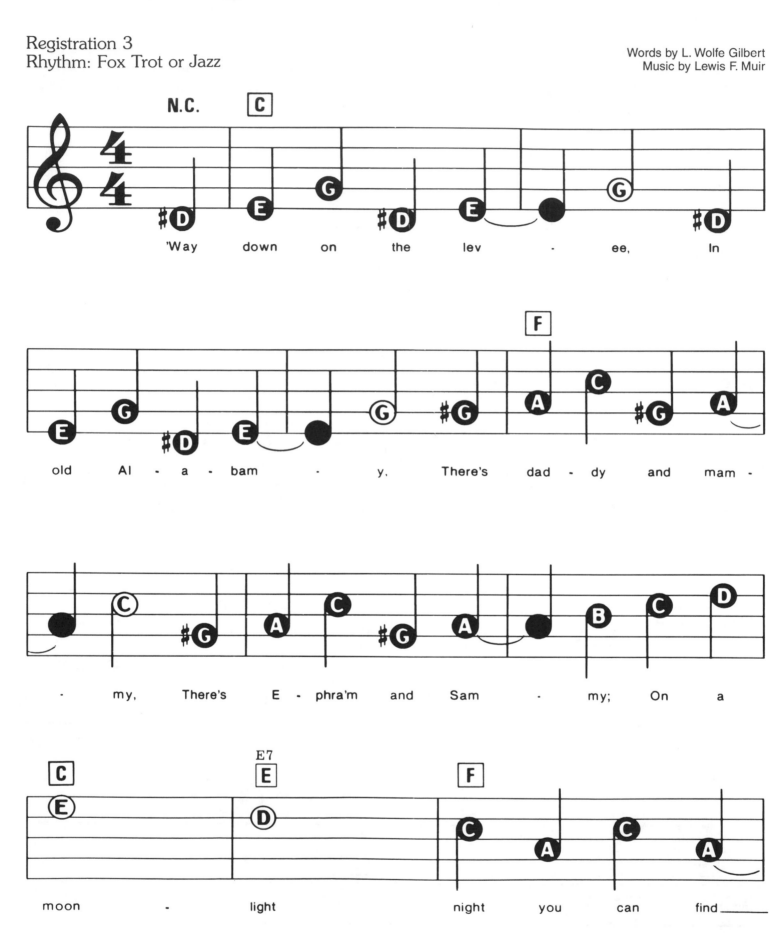

Copyright © 1994 by HAL LEONARD CORPORATION
International Copyright Secured   All Rights Reserved

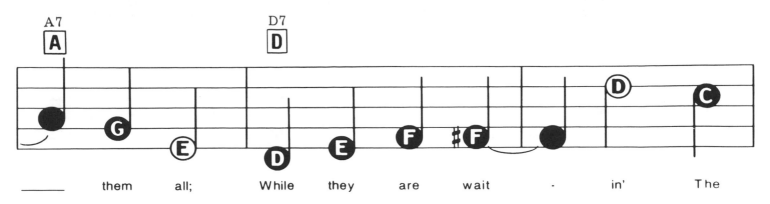

them all; While they are wait - in' The

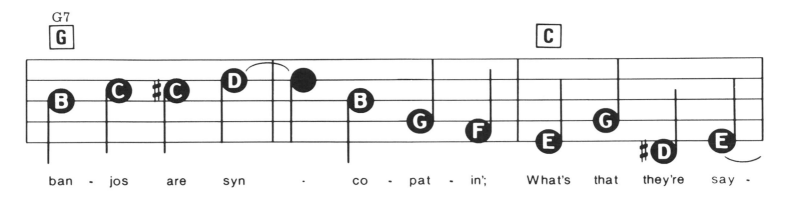

ban - jos are syn - co - pat - in'; What's that they're say -

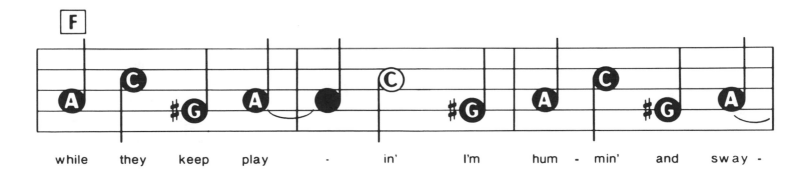

- in'? Oh, what's that they're say - in'? The

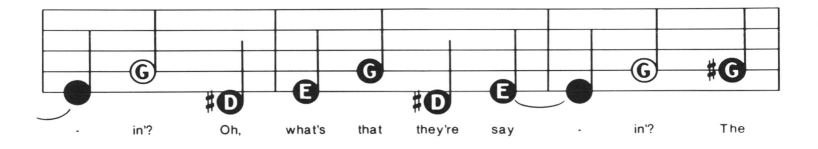

while they keep play - in' I'm hum - min' and sway -

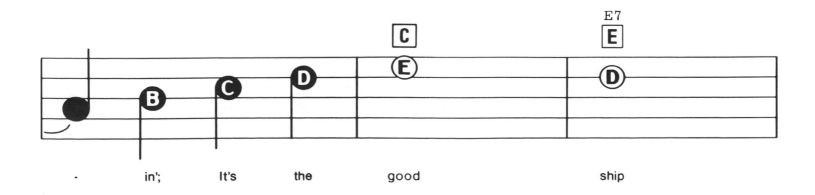

- in'; It's the good ship

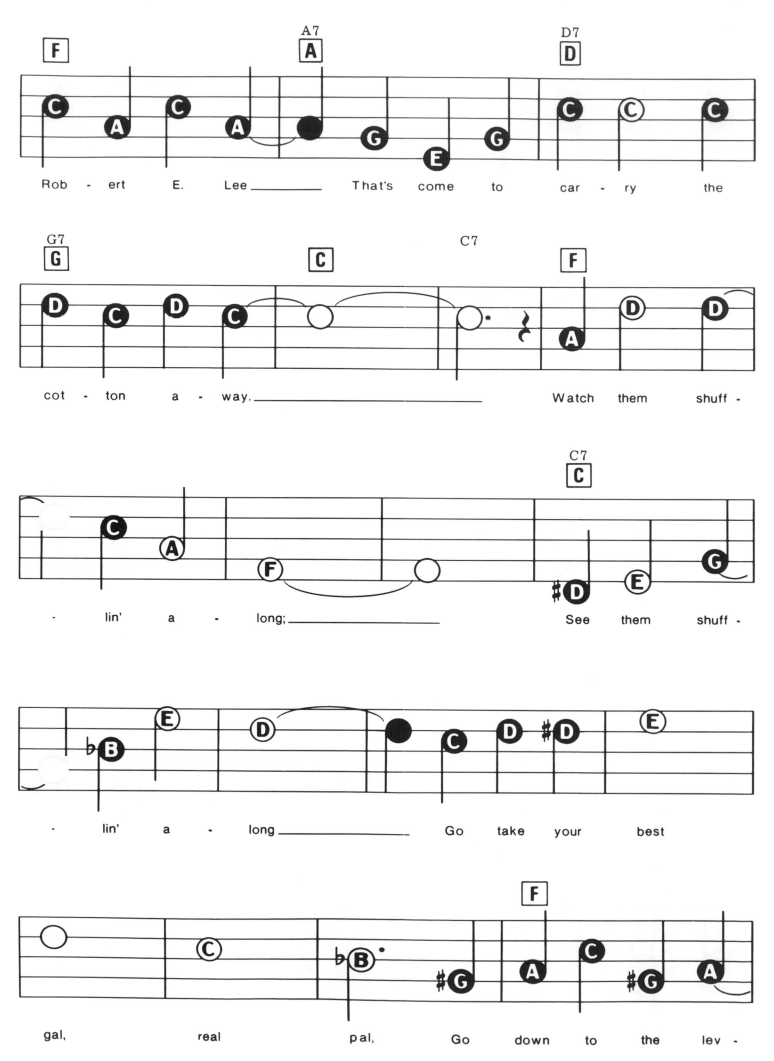

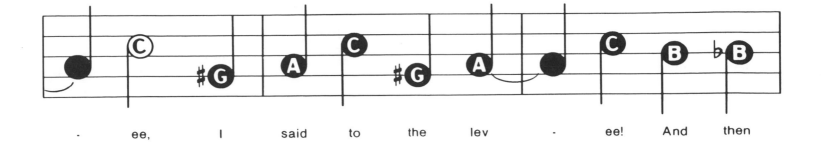

- ee, I said to the lev - ee! And then

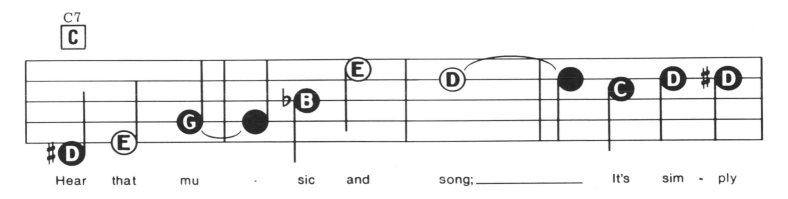

join that shuff - - lin' throng;_____

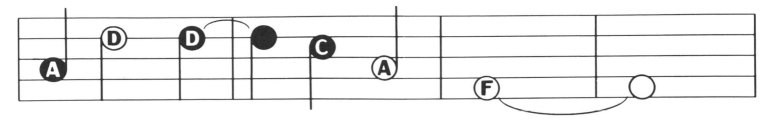

C7

Hear that mu - sic and song;_____ It's sim - ply

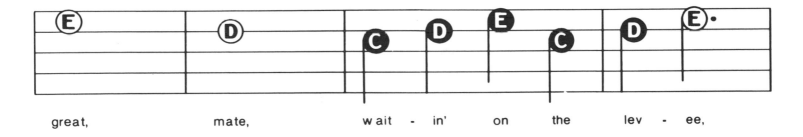

great, mate, wait - in' on the lev - ee,

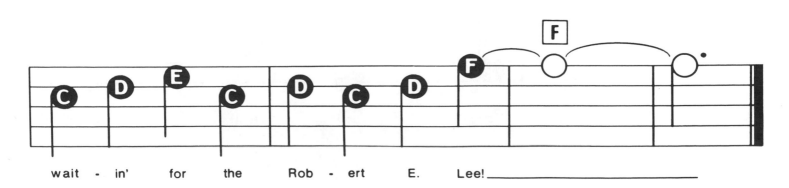

wait - in' for the Rob - ert E. Lee!_____

When Irish Eyes Are Smiling

Registration 3
Rhythm: Waltz

Words by Chauncey Olcott and George Graff, Jr.
Music by Ernest R. Ball

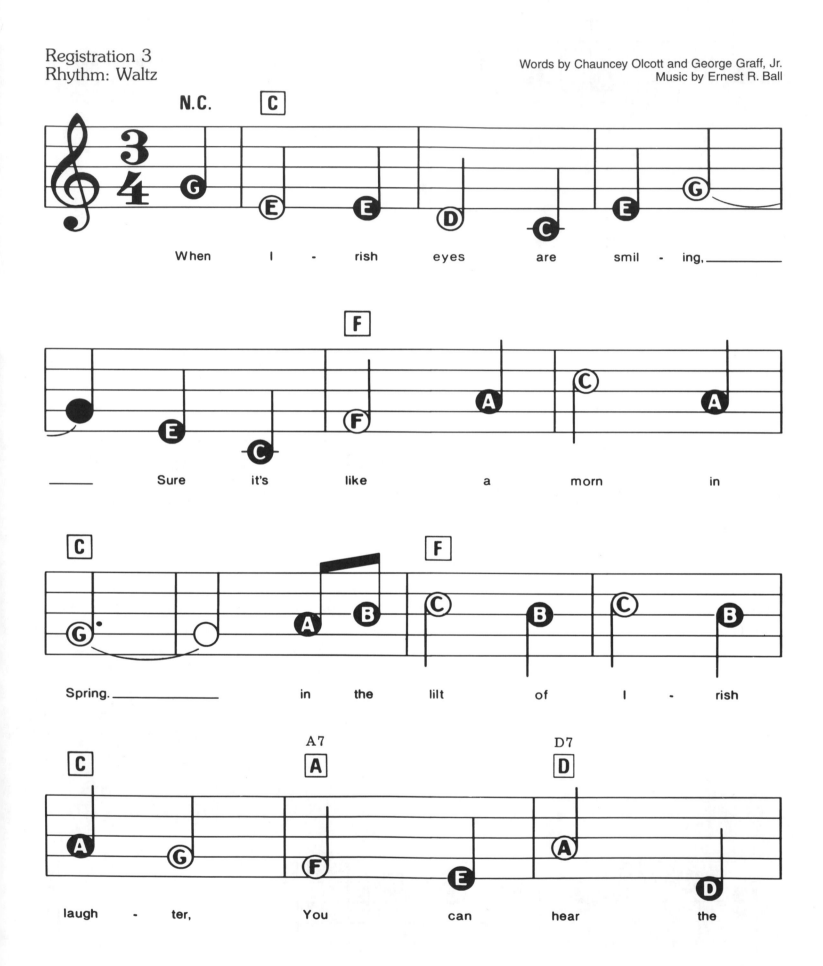

Copyright © 1994 by HAL LEONARD CORPORATION
International Copyright Secured   All Rights Reserved

243

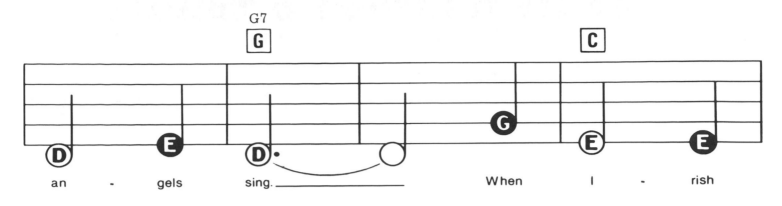

an - gels sing._____ When I - rish

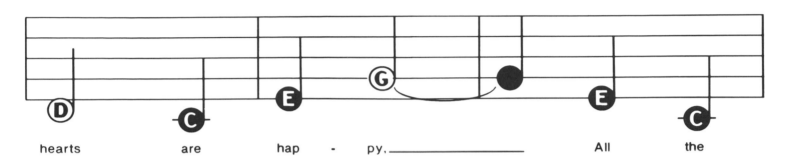

hearts are hap - py,_____ All the

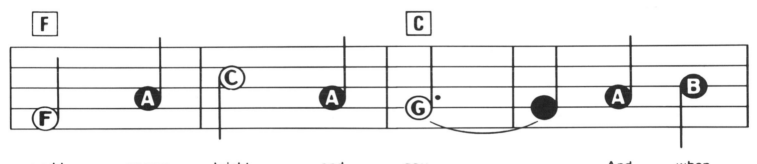

world seems bright and gay,_____ And when

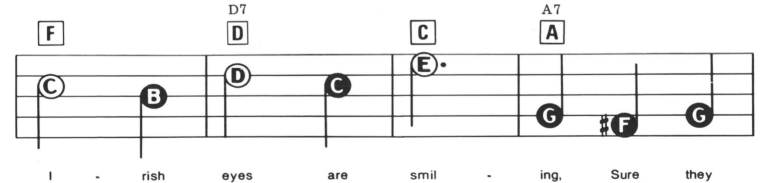

I - rish eyes are smil - ing, Sure they

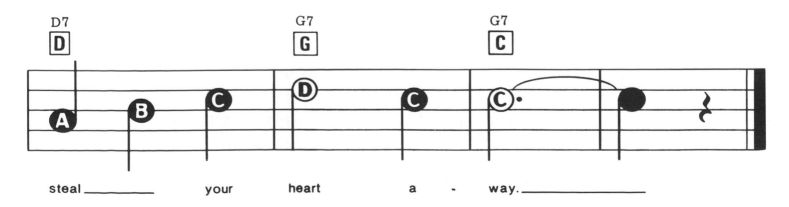

steal_____ your heart a - way._____

When You Wore a Tulip
(And I Wore a Big Red Rose)

Registration 9
Rhythm: Fox Trot or Pops

Words by Jack Mahoney
Music by Percy Wenrich

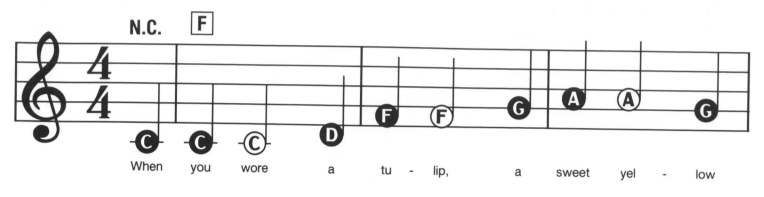

When you wore a tu - lip, a sweet yel - low

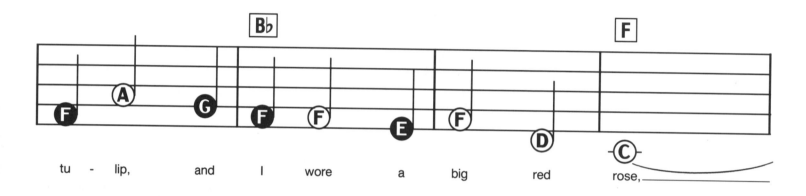

tu - lip, and I wore a big red rose,

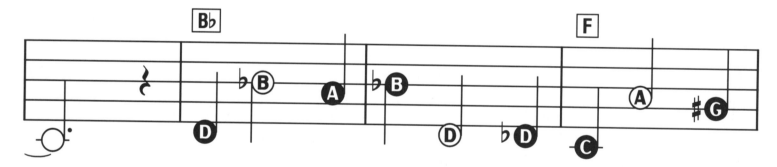

when you ca - ressed me 'twas then heav - en

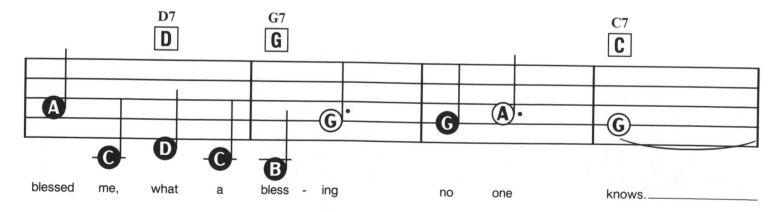

blessed me, what a bless - ing no one knows.

Copyright © 1996 by HAL LEONARD CORPORATION
International Copyright Secured   All Rights Reserved

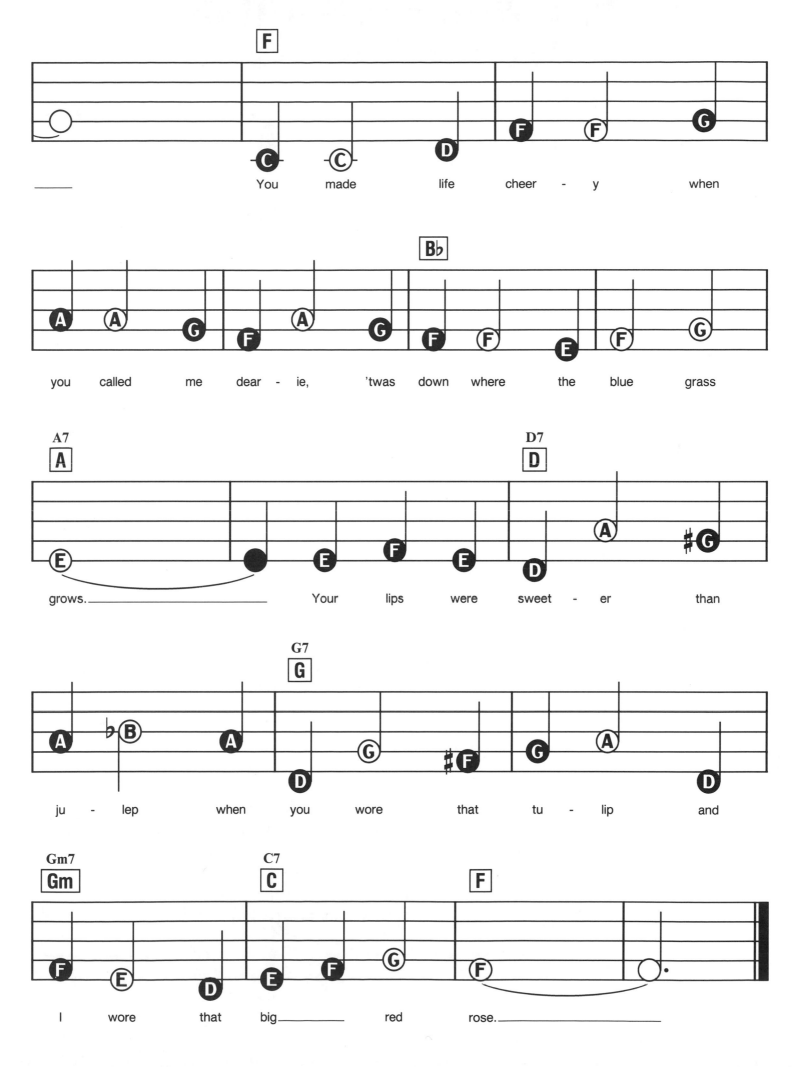

The World Is Waiting for the Sunrise

Registration 5
Rhythm: Fox Trot or Swing

Words by Eugene Lockhart
Music by Ernest Seitz

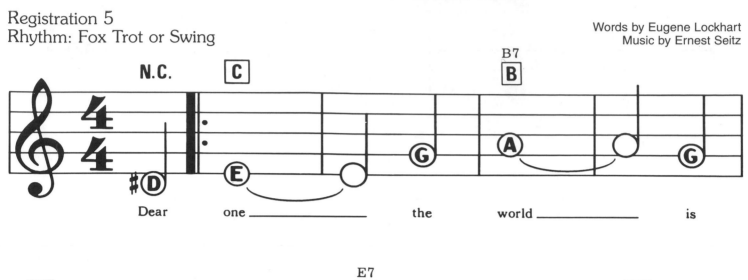

Dear one _____ the world _____ is

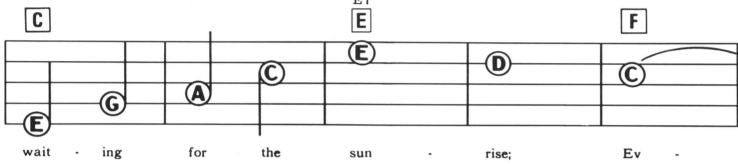

wait - ing for the sun - rise; Ev -

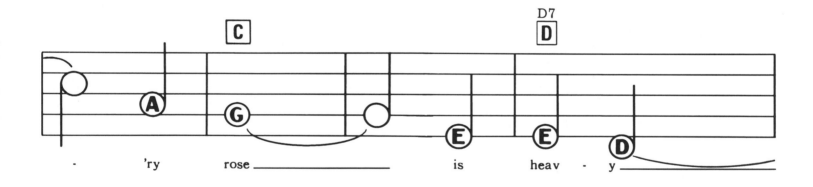

- 'ry rose _____ is heav - y _____

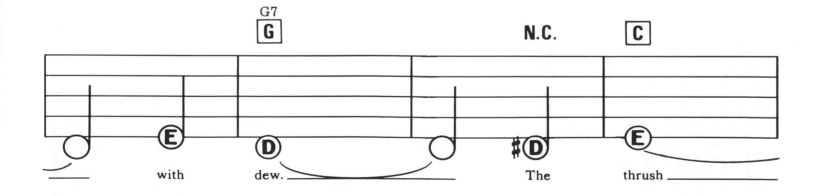

_____ with dew. _____ The thrush _____

Copyright © 1996 by HAL LEONARD CORPORATION
International Copyright Secured   All Rights Reserved

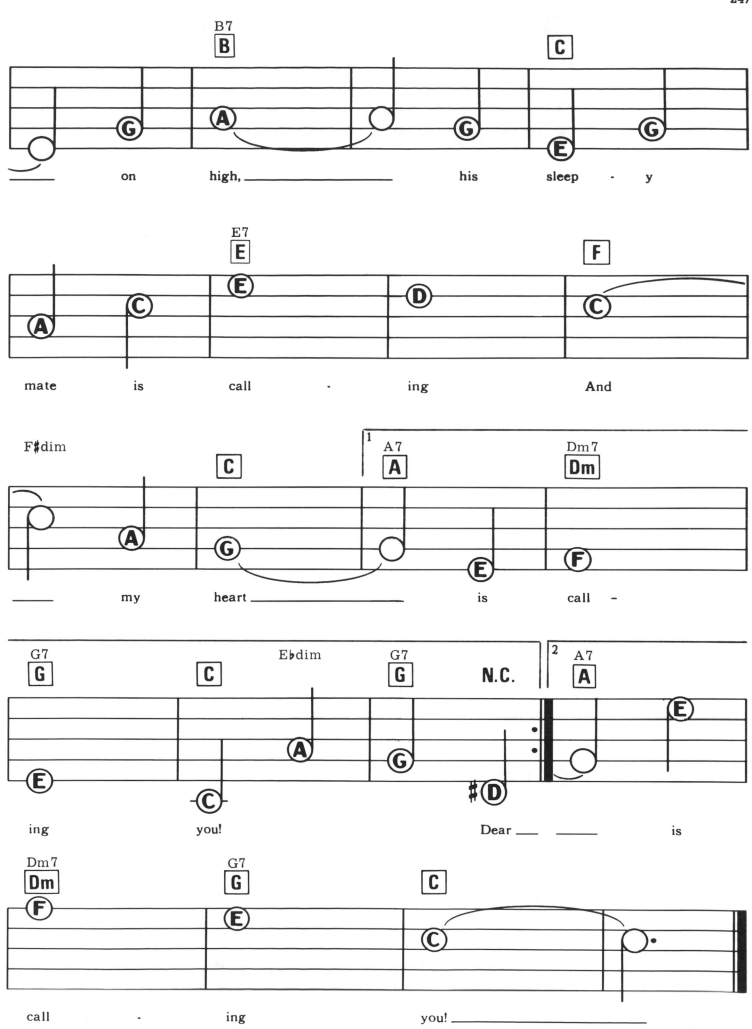

Registration Guide

- Match the Registration number on the song to the corresponding numbered category below. Select and activate an instrumental sound available on your instrument.
- Choose an automatic rhythm appropriate to the mood and style of the song. (Consult your Owner's Guide for proper operation of automatic rhythm features.)
- Adjust the tempo and volume controls to comfortable settings.

Registration

1	Flute, Pan Flute, Jazz Flute
2	Clarinet, Organ
3	Violin, Strings
4	Brass, Trumpet
5	Synth Ensemble, Accordion, Brass
6	Pipe Organ, Harpsichord
7	Jazz Organ, Vibraphone, Vibes, Electric Piano, Jazz Guitar
8	Piano, Electric Piano
9	Trumpet, Trombone, Clarinet, Saxophone, Oboe
10	Violin, Cello, Strings